A GUIDE TO ANGLO-IRISH LITERATURE

By the same author
A SHORT GUIDE TO ENGLISH STYLE
CLAY IS THE WORD (Patrick Kavanagh)
WILLIAM ALLINGHAM

ALAN WARNER

A GUIDE TO ANGLO-IRISH LITERATURE

GILL AND MACMILLAN

ST. MARTIN'S PRESS, NEW YORK

First published 1981 by
Gill and Macmillan Ltd
Goldenbridge
Dublin
with associated companies in
London, New York, Delhi, Hong Kong,
Johannesburg, Lagos, Melbourne,
Singapore, Tokyo

7171 1003 6

First published in the United States of America in 1981 by
St. Martin's Press, Inc.,
175 Fifth Avenue, New York, NY 10010

Library of Congress Card Catalog Number 81 - 52946

ISBN   0 − 312 − 35290 − 5

Typeset by Lagamage Co. Ltd.
Printed and bound in Great Britain by
Redwood Burn Ltd., Trowbridge, Wiltshire.

In Memoriam

PHYLLIS WARNER

b. Belfast 1913 — d. Derry 1965

Acknowledgments

The author and publishers are grateful for permission to reprint the following copyright material: extracts from *Austin Clarke's Collected Poems*, reprinted with the permission of The Dolmen Press Ltd; Mary Gilmore's poem 'Nationality' from *The Passionate Heart and Other Poems*, reprinted with the permission of Angus & Robertson (UK) Ltd; extracts from Seamus Heaney's *Wintering Out, North, Death of a Naturalist,* and *Field Work*, reprinted by permission of Faber and Faber Ltd, London, Oxford University Press, New York, and of Farrar, Straus and Giroux Inc., copyright © 1976, 1979; extracts from John Hewitt's volumes of poems, reprinted with the permission of the poet; extracts from *Patrick Kavanagh's Collected Poems*, reprinted with the permission of Mrs K.B. Kavanagh; James Stephens' poem 'A Glass of Beer' from *Collected Poems of James Stephens*, reprinted with the permission of Mrs Iris Wise and Macmillan, London and Basingstoke; also of Macmillan Publishing Co. Inc., Copyright 1918 by Macmillan Publishing Co. Inc., renewed 1946 by James Stephens.

Contents

PART FOUR
Yeats and Synge

PART FIVE
Some Living Writers

Preface

This book offers a personal and selective guide to Anglo-Irish literature. I hope I have indicated adequately the scope of the subject, but I have made no attempt to cover it all myself. There are a growing number of books about Anglo-Irish literature, and soon the scholars will be providing us with comprehensive critical and historical studies of all the significant writers. My purpose is to introduce this field of literature, and to indicate some of the problems involved in studying it. At the same time I hope to stimulate interest in a number of writers who are not yet widely read, even in Ireland.

The greatest Anglo-Irish writers — Yeats, Joyce, Synge, O'Casey — are already widely known. At first I planned to omit these big names because so much has already been written about them. On second thought I decided to include them, but not to attempt any comprehensive treatment of their work. So I have discussed their work in a highly selective way. I have tried, within the limits of this guide, to be a little more comprehensive in my treatment of those writers who are less well known. Among these my selection is largely a personal one. I have chosen those writers who delighted or intrigued me, and it seems to me a sensible assumption that I am most likely to interest my readers in the writers who have fully engaged my own interest.

I thought it wiser to consider a few writers in some detail, rather than devote a few paragraphs each to many writers. This allows me to quote freely from the writers I have chosen, so that my readers can judge for themselves whether or not they will be interested in them. At the same time, in order to extend a little further the range of my guide, I have included

1

some brief supplementary notes on some of the writers not selected for individual treatment.

In the last part of the book I have attempted to deal with some living writers. Here the problem of selection proved extremely difficult, and for a time I thought the only fair way was to leave them all out and confine my attention to the dead. But death makes an untidy line of demarcation. O'Faolain, still happily alive and writing, was born before O'Connor and Kavanagh. Flann O'Brien, who died untimely, was born much later than many living writers. In the end I settled for what must inevitably be a somewhat arbitrary personal selection. To have included all the living writers who are worthy of inclusion would have made this book too long. Quite apart from this, I might as well candidly admit that I have not read them all.

The small island of Ireland has produced a remarkable number of gifted writers. I hope that, at the end of this book, my readers will not only have a clearer view of Anglo-Irish literature, but some sense of the special savours and flavours to be found within it.

PART ONE

Introduction

1

The Scope of Anglo-Irish Literature

At first sight it might seem a simple matter to define the scope of Anglo-Irish literature. Daniel Corkery said that it was 'literature written in English by Irishmen' and this definition was adopted at the first meeting of the International Association for the Study of Anglo-Irish Literature. It is convenient to have a wide definition that will allow for the diversity of interests of an international body of scholars, but when we examine the writings of those who have discussed Anglo-Irish literature we soon become aware of problems.

In the foreword to his book on *Ireland's Literary Renaissance* Ernest A. Boyd remarks: 'Such names as Oscar Wilde and Bernard Shaw belong as certainly to the history of English literature as Goldsmith and Sheridan.' Goldsmith, Sheridan, Wilde and Shaw were all Irishmen who wrote in English, yet we cannot easily set them alongside Yeats, Synge and Sean O'Casey. Shaw did write a play about Ireland (*John Bull's Other Island*) but the bulk of his work has an English or European rather than an Irish dimension. Wilde's best known play, *The Importance of Being Earnest*, is set in London and deals with upper class English society and there is nothing Irish or Anglo-Irish about it.

Do we then need a narrower definition of Anglo-Irish literature than the one given above? Those who write about Anglo-Irish literature clearly feel the need for a more specific Irish dimension. Boyd himself suggested one, though he wisely does not attempt to define it: ' . . . the term Irish (or Anglo-Irish) can most properly be reserved for the literature which, although not written in Gaelic, is none the less informed by the spirit of the race.' Unfortunately the concept of 'the spirit of the race' is so wide and vague that no two Irishmen are likely to agree about it.

But more modest attempts to describe Anglo-Irish literature also move towards some kind of Irish dimension. Sean Lucy, speaking about Anglo-Irish poetry, although accepting Corkery's definition, goes on to add to it the notion of 'the Irish experience'. He says that the story of Anglo-Irish poetry is 'part of the quest of the English-speaking Irish for an identity, the reshaping of English to express the Irish experience.'

Roger McHugh, in a talk on Anglo-Irish poetry, gives his own clear definition to the literature he is dealing with:

> Let me say exactly what I mean when I use the term Anglo-Irish literature. I mean the kind of literature written in English which is as indigenous to and relates to this country as American literature to America.

'Expressing the Irish experience', literature 'indigenous to and relating to Ireland' — the two phrases express the same concept of an Irish dimension. In one form or another the concept is present in most discussions of Anglo-Irish writing. Frequently the Irish dimension is seen in terms of nationality. Stephen Gwynn, in his book on *Irish Literature and Drama,* speaks of 'the national literature of Ireland in English' and he sees Tom Moore's *Irish Melodies* as the true beginning of 'a national Irish literature in Ireland's second language.'

W.B. Yeats, whom many people consider to be the most distinguished of all Anglo-Irish writers, was also the moving spirit of the Irish literary movement at the end of the last century. He openly campaigned for a national literature in English:

> Can we not build up a national tradition, a national literature which shall be none the less Irish in spirit from being English in language? Can we not keep the continuity of the nation's life not by doing what Dr Hyde has practically pronounced impossible but by translating or re-telling in English, which shall have an indefinable Irish quality of rhythm and style, all that is best of the ancient literature.

Yeats wrote these words in a letter to the newspaper *United Ireland* on 17 December 1892. He wrote shortly after Douglas Hyde, who was later to found the Gaelic League, which aimed at restoring Irish as the national language of Ireland, had delivered a passionate plea for the disappearing Irish language in a speech to the National Literary Society in Dublin, entitled 'On the necessity for de-Anglicising the Irish people'.

Yeats, together with his friends and helpers, devoted much time and effort to the promotion of a national Irish literature in English. He looked both to the past and to the future. He tried to stimulate interest in the Anglo-Irish writers of the nineteenth century, such as Ferguson, Mangan, Carleton and Allingham. He wrote articles on these writers and sent lists of Irish books to the newspapers. At the same time he encouraged living writers to seek Irish themes and he chose Irish themes himself. He was active in encouraging Irish national literary societies. A number of these sprang up in the nineties at the same time as branches of the Gaelic League were being established. The movement began in London with the Southwark Irish Club. In 1891 Yeats and his friends used this as the basis for a new and more ambitious movement, the Irish Literary Society, London. The movement spread to Dublin, where a National Literary Society was started in 1892. The Appeal issued by the provisional committee of this Society makes its aim to promote a national literature quite clear:

> In recent years we have heard much of the material needs of Ireland, and little or nothing of her intellectual or literary needs ... Without an intellectual life of some kind we cannot long preserve our nationality. Every Irish national movement of recent years has drawn a great portion of its power from the literary movement started by Davis, but that movement is over, and it is not possible to live for ever upon the past. A living Ireland must have a living literature.

Yeats and his friends in the nineties were still living in the glow of the romantic nationalism that powerfully influenced European thought and feeling in the nineteenth century. Today nationalism is out of date and out of favour. The Irish Literary movement is now frequently viewed with mockery. Patrick Kavanagh, who needed elbow room for his own kind of truth and experience, reacted vigorously against what he called 'the Irish thing', and he resented being labelled an Irish poet. His lead was followed by younger men. Anthony Cronin wrote in *The Irish Times* (3 November 1976):

> Once upon a time there was a thing called The Irish Literary Revival, which was connected with another thing called The Celtic Twilight, which was more like a fog. It descended (if that be the word) a long time ago, but it hasn't cleared away yet and the smell continues to pollute the air . . .
>
> Now, such as it was, the Irish Literary Revival was an offshoot of British needs. Materialistic, moneyed, torpid late Victorian society wanted an anti-materialist Land of Heart's Desire whose existence could be checked on the map and whose literary representatives could be produced in drawing rooms once their boots had been cleaned to prove how charming and delightful it all was. Yeats and his friends elected to supply such a never-never land.

The British have been blamed, perhaps rightly, for most of Ireland's troubles, so it was perhaps inevitable that when opinion turned against the Irish Literary movement, they should be blamed for this too.

Michael Smith, writing in *The Lace Curtain* (no. 3), joins in the condemnation.

> For there is, it seems to me, something ineffably bourgeois and artificial about the Celtic and late-Celtic Twilight, about all its blather of fairies and unintentionally ridiculous or imaginatively untenable entities of Gaelic mythology and folk-lore, about its bad, fifth-rate nature poems and its sham imbecilic peasant poems.

It is natural enough that contemporary Irish writers and critics should reject a self-conscious literary movement belonging to the early years of this century, and that they should be unsympathetic to Yeats's attempts to formulate and define a national literature. But no consideration of Anglo-Irish literature can afford to ignore the Irish Literary Revival. Indeed the concept of Anglo-Irish literature only emerges after the Revival. The term 'Anglo-Irish' is not used in the nineteenth century to describe the work of Irish writers in English.

Although we may be uneasy about nationalism we cannot ignore its force or dispute the fact that it influences literature as well as politics. One important aspect of Anglo-Irish literature is the national aspect. It must be accepted and examined. Discussion of nationality can be difficult, because it is impossible to define very clearly, and it can be embarrassing, because nationalism often takes violent and irrational forms. But there is really no need for a world that now thinks in international terms to be suspicious of nationality. Local and national ties and affections still bind citizens of the wider world. The point is made neatly in a poem by an Australian writer, which is entitled 'Nationality'.

> I have grown past hate and bitterness
> I see the world as one;
> Yet, though I can no longer hate,
> My son is still my son.
> All men at God's round table sit,
> And all men must be fed;
> But this loaf in my hand,
> This loaf is my son's bread.
>
> (Mary Gilmore b. 1865)

Yeats's own definition of a national literature brings us back to the notion of an 'Irish experience', the phrase used by Sean Lucy. Yeats called it 'the work of writers who are moulded by influences that are moulding their country; and who write out of so deep a life that they are accepted there in the end.' The second half of this sentence reminds us that Yeats fought his battle for a national literature on two fronts. On the one hand he had to contend with those, in England and in Ireland, who were hostile to the development of 'an individual national life' in Ireland; on the other hand he had to fight a rearguard action against those who wanted a national *propaganda* rather than a national literature.

We cannot think of Goldsmith, or of Wilde, as being moulded by influences that were moulding Ireland. The question of Irish nationality did not arise for Goldsmith. Not only did he spend most of his life outside Ireland, but, like most of his fellow Anglo-Irishmen of the eighteenth century, he saw Ireland as a kind of province of England not a separate nation. Even Swift, though he fought passionately for Ireland against English indifference and injustice, was not really aware of Irish nationality. Yeats claimed that Swift found his nationality through the *Drapier's Letters,* but Yeats is a passionate partisan trying to establish a national tradition stretching back through Burke, Berkeley and Swift, to Molyneux.

Oscar Wilde was born in Dublin (1856) and his mother who was an Irish patriot, and wrote poems under the pen name of 'Speranza', gave him several Irish names – Oscar, Fingall, O'Flahertie, Wills. He was educated at Portora Royal School, Enniskillen, and then at Trinity College, Dublin, before going on to Oxford. His witty and amusing plays were written in the nineties, the decade when Yeats and his friends started the Irish Literary Society. In fact Wilde joined the Society. W.P. Ryan, who published an account of the Irish Literary Revival as early as 1894, has recorded this fact:

> When it was suggested that Oscar Wilde should be invited to join the Society, one who knew him said that he would certainly put off the matter with a quip or a paradox, which however would be a good one, and worthy of being entered in the minute-book. This friend was a false prophet for Oscar Fingal O'Flaherty Wills Wilde was soon an honoured name on our register.

Although Wilde joined the Society, it cannot be said that he was influenced by it, or that he was moulded by influences that were moulding Ireland. At the same time we can hardly exclude Wilde from the ranks of the Irish writers. If we do then what about Goldsmith, Sheridan, Shaw, and Samuel Beckett?

At this point it may help to recall a definition of Irishness suggested by Conor Cruise O'Brien. 'Irishness', he wrote 'is not primarily a question of birth or blood or language; it is the condition of being involved in the Irish situation, and usually of being mauled by it.'

'Being involved in the Irish situation' is clearly linked with the concept of 'the Irish experience' and 'being moulded by influences that were moulding Ireland'. From this aspect it is difficult to see any Irishness in the work of Goldsmith,

Sheridan, Wilde and Beckett, and even Shaw was only temporarily and partially involved in the Irish situation.

One way out of the difficulties encountered in the attempt to separate Anglo-Irish from English writers would be to establish two broad categories, though they will of course shade into each other. In the first category, which we might call 'insiders', are those writers who are clearly involved in the Irish experience and situation; in the second category, 'outsiders', are those who are not involved in spite of their Irish birth and even though they may be found to have some Irish qualities or characteristics.

Clearly Yeats and his friends are 'insiders', deeply involved at various levels in the Irish experience. So, in their different ways, are William Carleton and Samuel Ferguson. So is Patrick Kavanagh, in spite of his attack on self-conscious cultural 'Irishness'. The Irish experience takes many different forms. Some are political and cultural, others are social and geographical. Kavanagh writes from an experience of the little fields of Monaghan, and later the streets of Dublin. Somerville and Ross, though suspicious of and indeed hostile to Irish nationalism, are deeply rooted in an Irish world. But their world is very different from that of Carleton or Kavanagh. They belonged, as did many other Anglo-Irish writers, to the Anglo-Irish social class; their world was that of the Big House. But Anglo-Irish literature is not the preserve of the Anglo-Irish class, nor is it confined to the Big House. Confusion over this has been the cause of some hostility to Anglo-Irish literature.

It is hardly possible to find any Anglo-Irish writers who write from the inside before 1800. Those earlier writers who were really inside the Irish situation wrote in Irish. Goldsmith, Berkley, Burke, wrote very little out of an Irish experience, and although Swift has an intense and passionate involvement in the Irish situation in a few of his writings, the main bulk of his work lies outside the Irish orbit.

The year 1800 saw the publication of Maria Edgeworth's *Castle Rackrent.* This book clearly comes out of an Irish experience, but Maria Edgeworth is only partly an 'insider' in the field of Anglo-Irish literature. She wrote three other Irish novels, *The Absentee, Ennui* and *Ormond,* but the rest of her work, indeed the bulk of it, belongs to an English mode and is unrelated to her Irish experience. She is thus the first of an important group of Anglo-Irish writers: those who have an Irish segment in their work, where they are deeply involved with the Irish situation, but whose work ranges outside Ireland and the Irish experience. In this group we must put George Moore, Joyce Cary and Louis MacNeice.

This book, because it is only an introductory guide, will be mainly concerned with the work of 'insiders', but this does not mean that the 'outsiders' are unimportant. Their importance, however, will be in areas outside the Irish experience, though it may be possible to see some Irish characteristics in them. Bernard Shaw, for example, was inescapably an Irishman. His attitude to English ideas and opinions is not that of an Englishman. He was something of a stranger in London and he felt socially insecure. We find him reading in the British Museum, not only Karl Marx, but also books on English etiquette.* His speech was Irish and he thought of himself as an Irishman. In his old age he wrote to Sean O'Casey: 'Sixty-six years of English air have not made an Englishman of me, because I started with twenty years of Irish air.'

In dealing with Anglo-Irish writers we must be careful not to fall into the trap of judging them according to their 'Irishness'. Quite apart from the fact that it is impossible to establish a scale of 'Irishness', the most important thing about a writer is his ability to write and to illuminate human experience. The first criterion for including any name in a list of Anglo-Irish writers must be that the writer is worth reading. But this granted, it does make sense to group together those writers who write from inside an Irish experience, who create an Irish world in their writings. Their gifts, and their limitations, will be more clearly brought into focus if they are studied alongside their fellows.

So far I have been defining the scope of Anglo-Irish literature to embrace first those Irishmen or Anglo-Irishmen who wrote, in English, out of their Irish experience, and second

---

* Yeats had something of the same feeling of social insecurity. He records in a letter to Katharine Tynan how he was deeply troubled about the size of the tip he should give to the manservant who waited on him when he stayed in York Powell's rooms at an Oxford College.

those who wrote, but rarely or not at all out of their Irish experience. But are there no national characteristics that may help us to define and formulate the body of Anglo-Irish literature?

A number of such characteristics have been suggested. They may be stimulating aids to the discussion of Anglo-Irish writers, and valid for many of them, but they are too uncertain or too limited to be useful as guides to classification. Thomas MacDonagh in his book, *Literature in Ireland* (1916), traces an Irish mode in Anglo-Irish poetry and compiles a brief anthology of poems revealing the influence of Gaelic versification, or Irish music, or the Irish way of speech. But clearly many significant Anglo-Irish poets could find no place in such an anthology. Brendan Kennelly, in his introduction to the *Penguin Book of Irish Verse,* singles out as the most memorable characteristic of all Irish poetry, 'a hard, simple, virile, rhetorical clarity.' Sean Lucy finds at the centre of most Irish people 'what might be called *a dramatic self-awareness.* This has deeply marked Irish and Anglo-Irish poetry, in subject, in mood, in imagery, in technique, and in speech rhythms.' Andrew Carpenter, in a lecture given to the third conference of I.A.S.A.I.L. at University College Galway in 1976, made a similar point in suggesting that Anglo-Irish writers were always attempting self-scrutiny. Because they lacked the basic security of English writers, there was often tension, ambiguity, irony and double vision in the tone of their writing.

All the suggestions above make valuable and fruitful points of departure for the discussion of particular books and writers. But they clearly cannot be used to separate Anglo-Irish from English or American or Russian writers. So we must turn back again to the simple and comprehensive definition offered by Daniel Corkery: 'literature written in English by Irishmen', remembering that there can be considerable argument about who is or is not an Irishman.

As far as this book is concerned I shall be dealing with those Anglo-Irish writers whom I have called 'insiders', those deeply involved in an Irish situation and writing out of their Irish experience. There are enough of them whose work can be taken seriously as literature to make a separate study of them worthwhile. They do not form a coherent tradition, and although there are facets of nationality in the work of many, it is debatable how far they can be said to provide the national literature of Ireland in English. In spite of this, when they are studied together, they illuminate each other, and they illuminate also the past and present history of Ireland. The Irish imagination, as revealed in its literature in English, is wide-ranging and powerful, humorous and inventive. Not only the Irish themselves but anyone who has the necessary freedom of the English language will find enjoyment and illumination in Anglo-Irish literature.

2

The Growth of
Anglo-Irish Literature

It is difficult, if not impossible, to approach Anglo-Irish
literature without some knowledge of Irish history. But Irish
history, like some Irish bogs, is nearly bottomless, and it is
difficult to give any quick survey of it. John Hewitt, in his
poem, *An Irishman in Coventry,* offers a short dark summary:
'This is our fate: eight hundred years' disaster/crazily tangled
as the Book of Kells.' And in *Conacre* he refers to Ireland as
'This mad island crammed with bloody ghosts'. Professor
Owen Dudley-Edwards, contributing an historical chapter to
a book on Ireland, chose as his title 'The Burden of History'.
Ireland is still powerfully burdened and haunted by the past.
I realised this with a shock when I came to live in Ulster in
1960. One of the first things I saw was a huge slogan painted
on a bridge – 'REMEMBER 1690'. My first reaction was
astonishment. I had just come from East Africa, where
people can hardly remember anything that happened before
1900, and I wanted to cry out: 'For God's sake, forget 1690
and remember 1960.' Now, after twenty years in Ulster, I
accept such slogans as commonplace, and even the wittier
ones, such as 'PAISLEY FOR POPE', hardly rouse a reaction.

In trying to sketch briefly the growth of Anglo-Irish literature I must offer some potted history; but I am aware of the
complexities of the subject that defy any simple potting, and
I urge my readers to consult some of the history books listed
in the bibliography at the end of this guide.

The language of early literature in Ireland was, of course,
Irish, a Gaelic language. The Gaels, coming from Gaul, reached Ireland about the first century B.C. The coming of
Christianity brought Latin to the churches and monasteries
but Irish remained the secular language. The Norsemen, who

15

invaded Ireland between the end of the eighth century and the beginning of the eleventh, left no language or literature, though they gave their names to some of the towns they founded, such as Dublin (Dyfflin, the Black Pool, anglicised as Dublin), Waterford and Carlingford. After the Anglo-Norman invasions of the twelfth century, English was gradually introduced to some areas of Ireland, though the language of the first settlers was Norman French. Many of the Norman invaders married into Irish families and became assimilated to an Irish way of life and speech. The English government tried to prevent the English colony in Ireland from becoming absorbed into the Gaelic world. The Statutes of Kilkenny were aimed at discouraging the use of the Irish language and the adoption of Irish customs. It is interesting to recall that the third earl of Desmond, at one time a leader of the English colony, was also celebrated for his skill as a poet composing in Irish.

Gradually English spread as the settlers moved further into Ireland, and as successive waves of conquest brought more speakers of English to settle in Ireland, but there is little significant literature in English until the eighteenth century, when the Protestant Ascendancy was firmly established. Until about the end of that century Irish was still the chief language of literature in Ireland. But by the nineteenth century the position had changed. English was now the generally accepted language of literature. Irish was everywhere in decline, and its decline was hastened by the disaster of the Great Famine and the establishment of English-speaking schools.

The long and troubled history of Ireland stems from the attempts made by successive English governments to bring Ireland under their control and make it a kind of English province. These attempts were never wholly successful. The deep divisions between the two sides were made infinitely worse by the religious differences resulting from the English Reformation. The early colonists had been Catholics, but Henry VIII and Queen Elizabeth tried to force Protestantism upon Ireland. In 1641, during the English Civil War, the Irish Catholics rebelled and many Protestants were killed. A few years later Cromwell carried out a ruthless suppression of the rebels, and large tracts of land were taken from their owners and given to Cromwell's soldiers and supporters.

There was another rebellion in 1689 led by King James II who had been dispossessed of his English throne because he was a Catholic. The Irish forces were defeated at the Battle of the Boyne, and later the harsh Penal Laws were passed to protect the Protestant Ascendancy. A different kind of revolt occurred at the end of the eighteenth century, when the United Irishmen, largely led by Anglo-Irish Protestants, attempted a revolution with French support. In the nineteenth century the struggle for freedom took mainly a political shape. There was first the successful struggle for Catholic Emancipation, then the unsuccessful struggle for Repeal of the Union with England. There followed the Parliamentary struggle of the Irish members at Westminster, led by Parnell, for Home Rule.

Finally, in the twentieth century the most eager nationalists took up arms against British rule, first in 1916, when a small band of idealists, led by Patrick Pearse, faced hopeless odds, and later in a guerilla war against British power that lasted from 1918 to 1921. In 1921 a Treaty was signed giving a large measure of independence to twenty-six counties of Ireland, but separating off Northern Ireland, which was given its own Parliament, while still remaining part of the United Kingdom. Unfortunately this was not the end of Ireland's troubles, as we know from contemporary history. But I must return to the past.

A key date both in Irish history and in the history of Anglo-Irish literature is the year 1800. In that year the Act of Union was passed, abolishing the partly independent Irish Parliament and bringing Ireland into political union with England. Henceforth the members elected for Irish counties took their seats at Westminster, and the fine Parliament building in Dublin became the headquarters of the Bank of Ireland.

In a remarkable poem entitled 'Act of Union' Seamus Heaney imagines the act as a sexual one and extends it as a kind of myth representing the whole fate of Ireland. He envisages a rape of soft bogland Ireland by male, colonial England, and the act brings to birth 'an obstinate fifth column', a legacy of trouble and pain.

The last years of the eighteenth century, before the Act of Union took place, had been the best years of the Protestant Ascendancy. Faced with defeat in America, and a lack of troops in Ireland, the English government granted a measure of independence to the Irish Parliament in 1782. There was a mood of optimism and a sense of national unity, and Dublin flourished as one of the great capital cities of Europe. Many of the fine Georgian buildings that give Dublin its character and distinction date from this period.

But in the minds of some men thoughts and hopes for Irish independence went much deeper. The revolutionary examples of America, and later of France, sent ripples to Ireland. In 1791 the United Irish Society was founded in Belfast under the leadership of Wolfe Tone, and what began as a middle class debating society ended with the more radical members forming a secret society, planning rebellion and seeking help from France. The result was the abortive rebellion of 1798, which hastened the Act of Union. But as the years passed the Irish imagination was stirred by memories of the events of 1798. Ballads grew up about the Croppy Boys, and John Kells Ingram wrote a poem for *The Nation* in 1843 that became known all over Ireland. Entitled 'The Memory of the Dead', it opens with the line, 'Who fears to speak of ninety-eight?' Much later Yeats chose the landing of French troops in Killala Bay as the subject of his patriotic play, *Cathleen ni Houlihan*. His play encouraged the young patriots of his time to join in the Easter Rising, as Yeats reflected in his old age:

Did that play of mine send out
Certain men the English shot?

1800 is not only a key date in Irish history; it is also the real starting point for Anglo-Irish literature. In that year Maria Edgeworth published *Castle Rackrent,* the first Anglo-Irish novel, which I will discuss in some detail in Part II. Six years later Lady Morgan had a great success with *The Wild Irish Girl.* In 1820 Thomas Moore's *Irish Melodies* appeared. Irish themes and scenes and Irish people became increasingly acceptable to the general reading public and some Irish writers began to discover a rich heritage of Gaelic myth and legend that came near to rivalling the Classical myth and legend, the imaginative source of much European writing.

Before moving forward from 1800 to look at the growth of English writing in nineteenth century Ireland, I would like to look back for a moment at the previous century. Hugh A. Law, in his account of Anglo-Irish literature, finds its origins in the writings of William Molyneux, Swift and Berkeley, all of whom protested against the exploitation of Ireland by England. There is some justification for this view, though it tends to identify literature with political protest. The three writers named all belonged to the Protestant Ascendancy, and had no thoughts of Irish independence, yet their questioning and defiance of English authority served as an example and inspiration to others.

In 1698 William Molyneux wrote a famous pamphlet: 'The Case of Ireland's being bound by Acts of Parliament in England stated'. It belongs more to the history of politics than of literature, but it lingered in the imagination of Irishmen. Grattan referred to it in a famous speech in 1782, when he was proposing the emancipation of the Irish Parliament: 'Spirit of Swift! Spirit of Molyneux! your genius has prevailed! Ireland is now a nation.'

Swift, like Molyneux, led a political protest against the English government's treatment of Ireland, yet he took a near colonial view of the country and hated the people whose cause he championed. If he had been given a decent ecclesiastical position in England, he would never have become Dean of St Patrick's in Dublin. When he was on his way back to Dublin from London in 1727 he was forced to wait some days in Holyhead. He chafed, and wrote some verses in which he says:

> I never was in haste before
> To reach that slavish hateful shore . . .

But now, because Stella is ill and in danger, he curses the contrary wind that

> With rage impatient makes me wait
> A passage to the land I hate.

Another poem entitled 'Ireland' and written on the same occasion begins:

> Remove me from this land of slaves
> Where all are fools and all are knaves,
> Where every knave and fool is bought
> Yet kindly sells himself for nought . . .

In spite of this Swift championed the Irish interest. Not only did he attack the British Government's proposals to issue a patent for copper coins to William Wood (who had paid handsome bribes to the King's mistress) in the famous *Drapier's Letters,* but he wrote a scathing satire on those he held responsible for the poverty and misgovernment of Ireland. 'A Modest Proposal for Preventing the Poor Children of Ireland from Being a Burden to their Parents or Country' is the finest of his ironical essays. In a calm and rational tone of business calculation he advances the proposition that Irish infants should be sold for meat 'to persons of quality and fortune'. By pretending to ally himself with the attitudes of landlords, squires and merchants, who saw the poor mainly as a nuisance, he exposes their inhumanity. 'I grant this food will be somewhat dear, and therefore very proper for landlords, who as they have already devoured most of the parents seem to have the best title to the children.'

Swift has certainly earned a place in the annals of Anglo-Irish literature, but there is already a considerable literature devoted to him, and he lies a little outside the mainstream of this book.

George Berkeley was born and spent most of his life in Ireland. He was Bishop of Cloyne from 1734 to 1752 and he was deeply concerned about the poverty and backwardness of Ireland. Although his fame chiefly depends upon his philosophical writings, he did also write from his Irish experience. In *The Querist* he raised many pertinent questions about the way things were managed in Ireland. Here are some of his queries:

> 106 Whether the dirt and famine and nakedness of the bulk of our people might not be remedied, even though we had no foreign trade?

169 Whether it is possible the country should be well
improved, while our beef is exported and our labourers live upon potatoes?

235 Whether a scheme for the welfare of this nation
should not take in the whole inhabitants? And
whether it be not a vain attempt to project the flourishing of our Protestant gentry, exclusive of the bulk
of the inhabitants?

594 Whose fault is it if poor Ireland still continues poor?

Swift and Berkeley, and also Burke and Goldsmith, were
exalted to a high place in Yeats's imagination of the Irish
past. He thought of the eighteenth as 'that one Irish century
that escaped from darkness and confusion'. But Yeats is
building images of these writers for his own purposes as a
poet. They did not see themselves as part of an Irish tradition,
and they had little real sense of Ireland's past. This was something that would slowly grow in the following century.

Moving on now into that later century I would like to recall
one important aspect of the romantic movement that was
exerting a strong influence at this time, namely the revival of
interest in the past, in early literature, ballads and folk music.
The publication of the Ossian cycle of heroic poems, from
1760, by James Macpherson, although they were his own
work and not that of a genuine early bard, as he pretended,
did a great deal to stimulate interest in the Gaelic past. In
1789 Charlotte Brooke published her collection of poems
from the Irish, *Reliques of Irish Poetry*. Edward Bunting
collected Irish music and in 1796 he produced *The Ancient
Music of Ireland*. The Royal Irish Academy had been founded in 1786, and during the nineteenth century a growing
band of scholars and translators were to make available to
English readers the Irish literature of the past.

James Hardiman's *Irish Minstrelsy* (1831) offered English
translations of Irish songs and poems. The chief translator
was Thomas Furlong, whose English versions were refined
and Victorian, frequently missing the natural vigour and
directness of the originals. But the book served as a source
for other and better poets and translators, such as Ferguson
and Mangan. Ferguson criticised some of the translations and
offered his own versions which were considerably better.

In the course of the nineteenth century the revolutionary urge towards Irish independence (which led to an abortive rising in 1848, and later to the formation of the Fenian Brotherhood) combined with the romantic urge to suggest the promotion of an Irish national literature in English. Thomas Davis, with his fellow editors of *The Nation* (founded 1842), Charles Gavan Duffy and John Blake Dillon, tried to foster such a literature, but their political motivation was too patent. Yeats, who led the second and more successful attempt to create an Irish national literature in English, criticised Davis for a naiveté that produced propaganda rather than poetry, writing in his introduction to *A Book of Irish Verse*:

> No man was more sincere, no man has a less mechanical mind than Thomas Davis, and yet he is often a little insincere and mechanical in his verse. When he sat down to write he had so great a desire to make the peasantry courageous and powerful that he half believed them already 'the finest peasantry upon the earth'... and today we are paying the reckoning with much bombast.

Yeats wanted a literature that should be truly national and local but of the highest possible quality, a literature that should not be provincial in outlook but aware of the great masters of other nations, such as Homer and Balzac and Ibsen. He also wanted people to be aware of an Irish tradition of writing, and he consciously set out to promote this tradition. He helped to found the Irish Literary Society, and he wrote articles in Irish journals on the neglected Irish writers of the nineteenth century, Ferguson, Mangan, Carleton and Allingham. He reviewed current Irish writers and he drew up lists of the best Irish books.

The result of his enthusiasm and effort was a literary movement in Ireland in which there was a conscious turning to Irish themes in legend and history, and a conscious reflection of Irish life. Yeats helped to turn Synge away from French and Italian poetry to the Aran islands; he encouraged him to express a life that had never been expressed. The result was Synge's fine journal, *The Aran Islands,* and his peasant plays. The result of Yeats's work and that of his collaborators, Lady

Gregory, Edward Martyn, George Moore and others, was the growth of an Irish dramatic movement in a country where there had previously been no native drama at all.

Yeats wanted to revive poetic drama, and at one time he thought in terms of a little theatre in the London suburbs, but after a famous conversation in Duras House, Co. Galway, in the summer of 1897, between Yeats, Lady Gregory and Edward Martyn, the Irish Literary Theatre was born. The appeal for guarantors reveals their idealistic aim:

> We propose to have performed in the Spring of every year certain Celtic and Irish plays, which whatever be their degree of excellence will be written with a high ambition, and so to build up a Celtic and Irish school of dramatic literature . . . We will show that Ireland is not the home of buffoonery and easy sentiment, as it has been represented, but the home of an ancient idealism . . .

Sufficient guarantors came forward and the Irish Literary Theatre was formally established in 1899. At first English actors and actresses were used, but later W.G. Fay's company of Irish players combined with the new theatre group to form the National Theatre Society, and finally they found a permanent home in the Abbey Theatre, where they opened on 27 December 1904, with Yeats's *On Baile's Strand* and Lady Gregory's *Spreading the News*.

In the years that followed, the Abbey Theatre, as it henceforth came to be known, produced mainly Irish plays, with an occasional translation of a European classic. It survived a week of riots when Synge's *Playboy* was first performed, and it soon achieved world-wide fame. In 1911 and 1912 the company went on tour to America, and in spite of some opposition from nationalist circles, the tour was a great success, and universities in America began to study the new Irish drama.

With a few exceptions, notably William Carleton, the Anglo-Irish writers of the nineteenth century were drawn from the Anglo-Irish social class, from the families of the Protestant Ascendancy, some of whom lived in large houses on large estates. The Big House plays a significant part in Anglo-Irish fiction from Castle Rackrent itself to Springfield

House in Aidin Higgins' *Langrishe Go Down*. For this reason I have called Part II of this guide 'Views from the Big House.'

In the nineteenth century both the Protestant Ascendancy and their big houses were in decline. Catholic Emancipation, the Famine, land reforms, the gradual spread of education and the struggle for independence helped to bring forward writers from very different backgrounds. In the twentieth century Frank O'Connor and Patrick Kavanagh improvised an education for themselves. Brendan Behan got a good part of his at Borstal, where he was sent for his adolescent IRA activities. In his play *The Hostage* Behan offers an amusing definition of an Anglo-Irishman. His characters are discussing 'Monsewer', who speaks Irish, plays the pipes, and uses a Dublin brothel as a hideout for an IRA group:

Meg: Aren't you after telling me he was an Englishman?

Pat: He was an Anglo-Irishman.

Meg: In the name of God, what's that?

Pat: A Protestant with a horse.

Ropeen: Leadbetter.

Pat: No, no, an ordinary Protestant like Leadbetter, the plumber in the back parlour next door, won't do, nor a Belfast Orangeman, not if he was as black as your boot.

Meg: Why not?

Pat: Because they work. An Anglo-Irishman only works at riding horses, drinking whisky and reading double-meaning books in Irish at Trinity College.

It won't do to press Behan's definition too far, but he indicates the significant class distinctions that existed among Protestants, and he has a valid point in calling attention to the horse. In the past, at any rate, the possession of a horse was important. Under the penal laws Catholics were not permitted to own horses of greater value than £5. A famous Irish poem, 'The Lament for Art O'Leary', expresses the passionate grief of a wife whose husband, Arthur O'Leary, a colonel in the Austrian army, was outlawed and killed in Co. Cork for refusing to sell his famous mare to a Protestant for £5. Edith Somerville was a skilled horsewoman and became M.F.H. of the West Carbery Fox Hounds. Horses play a significant part in the R.M. stories and in the fiction of other Anglo-Irish writers.

The scene changes markedly in the twentieth century, though Yeats continued to admire horsemen. I doubt if Sean O'Casey was ever on horseback, and bicycles are more important than horses in the world of Flann O'Brien.

With or without horses the Anglo-Irish ceased to be an important social group after the establishment of the Free State, but the influence of their attitudes and their ways of seeing Ireland remained in literature. Yet at no time did it provide a strong enough tradition to dominate Anglo-Irish writing. In fact there is no strong central force binding together all the disparate trends in English writing in Ireland. To a large extent each man ploughs his own furrow, though some writers, like O'Connor and O'Faolain, O'Flaherty and Peader O'Donnell, share a common background and adopt similar modes of writing. Yet the five Dubliners I have chosen in Part IV all see Dublin in different ways and have little in common as writers; and it would be difficult to fit any two of the seven writers I have chosen in Part VI into a common pattern or tradition. Even Yeats and Synge, although they shared a common faith in folk-literature and deplored the vulgarity of the newspapers, took very different ways as writers. And yet, in spite of all this divergence, some general 'sense of Ireland' does emerge from the work of Anglo-Irish writers, as I hope to show in the next chapter.

3

A Sense of Ireland

As I embark on a chapter intended to point out some of the characteristic features of Anglo-Irish writing, I hear the voice of Blake over my shoulder: 'To generalize is to be an idiot.' What can there possibly be in common between novelists like Maria Edgeworth, William Carleton and Francis Stuart? Or between poets like Yeats and Patrick Kavanagh, playwrights like Synge and Denis Johnston? If we put the questions in this way the answer is 'very little'; but if we take a wider view of Anglo-Irish writing, without such sharp juxtapositions, we do find some recurring characteristics, some features shared in common, not by all the writers, but by many of them. If we keep in mind that 'Irishness' and 'a sense of Ireland' is not one thing but a multiple prism that reflects different things at different times and in different lights, then we may avoid Blake's charge of idiocy.

I said in the first chapter that there were no obvious features of style that clearly distinguished Anglo-Irish literature from English literature, but nevertheless there are some modes of imagination and expression that recur more often in the former. To begin with, the influence of an oral tradition is more clearly marked. It is natural that this should be so. The shanachie, or story teller, survived in Ireland into the twentieth century. One of the last notable ones was Timothy Buckley, the Tailor of Gougane Barra in West Cork. Eric Cross recorded his way of life, his personality and many of his stories in his delightful book, *The Tailor and Ansty*. Here the speaking voice comes clearly off the printed page. We would naturally expect this in stories recorded from oral versions. But we find it also in stories written for a reader's eye. Frank O'Connor and Michael McLaverty spring to mind.

26

O'Connor's well known story 'First Confession' begins: 'All the trouble began when my grandfather died and my grandmother — my father's mother — came to live with us. Relations in the one house are a strain at the best of times . . .' McLaverty's 'Evening in Winter' starts in a similar easy, colloquial way that suggests the speaking voice: 'Charley was six at the time, or maybe seven. His Mammie was beside him in a white apron, her hands on her lap doing nothing.'

In most of her novels Maria Edgeworth used a narrative style remote from common speech, a style that suggests a carefully wrought written pattern, employing periodic sentences and neatly balanced constructions. In the following passage from *Ennui* she is comparing the characters of two ladies, Lady Geraldine and Cecilia Delamere:

> With as much generosity as Lady Geraldine could show in great affairs, she [Cecilia] had more forbearance and delicacy of attention on everyday occasions. Lady Geraldine had much pride, and it often gave offence; Cecilia, perhaps, had more pride, but it never appeared, except upon the defensive; without having less candour, she had less occasion for it than Lady Geraldine seemed to have; and Cecilia's temper had more softness and equability. One had the envied art of appearing to advantage in public — the other, the more desirable power of being happy in private. I admired Lady Geraldine long before I loved her; I loved Cecilia long before I admired her.

In her preface to *Castle Rackrent* Maria Edgeworth uses a similar carefully wrought style, but in the story itself she was inspired to adopt the oral mode that would have been natural to her story teller, Thady Quirk. Although she avoids a full Irish dialect, that might have been difficult for her English readers, she succeeds in creating a vivid spoken idiom that is the right mode of discourse for the story she has to tell. This makes *Castle Rackrent* not only the most Irish but the liveliest and best of her novels.

Somerville and Ross, and George Moore, do not attempt to write complete stories or novels in an oral mode (with the possible exception of Moore's *Ulick and Soracha*) but, in their different ways, they make considerable use of the spoken word. Somerville and Ross had an accurate ear for the tones and turns of speech of the people around them, and many of the liveliest parts of the R.M. stories come to us in the voice of Slipper.

When we turn from the Big House writers to those who came from the common people we naturally find an indigenous oral mode. Carleton told stories before he wrote them down, and through his parents and the people around him he was still in touch with the oral tradition of Irish story tellers and folk singers. Although the adoption of Victorian literary modes confused and spoilt his writing, the basic oral idiom remains. In the prose of Patrick Kavanagh the tones and turns of country speech persist strongly. Joyce has a marvellous ear for Dublin speech, and though he has all styles at his command, in *Ulysses* the oral idiom is strongly present throughout the book. It is strong, too, in the work of Flann O'Brien, and it is scarcely necessary to mention the work of dramatists like Synge and Sean O'Casey, where we would naturally expect to find it.

Accompanying the strong and persistent oral influences in Anglo-Irish writing is a love of words and word play and a tendency to extravagance and flamboyance. Not only did Elizabethan usages persist in Ireland when they had died out in England, but the Elizabethan delight in what Dylan Thomas called 'the colour of saying' remained strong, encouraged perhaps by similar trends in Irish speech. In his book, *Ulster and Elizabethan English,* Professor Braidwood points out the parallel between Elizabethan English and Anglo-Irish English:

> The Elizabethans (or better the Tudors) discovered that the hitherto despised vernacular could be used with magnificent rhetorical effect, could even, because a living language of greater flexibility and inventiveness, surpass the traditional Latin. . . . Today probably only the Irishman, especially the southern Irishman, and some Welshmen, work in Elizabethan linguistic, mastering the language, where the rest of us, with pusillanimous notions of correctness and good taste hammered into us at school, let the language master us . . .

If ever an age had the gift of the gab, that age was the Elizabethan. If ever a nation had the gift of the gab, that nation is the Irish. It is not suggested for a moment that the Irish inherited the gift from the Elizabethans, for the Irish gift is of ancient origin and the nation has long been notorious for loquacity.

In his enthusiasm for a literary movement in Ireland Yeats made much of the traditional Irish love of rhetoric. In *Plays and Controversies* he quoted his father's words:

It is natural to an Irishman to write plays; he has an inborn love of dialogue and sound about him, of a dialogue as lively, gallant, and passionate as in the times of great Eliza. In these days an Englishman's dialogue is that of an amateur — that is to say it is never spontaneous. I mean in *real life*. Compare it with an Irishman's, above all a poor Irishman's reckless abandonment and naturalness, or compare it with the only fragment that has come down to us of Shakespeare's own conversation . . .

It is possible to exaggerate the natural liveliness and colour of Irish speech, but it does have a basis in reality. I still recall the words of my aunt in Co. Cork, when she was praising a vigorous, thriving baby: 'He's that strong, he'd suck the cork out of a whisky bottle.' Not long ago, when I was waiting for a bus in Dublin, I heard one woman say to another: 'She has the leather worn off her shoes with walkin' the streets.' In a Donegal pub I listened to a man explaining how rich and quick-growing the grass was in Co. Meath. To illustrate his point he said: 'If you laid your stick down in the grass in the evening you wouldn't find it in the morning.' These fragments of living speech are commonplace enough, and anyone who has lived in Ireland could easily recall similar or better examples, but they do indicate a natural delight in vivid expression that finds its counterpart in Anglo-Irish writing. Like the Elizabethan writers, many Anglo-Irish writers take pleasure in playing with words. At one end of the scale this gives us the apt malapropism, at the other end we have the elaborate word-making of *Finnegans Wake*. It is not surprising that the creator of Mrs Malaprop was an Anglo-Irish writer. Her misuse of words is highly entertaining, but some later malapropisms have a touch of genius. Captain Boyle's 'chassis' for 'chaos' — has almost passed into the language. One of my special favourites is the Tailor's use of 'alabastery'. He is driven to use it one day after the startling discovery that a passing woman didn't know the difference between a bull and a cow:

> 'She didn't know a bull from a cow. That is what started me thinking. Thon amon dieul! but I swear the world's gone to alabastery. It's queerer it's getting every day. Would you believe it that there are people nowadays who don't know wheat from barley and yet eat bread . . .?'

'Alabastery' seems to combine the suggestions of fragility, associated with alabaster, with those of corruption, wrongdoing, degeneracy and name-calling associated with 'bastardy'.

The Irish imagination plays not only with words, but with ideas and planes of reality. An element of fantasy is found widely in Anglo-Irish writing, together with a love of the marvellous and supernatural. The Gaelic tradition bears strongly in this direction and a story was expected to contain wonders. When Frank O'Connor showed some of his own stories to the Tailor, he complained that they were lacking in marvels.

With or without marvels, there is a generous measure of fantasy in Anglo-Irish writing. Certain names will spring to mind at once. Joyce, with the huge fantasy of nighttown in the Circe episode of *Ulysses;* James Stephens, with his philosophers, leprechauns, Greek and Celtic Gods; Flann O'Brien, potently mixing Dublin cowboys with Finn McCool and mad Sweeney, and St Augustine with James Joyce; Mervyn Wall writing of medieval monks, witches and devils.

There is fantasy of a different kind in the plays of Yeats. In his reaction against both the commercial theatre of England and the social realism of Ibsen he wanted 'an art of the theatre that shall be joyful, fantastic, extravagant, whimsical, beautiful, resonant and altogether reckless' (*Plays and Controversies*). His first play, *The Countess Cathleen*, tells of a noble countess who sells her soul to the devil for gold to relieve the famine stricken peasantry. The opening lines speak of a strange, dark world:

—at Tubber-Vanach
A woman met a man with ears spread out,
And they moved up and down like a bat's wing.

In *Purgatory,* written in the last year of his life, the language is closer to everyday speech, but the action is strange and un-earthly. The souls of the dead return to re-enact the crises of their past lives in a ruined house, suddenly lit up.

Yeats was fascinated by magic and the occult, and the elements of dream and fantasy are found everywhere in his poetry, where sometimes 'Magical unicorns bear ladies on their backs' (*Meditations in Time of Civil War*).

Even in the more down-to-earth writers, who do not offer us marvels, there is often a strong spice of fantasy. We find it in the R.M. stories and in Frank O'Connors tales, and it is clearly evident in the plays of Synge and Lady Gregory.

In the first chapter I spoke of those writers whom I called 'insiders' being involved in the Irish situation, 'being moulded', to use Yeats's words, 'by influences that were moulding Ireland.' Most Anglo-Irish writers are caught up in a love-hate relationship with Ireland, in a way that is unlikely to happen between English writers and England. English writers are not haunted by history in the way that Irish writers are. History is more remote. The last civil war in England was over three hundred years ago, but in Ireland there are still many who remember the civil war (after the Treaty was signed in 1921) and the 'troubles' that preceded it. Even the younger writers, who were born after the partition of Ireland and the civil war, find themselves turning to the past with the backward look that is so common in Ireland. Seamus Heaney, for example, the youngest writer I have chosen for detailed dis-cussion in this book, has a deep and troubled awareness of the Irish past. His first collection, *Death of a Naturalist,* which deals mainly with his farm and country background, also contains two poems recalling the grim horrors of the great Famine. In his later volume, *North*, Part I is dominated by the past and Part II deals with the legacy of history in contemporary Ulster.

It is interesting to compare Heaney with the English poet, Philip Larkin. No shadows from English history fall on to Larkin's pages, and he has little sense of roots. In the poem 'I Remember, I Remember', he ironically dismisses any significance in the town of his birth, Coventry, when he later passes through it by train:

> 'Was that,' my friend smiled, 'where you "have your
>   roots"?'
> No, only where my childhood was unspent,
> I wanted to retort, just where I started . . .
> 'You look as if you wished the place in Hell,'
> My friend said, 'judging from your face.' 'Oh well,
> I suppose it's not the place's fault,' I said.

Heaney's attitude to the place of his birth is entirely different, as he himself explains (see page 261). He sees it as deeply significant. It was symbolically placed in 'the split culture of Ulster'.

No Anglo-Irish writer adopts towards Ireland, or a part of Ireland, the attitude of indifference that Larkin assumes towards Coventry. There may be hatred, but it is the kind of hatred that is the reverse side of love. Patrick Kavanagh understood this when he wrote in *The Irish Times* (13 Nov. 1943): 'The artist may hate his subject with that kind of furious enthusiastic hate which is a form of love, and which equally with love is a giver of life in literature.'

It is in the North of Ireland that the darkest shadows of history fall today. Another northern writer, Ben Kiely, catches the shadow in an ironic line from his recent novella, *Proxopera,* which deals with a terrorist incident: 'Ireland of the welcomes and the bomb in the pub and the bullet in the back'. His words recall those written by Louis MacNeice in his 'Autumn Journal' more than forty years earlier:

> The land of scholars and saints:
> Scholars and saints my eye, the land of ambush,
> Purblind manifestoes, never-ending complaints,
> The born martyr and the gallant ninny;
> The grocer drunk with the drum,
> The land-owner shot in his bed . . .

It may be naive to regard Ireland as a land of saints and scholars, but religion plays an important part in the Irish experience. In Ireland the suicide rate is very low and the rate of church attendance is very high. 'Nothing thrives in Ireland,' said George Moore, 'like a convent, a public house and a race-meeting.' Anglo-Irish literature includes some pious fiction, like the novels of Canon Sheehan, who wrote with affection and humour about the dedicated lives of parish priests and curates. There are also some fine studies of priests and members of religious orders. Kate O'Brien's *The Land of Spices* comes to mind, which tells the story of a sensitive and intelligent mother-superior of a convent. A novel by Francis MacManus, *The Greatest of These,* portrays a bishop healing a breach with a parish priest in a spirit of deep Christian charity. Another truly religious figure of a different kind is Father Mellowes in Francis Stuart's *Redemption.* Francis Stuart, whose work I will discuss later, is in fact a deeply religious writer.

One aspect of religion in Ireland, found in both Catholic and Protestant camps, is a severe puritanism. This sometimes took the form of personal asceticism. An extreme case was that of Matt Talbot, a Dublin labourer, whom the Church officially declared 'Venerable' in 1976. (He was already 'A Servant of God'.) Talbot was a heavy drinker in his youth but 'about 1884 he took a pledge of total abstinence and his whole life changed. . . . He slept on a wooden plank with a wooden block for pillow, restricted his food most days to dry bread and cocoa without milk or sugar, and began to attend Mass daily, rising before 4 a.m. for this purpose . . . ' In 1925 he collapsed and died on the way to early Mass. 'It was then discovered that he wore a chain on his waist and a lighter chain on one arm, on the other arm a cord, and a chain below one knee, immediately below the knee-cap. . . . He gave most of his wages to charity, and sought to conceal his prayers and fasts.' (Boylan, *A Dictionary of Irish Biography*).

Austin Clarke, who fought a long battle against Irish puritanism in his poetry, tells us in his autobiography, *Twice Round the Black Church,* of the attempts made to subdue nature by Father Boyle, the Prefect of Studies at Belvedere College. The conditions of community life made it difficult for him to fast, so he turned to other mortifications:

> Flagellation can be overheard and so Father Boyle devised silent methods of subduing nature. . . . Most of his experiments in pain were not, however, practical: he tried to cut the holy name of Jesus on his chest with a razor blade but suffered too much loss of blood, and the application of a heated iron caused ugly dangerous sores. His last attempt was almost fatal. He was giving a retreat in a convent near Greystones and one evening, passing a lonely wood, saw a bed of nettles. Hastily stripping, he jumped into the bed, rolled among the nettles and was severely poisoned.

A commoner manifestation of the puritan spirit was the attempt to purify literature and conduct, especially from the lurking dangers of sex. Hence the notorious Censorship Board of the forties that banned so much worth-while Anglo-Irish literature. Even *The Land of Spices*, mentioned above, was banned because of one reference to a homosexual relationship. Hence, too, the ban on dancing imposed by some bishops, and enforced by their parish priests. In *Kavanagh's Weekly*, No. 7, Patrick Kavanagh recalled an occasion in his youth when a large crowd, dancing on a beautiful summer evening at Annavackey Cross, were dispersed by clerical command:

> The melodeons were playing and life itself was dancing, when up the road on his bicycle came a little black priest who could not have been long out of college. This little man got up on the fence and ordered us to disperse, which we did. I was ashamed of those young boys and girls, who knew so little about their own religion not to realize that this little man was acting from impulses that were pernicious.

As we might expect, the power and authority of the Catholic Church in Ireland has evoked strong protest. An anti-clerical stance is a familiar attitude in Anglo-Irish literature, from George Moore onwards. In *Juno and the Paycock*, Boyle delivers himself of a solemn cliché to his butty, Joxer: 'I'm goin' to tell you somethin', Joxer, that I wouldn't tell to anybody else — the clergy always had too much power over the people in this unfortunate country.'

Joyce's Stephen Dedalus refused to serve a religion in which he no longer believed, and an attitude of resistance and dissent is a strong element in Anglo-Irish literature during the first half of the twentieth century. Nowadays we can afford to laugh at the excesses of religious zeal. It may be too soon to say, with John Montague in his 'Patriotic Suite', that

> Puritan Ireland's dead and gone,
> A myth of O'Connor and O'Faolain

but it has profoundly changed. We should also remember that, while O'Connor and O'Faolain fought manfully against a narrow censorship and a narrow religion, they were not simply anti-clerical writers. They treat some aspects of puritanism with satire and irony, but they both understand and sympathise with priests, and they write revealingly of the religious dimension in Irish experience.

The elements that combine to create a sense of Ireland do not all cast dark shadows. There are lighter and more amusing aspects. The word 'Irish' has acquired a humorous though unflattering dictionary definition. I quote from *Chambers Twentieth Century Dictionary* (new ed. 1972): 'characteristic of Ireland, esp. blundering, self-contradictory, bull-making'. The Irish bull was not always Irish. The term 'bull', meaning an illogicality, came into use in the early seventeenth century and the *Shorter Oxford Dictionary* tells us that the epithet 'Irish' is a late addition. It seems to have attached itself to the 'bull' at the end of the eighteenth century, which tells us something of the attitude of the English to the Irish at that time. A bull can be a blunder, but it can also be a shaft of wit. The truth is often paradoxical, as we can discover from the New Testament. As Sir John Mahaffy once remarked: 'An Irish bull is always pregnant.'

Although it was not begotten in Ireland, the bull has found good pasture there. A dispossessed people with few capable leaders finds a natural defence in wit and humour, also in naivety and simplicity. If you can appear to be a fool, you are less likely to be punished as a knave. I am not denying that there are simpletons and fools in Ireland, but simply pointing out that the role of simpleton was often a useful one to adopt.

Associated with Irish simplicity and blundering is the Irish habit of improvisation. An 'Irish' gate may be anything except a gate designed for the purpose — a few strands of wire, a hurdle laced with furze bushes, the head of an old iron bedstead, even an old cart. It was a maxim with Sir Tallyhoo O'Shaughlin in *Castle Rackrent* that a car [i.e. cart] was the best gate. Unfortunately he killed himself by trying to jump over one on horseback.

An astute German observer of things Irish, Heinrich Böll, in his *Irish Journal*, noticed the ubiquitous use of the safety-pin in Ireland. He saw this 'Celtic clasp' as the symbol of Irish improvisation. Certainly improvisation plays its part in Anglo-Irish literature. One of the finest passages in Maria Edgeworth's *Ennui* is a vivid account of an improvised carriage. Lord Glenthorn, on a tour of Ireland in his private carriages, is obliged to hire a local vehicle for his servants, when their carriage breaks down:

> From the inn-yard came a hackney chaise, in a most deplorably crazy state; the body mounted up to a prodigious height, on unbending springs, nodding forwards, one door swinging open, three builds up, because they could not be let down, the perch tied in two places, the iron of the wheels half off, half loose, wooden pegs for linch-pins and ropes for harness. The horses were worthy of the harness; wretched little dog-tired creatures, that looked as if they had been driven to the last gasp, and as if they had never been rubbed down in their lives; their bones starting through their skin; one lame, the other blind; one with a raw back, the other with a galled breast; one with his neck poking down over his collar, and the other with his head dragged forward by a bit of a broken bridle, held at arms' length by a man dressed like a mad beggar, in half a hat and half a wig, both awry in opposite directions; a long tattered great coat, tied round his waist by a hay-rope; the jagged rents in the skirts of this coat showing his bare legs, marbled of many colours; while something like stockings hung loose about his ankles. The noises he made, by way of threatening or encouraging his steeds, I pretend not to describe.

In an indignant voice I called to the landlord — 'I hope these are not the horses — I hope this is not the chaise, intended for my servants.'

The innkeeper, and the pauper who was preparing to officiate as postillion, both in the same instant exclaimed —

'*Sorrow* better chaise in the country!'

'*Sorrow*!' said I — 'what do you mean by sorrow?'

'That there's no better, plase your honour, can be seen. We have two more to be sure — but one has no top, and the other no bottom. Anyway there's no better can be seen than this same.'

Lord Glenthorn is a stranger in Ireland. His surprise and indignation is treated with humorous irony by the author. In spite of his protests, and the protests of his English valet and French cook, they are obliged to accept the chaise offered them:

In vain the Englishman, in monotonous anger, and the Frenchman in every note of the gamut, abused Paddy: necessity and wit were on Paddy's side; he parried all that was said against his chaise, his horses, himself, and his country, with invincible comic dexterity, till at last both his adversaries, dumbfounded, clambered into the vehicle, where they were instantly shut up in straw and darkness.

Improvisation may well suit the Irish temperament but there were also historical reasons for it. Plain poverty was one. Another was the fear of attracting the sharp eye of the landlord or his agent. If a brand new gate was erected, suggesting improvement and prosperity, the landlord might increase the rent. It was safer to make do with a few strands of old wire or a furze bush.

Bulls, blunders, simplicity, improvisation — all these may be seen as aspects of provincialism. Irish people lived far from the centres of government, fashion or learning. Among the peasants we find simpletons and comic blunderers. Among the landlords we find eccentrics. A rural squire could be, and often was, a law to himself. He could lock up his wife for seven years, like Sir Kit Rackrent (or Colonel Maguire, who is actually cited by Maria Edgeworth), or indulge in formidable drinking bouts, such as those described by Sir Jonah Barrington in his chapter on 'Irish Dissipation in 1778'. Eccentrics are plentiful, both in reality and in fiction, from the Rackrent squires to the characters in Flann O'Brien's novels.

I seem to be in danger of reviving the myth of the rollicking squire and the clowning peasant, that flourished in the nineteenth century. This, in the words that George Birmingham uses to introduce the *Recollections of Jonah Barrington,* is 'The Ireland of Charles Lever . . . an Ireland of gay irresponsibility, of heavy drinking and good fellowship, of sport and sympathy with the sporting side of lawlessness, of nimble wit and frivolous love-making, of courage, honour, hard fighting and hard riding, of poverty turned into a jest.'

All this is a far cry from the Ireland of today, although there is plenty of fantasy, extravagance, improvisation and eccentricity in contemporary Anglo-Irish literature. But this literature is no longer provincial. Anglo-Irish writers are now part of an international scene.

In short it is nearly impossible to describe or define the Irish imagination as it appears in Anglo-Irish literature since 1800; and yet there is a colouring, arising partly from the subject matter, partly from ways of treating that subject matter, that makes this literature distinguishable from English writing in England or America or anywhere else where there is a literature in English. I have indicated some of the things that contribute to this colouring. I hope that the many passages quoted and discussed in the rest of this book will expand and illuminate the sense of Ireland that emerges from Anglo-Irish writing.

PART TWO

i. Views from the Big House

Chapter 4   Maria Edgeworth
Chapter 5   Somerville and Ross
Chapter 6   George Moore

ii. Views from smaller houses

Chapter 7   William Carleton
Chapter 8   Frank O'Connor
Chapter 9   Patrick Kavanagh

Supplement to Part Two. Notes on some other nineteenth century writers: poetry, prose, drama.

4

Maria Edgeworth

Maria Edgeworth, the eldest daughter of Richard Lovell Edgeworth, was born in England in 1767, but she came with her father to his Irish estate at Edgeworthstown, Co. Longford, when he settled down there in 1782. She helped her father in the management of the estate and kept accounts for him. Although she left Edgeworthstown from time to time to travel in England and on the continent, it became her home and base. She observed the life around her with sharp clear eyes, but also with affection and amusement. Naturally enough she saw the Irish scene from the viewpoint of her class, as an inmate of the Big House. Most of her father's tenants, and the servants of the house with whom she came in daily contact, belonged to the ranks of the 'lower Irish', as she frequently calls them. But the limitations of her class do not invalidate her observations and her skill in portraying the Irish scene.

One of the most vivid and interesting accounts of life in Ireland at the end of the eighteenth century is to be found in Richard Lovell Edgeworth's *Memoirs*. He began to write these, with Maria's assistance, in 1808, but he died before he finished them. Maria continued them, knowing that she was carrying out her father's wishes, and she gives her own accounts of events and scenes that affected the whole family. In the second volume of the *Memoirs,* which is her own work, she does not write in her usual manner as a novelist with a strong moralising tendency, but as a straightforward recorder of events and scenes. Even if she had never written any novels she would still be worth attention for her share in the *Memoirs*. She has a vivid and absorbing chapter on the rebellion of 1798, when the Edgeworths were forced to leave their home and seek refuge in the town of Longford. Shortly after the landing of French troops under General Humbert in Killala Bay, the news came to Edgeworthstown that rebels, armed with pikes, were pouring into the neighbourhood from Co. Westmeath. The reports were exaggerated but the family moved to Longford for safety, leaving behind them their English housekeeper. There was no room for her in the crowded family carriage, and she volunteered to stay until it was sent back for her. That evening a large body of rebels entered the village and were about to attack the house, but they were dissuaded by one of their leaders, whose wife had formerly been helped by the housekeeper. She had lent her the sum of sixteen shillings to pay the rent of flax ground. Instead of attacking the house the rebels sent a deputation of six men to interview the housekeeper:

> The six men went to the back-door, and summoned the housekeeper; one of them pointed his blunderbuss at her, and told her, that she must fetch all the arms in the house; she said she had none. Her champion asked her to say if she remembered him — 'No; to her knowledge she had never seen his face.' He asked if she remembered having lent a woman money to pay her rent of flax-ground the year before? 'Yes,' she remembered that, and named the woman, the time and the sum. His companions were thus satisfied of the truth of what he had asserted. He bid her not to be *frighted*, 'for that no harm should happen to her, nor any belonging to her; not a soul should get leave to go into her master's house; not a twig should be touched, nor a leaf harmed.'

Next morning the housekeeper was able to join the rest of the family in Longford. Here they experienced more troubles, and Mr Edgeworth was roughly handled by an Orange mob before being rescued by British officers with drawn swords. Finally, after the defeat of the rebel forces, the family returned home:

> When we came near Edgeworth-Town, we saw many well known faces at the cabin doors, looking out to welcome us. One man, who was digging in the field by the roadside,

when he looked up as our horses passed, and saw my father, let fall his spade and clasped his hands; his face, as the morning sun shone upon it, was the strongest picture of joy I ever saw. The village was a melancholy spectacle; windows shattered and doors broken. But though the mischief done was great, there had been little pillage. Within our gates we found all property safe; literally not a twig touched, nor a leaf harmed. Within the house everything was as we had left it — a map that we had been consulting was still open on the library table, with the pencil and slips of paper containing the first lessons in arithmetic, in which the young people had been engaged the morning we had been driven from home; a pansy, in a glass of water, which one of the children had been copying, was still on the chimney-piece. These trivial circumstances, marking repose and tranquillity, struck us at this moment with an unreasonable sort of surprise, and all that had passed seemed like an incoherent dream. The joy of having my father in safety remained, and gratitude to Heaven for his preservation. These feelings spread inexpressible pleasure over what seemed to be a new sense of existence. Even the most common things appeared delightful; the green lawn, the still groves, the birds singing, the fresh air, all external nature, and all the goods and conveniences of life, seemed to have wonderfully increased in value, from the fear into which we had been put of losing them irrecoverably.

Most of Maria Edgeworth's books have an explicit moral or educational aim. The titles alone are sufficiently indicative — *The Parent's Assistant* (1796), *Practical Education*, (1798), *Moral Tales* (1801). Even in the novels she frequently glides into the tone and manner of the moral essay. There is one remarkable exception, where the authorial voice is strictly confined to preface, epilogue and notes. For this reason *Castle Rackrent* has been rightly singled out as her greatest creative achievement; yet when I first read it I wondered why it had been so highly praised. It seemed no more than a mildly amusing brief chronicle of four eccentric and extravagant Irish squires. Then I read it again — and, because I found myself required to teach it, several more times. With each reading I found new levels and shades of wit and irony, and my respect for Maria Edgeworth increased. I now agree with the general view that the book is the first Anglo-Irish classic, and still one of the greatest.

On the surface the narrative is simple and straightforward. Thady Quirk, an illiterate old steward, devoted to the family he serves in Castle Rackrent, tells the story of four Rackrent squires, Sir Patrick, Sir Murtagh, Sir Kit and Sir Connolly. The story of Sir Patrick is brief and prefatory, and it mainly concerns his death following a birthday carouse. Sir Murtagh and Sir Kit, whom Thady served and loved (or professed to love), are dealt with more fully; but more than half the book is devoted to the History of Sir Connolly Rackrent, which was written later than the first part, and is sub-titled: 'Continuation of the Memoirs of the Rackrent Family'. All the squires, with the exception of Sir Murtagh, are idle, dissipated and extravagant, and they meet untimely deaths, while their neglected estate sinks deeper into debt and dilapidation, until finally Sir Connolly loses it altogether. Sir Murtagh, who marries a widow of the Skinflint family, with an eye on 'the great Skinflint estate', is a mean extortioner, who never keeps open house like Sir Patrick, but sends away his tenants on rent days without their customary glass of whisky. But if he is mean about hospitality, he is extravagant in his obsessive passion for litigation. He sells part of the estate in order to carry on his suit against the Nugents of Carrickashaughlin, but dies before he achieves success, bursting a blood vessel in the course of a quarrel with his wife over money.

The bare outline of the Rackrent story suggests a grimly moral tale of extravagance and ruin, but it is, in fact, richly comic. The author pretends that she is simply editing the oral memoirs of Thady Quirk, and she states in the preface: 'Several years ago he related to the editor the history of the Rackrent family, and it was with some difficulty that he was persuaded to have it committed to writing.' By using the persona of Thady, 'whose partiality to *the family* in which he was bred and born must be obvious to the reader,' and who speaks in his own vernacular idiom, the author marks a comic and ironic contrast between the loyal praises of the old retainer, so concerned for the honour of *the family*, and what he actually tells us of their selfishness and folly.

When Sir Kit succeeds Sir Murtagh he notices old Thady one morning and tosses him a guinea, as his horse rears up:

> I thought I never set my eyes on a finer figure of a man — quite another sort from Sir Murtagh, though withal *to me,* a family likeness — A fine life we should have led, had he stayed amongst us, God bless him! — he valued a guinea as little as any man — money to him was no more than dirt, and his gentleman and groom, all belonging to him the same — but the sporting season over, he grew tired of the place, and having got down a great architect for the house, and an improver for the grounds, and seen their plans and elevations, he fixed a day for settling with the tenants, but went off in a whirlwind to town, just as some of them came into the yard in the morning.

Sir Kit goes off to gamble at Bath, leaving his estate in the hands of an agent. 'The agent', Thady tells us, 'was one of your middle men who grind the faces of the poor, and can never bear a man with a hat upon his head — he ferreted the tenants out of their lives — not a week without a call for money — drafts upon drafts from Sir Kit — but I laid it all to the fault of the agent; for, says I, what can Sir Kit do with so much cash, and he a single man?'

The simple loyalty of Thady is used to make a devastating exposure of the utter selfishness and irresponsibility of Sir Kit. But the story remains comic, with threads of the bizarre, the grotesque and even the macabre. Sir Kit marries a Jewish heiress to raise money and pay his debts. When she refuses to part with her valuable diamond cross, he locks her up in her room for seven years. Meantime he makes advances to other women, and finally, when rumours of his wife's death get abroad, he is called to account by the brothers of the ladies he has philandered with. He fights three duels; kills the first man, fires over the head of the second, whose wooden leg sticks fast in a 'new ploughed field', and is himself killed by the third man, and brought home on a hand-barrow. His captive wife, once released, returns to England, for, says Thady, 'she had taken an unaccountable prejudice against the country and everything belonging to it'. There is a rich irony in Thady's final reflections upon her, when he gives her the blame and exonerates Sir Kit:

> But from first to last she brought nothing but misfortunes amongst us; and if it had not been all along with her, his honor Sir Kit would have now been alive in all appearance. — Her diamond cross was, they say, at the bottom of it all; and it was a shame for her, being his wife, not to show more duty, and to have given it up when he condescended to ask so often for such a bit of a trifle in his distresses, especially when he all along made it no secret he married for money. But we will not bestow another thought upon her. — This much I thought it lay upon my conscience to say, in justice to my poor master's memory.

Thady's special pleading for his worthless master is nicely exposed when we hear him describing her valuable diamond cross as 'such a bit of a trifle'; and when he excuses Sir Kit's barbarous treatment of his wife by saying that he 'all along made it no secret that he married for money', we find ourselves being asked to believe that insult lessens injury.

The ironic contrast between Thady's words, and the actual behaviour of the masters he professes to love and honour, provides the main comic element of the book, but some commentators have found a deeper and harsher irony in Thady's own behaviour. His simple loyalty is only a mask. He is secretly seeking to undermine them, and to get their estate for his son Jason, whose conduct he frequently deplores. In the words of James Newcomer (*Maria Edgeworth the Novelist* (1967), p. 151): 'The true Thady reflects intellect and power in the afflicted Irish peasant, who in generations to come will revolt and revolt again. He is artful rather than artless, unsentimental rather than sentimental, shrewd rather than obtuse, clear-headed rather than confused, calculating rather than trusting. There is less affection in our view of the true Thady, but now we have to feel a degree of admiration for him.'

It is true that Thady appears to co-operate with Jason, his clever, artful son, who ends up in possession of Castle Rackrent. When a good farm falls vacant, Jason obtains the lease at a very modest rent, assisted by his father: 'I spoke a good word for my son, and gave out in the country that nobody need bid against us.' Later on, when Sir Connolly is deeply in debt and just escapes arrest by his election to Parliament, Thady hob-nobs with the debtor's agent and introduces him to Castle Rackrent and to his son Jason. In spite of this damning evidence it seems to me wrong to inter- pret Thady as a calculating fifth-columnist, working to under- mine the Rackrents. Such an interpretation, influenced by the history of revolt in Ireland after 1798, is at odds with the general tone and texture of the book. There is ambiguity and inconsistency in Thady, but this is part of his character as Maria Edgeworth sees it. In her brief epilogue she calls attention to the mixture of qualities in the Irish character. 'All the features in the foregoing sketch were taken from the life, and they are characteristic of that mixture of quickness, simplicity, cunning, carelessness, dissipation, disinterested- ness, shrewdness and blunder, which in different forms, and with various success, has been brought upon the stage or delineated in novels.'

Thady is not consistent, and his behaviour is certainly ambiguous, but his character is wholly convincing and alive. By using him as a narrator Maria Edgeworth achieves a warmth and humour in this book that is not found in her more conventional novels and tales.

She wrote many other novels, but only three of them deal with Irish experience: *Ennui* (1809), *The Absentee* (1812) and *Ormond* (1817). The first two of these formed part of a series of *Tales of Fashionable Life*. *Ennui* is almost more a tract than a novel, showing how the Earl of Glenthorn, who suffers from the ennui of an idle, fashionable life, is cured by disinheritance and honest work. The plot is melo- dramatic and highly improbable (the Earl turns out really to be the son of an Irish peasant), but there are some lively and amusing scenes when the Earl and his servants travel through Ireland. *The Absentee* is more convincing but the patently overt moral aim of the book acts as a strait-jacket. Lord Colambre, the hero, son of Lord Clonbrony, the absentee landlord of a great Irish estate, decides to visit his father's property. He travels incognito and his eyes are opened to the iniquities of his father's agents. He helps a poor widow who is being defrauded of her lease, and finally reveals himself as the future master of the estate. He persuades his father and mother to return to their Irish home, and we leave him with the happy prospect of marriage to the lady he loves: 'Happy as a lover, a friend, a son; happy in the consciousness of having restored a father to respectability, and persuaded a mother to quit the feverish joys of fashion for the pleasures of domestic life; happy in the hope of winning the whole heart of the woman he loved . . . ' This brief outline is unfair to the variety of observation and humour in the novel, but virtue is so clearly defined and upheld that the reality of the book suffers.

In *Ormond* the moral aim is less obtrusive, though it is still there in the background. There is greater speed and complexity in the narrative, so that the occasional tendency to fall into a reflective essay on human behaviour does not impede the narrative movement. There is a greater variety of characters than in *Ennui* or *The Absentee,* and a fuller and more detailed presentation of the Irish scene. Harry Ormond, the hero, is a kind of Irish Tom Jones, 'a warm-hearted, generous, imprudent young man, with little education, no literature, governed more by feeling than by principle, never upon any occasion reasoning, but keeping right by happy moral instincts'. These words are used by Maria Edgeworth to describe the original Tom Jones at the point where her hero reads Fielding's novel with passionate absorption and admiration, and closes the book 'resolved to be what he admired and shine forth an Irish Tom Jones.' He is strongly tempted to seduce Peggy Sheridan, a gardener's daughter, but desists when he discovers that one of his favourite servants, Moriarty Carroll, is in love with the girl and hopes to marry her. Indeed, his natural generosity prompts him to do all he can to assist Moriarty's marriage. Maria Edgeworth comments on the episode. 'A fortunate escape. Yes; but when the escape is owing to good fortune, not to prudence; to good feeling, not to principle; there is no security for the future.'

The tone of this suggests a primness that is not really characteristic of the book. Maria Edgeworth is very sure of her own rational moral values, but she also likes Ormond as a fallible human being, and she makes her readers like him too. After the firm and clear statement of moral principle quoted above, she proceeds to praise Ormond in the very next paragraph:

> Ormond was steady to his promise towards Moriarty, to do him justice he was more than this, he was generous, actively, perseveringly generous, in his conduct to him. With open heart, open purse, public overture, and private negotiation with the parents of Peggy Sheridan, he at last succeeded in accomplishing Moriarty's marriage.

There is a greater variety of tone in *Ormond* than in the two earlier novels. She can be gay with King Corny of the Black Isles, witty with Sir Ulick O'Shane, pert and conceited with M. de Connal. Even in her descriptive passages there is often liveliness and wit. Introducing Sir Ulick to the reader she deftly sums up his succession of three wives: 'The first he loved and married imprudently, for love, at seventeen. The second he admired, and married prudently, for ambition, at thirty. The third he hated, but married from necessity, for money, at five-and-forty.' Although *Ormond* has not the inspired originality of *Castle Rackrent*, it deserves a place on the Anglo-Irish bookshelf.

5

Somerville and Ross

Somerville and Ross are widely separated in time from Maria
Edgeworth but they have some links with her. Edith Somerville and Violet Martin (she took the pen name of Martin
Ross) were cousins, and they had a distinguished great grandfather in common, Lord Chief Justice Bushe. His wife was a
friend of Maria Edgeworth, and in their book, *Irish Memories*
(1917), Somerville and Ross published some of the letters
that Maria wrote to her.

Irish Memories reveals not only their link with Maria and
their admiration for her, but also the world they shared in
common, in spite of the wide gap in time, the world of the
Big House. The Somervilles came from Drishane House at
Castletownsend in Co. Cork, the Martins from Ross House in
Co. Galway. The first chapter of *Irish Memories* contains
Violet Martin's reminiscences of Ross and her brother Robert:

> He was born on June 17th, 1846, the first year of the Irish
> famine, when Ireland brimmed with a potato-fed popula-
> tion, and had not as yet discovered America. The quietness
> of untroubled centuries lay like a spell on Connemara, the
> country of his ancestors; the old ways of life were unques-
> tioned at Ross, and my father came and went among his
> people in an intimacy as native as the soft air they breath-
> ed. On the crowded estate the old routine of potato
> planting and turf cutting was pursued tranquilly; the people
> intermarried and subdivided their holdings; few could read,
> and many could not speak English. All were known to the
> Master, and he was known and understood by them, as the
> old Galway people knew and understood; and the sub-
> divisions of the land were permitted, and the arrears of

rent were given time, or taken in boat-loads of turf, or worked off by day-labour, and eviction was unheard of. It was give and take, with the personal element always warm in it: as a system it was probably quite uneconomic, but the hand of affection held it together, and the tradition of centuries was at its back.

Somerville and Ross lived at a time when the old semi-feudal personal relationships between landlord and tenant had broken down, and they remember the past with nostalgic regret. Violet Martin recalls her father's dealings with a widow who could not pay her rent:

One instance will give, in a few sentences, the relation between landlord and tenant, which, as it would seem, all recent legislation has sedulously schemed to destroy. I give it in the words of one of the tenants, widow of an eye-witness.

'The widow A., down by the lake-side [Lough Corrib — about three miles away], 'was very poor one time, and she was a good while in arrears with her rent. The Master sent to her two or three times, and in the end he walked down himself after his breakfast, and he took Thady' (the steward) 'with him. Well, when he went into the house, she was so proud to see him, and "Your Honour is welcome!" says she, and she put a chair for him. He didn't sit down at all, but he was standing up there with his back to the dresser, and the children were sitting down one side the fire. The tears came from the Master's eyes; Thady seen them fall down the cheek. "Say no more about the rent," says the Master, to her, "you need say no more about it till I come to you again." Well, it was the next winter the men were working in Gurthnamuckla, and Thady with them, and the Master came to the wall of the field and a letter in his hand, and he called Thady over to him. What had he to show him but the Widow A.'s rent that her brother in America sent her!'

It will not happen again; it belongs to an almost forgotten *régime,* that was capable of abuse, yet capable too of summoning forth the best impulses of Irish hearts. The end of the *régime* was not far away, and the beginning of the end was already on the horizon of Ross.

Somerville and Ross had a deep love of, and respect for, the tradition of the Big Houses, but they were unsentimental about those who lived in them in their own times. Their finest novel, *The Real Charlotte*, has a sharp satiric edge. Bruff House is the home of an effete aristocratic family, cheated by their agent and no longer really respected by the local community. Sir Benjamin Dysart is a fairly harmless yet still malicious invalid, confined to a bath chair pushed by a man-servant. From his chair he threatens unsuspecting guests with his stick. His wife, who is described as 'a clever woman, a renowned solver of acrostics in her society paper, and a holder of strong opinions as to the prophetic meaning of the Pyramids,' is considerably relieved by her husband's confinement to a bath-chair:

> Lady Dysart had in her youth married, with a little judicious coercion, a man thirty years older than herself, and after a long and, on the whole, extremely unpleasant period of matrimony, she was now enjoying a species of Indian summer, dating from six years back, when Christopher's coming of age and the tenants' rejoicing thereat, had caused such a paroxysm of apoplectic jealousy on the part of Christopher's father as, combining with the heat of the day, had brought on a stroke. Since then the bath-chair and James Canavan had mercifully intervened between him and the rest of the world, and his offspring were now able to fly before him with a frankness and success impossible in the old days.

Lady Dysart is now happily freed to spend a warm summer morning working in the flower garden with her dutiful daughter Pamela:

> It was altogether a scene worthy in its domestic simplicity of the Fairchild Family, only that instead of Mr Fairchild, 'stretched on the grass at a little distance with his book,' a bronze-coloured dachshund lay roasting his long side in the sun; and also that Lady Dysart, having mistaken the young chickweed in a seedling pan for the asters that

should have been there, was filling her bed symmetrically with the former, an imbecility that Mrs. Sherwood would never have permitted in a parent.

The extracts I have quoted above (taken from chapter VIII, which presents the Dysart family to the reader) convey the dry, astringent flavour of the irony that runs through the book, sometimes reminiscent of Jane Austen. But the treatment of Charlotte Mullen, the central figure in the book, carries a more sombre weight. We are first introduced to her sullenly and unsentimentally watching over the death-bed of her aunt, and resisting the dying woman's wish to do more for 'little Francie', a younger niece, who has not been provided for in her will:

Miss Charlotte gave the fire a frugal poke, and lit a candle in the flame provoked from the sulky coals. In doing so some ashes became embedded in the grease, and taking a hair-pin from the ponderous mass of brown hair that was piled on the back of her head, she began to scrape the candle clean. Probably at no moment of her forty years of life had Miss Charlotte Mullen looked more startlingly plain than now, as she stood, her squat figure draped in a magenta flannel dressing-gown, and the candle light shining upon her face. The night of watching had left its traces upon even her opaque skin. The lines about her prominent mouth and chin were deeper than usual; her broad cheeks had a flabby pallor; only her eyes were bright and untired, and the thick yellow-white hand that manipulated the hair-pin was as deft as it was wont to be.

Somerville and Ross were writing *The Real Charlotte* at the time when Douglas Hyde was founding the Gaelic League and Yeats was rediscovering the world of Celtic legend. But all this was outside the world of Lismoyle, where the Dysarts and the Mullens lived. Indeed the novel was aptly described by Sean McMahon (writing in *Eire-Ireland,* winter 1968) as 'a kind of hand-book for the Ireland of the non-Celtic twilight.' Their Ireland was observed closely and faithfully, and described with power and humour. Their imagination may be limited by their class background, by a lack of sympathy with the peasantry, and with the growing national consciousness, but it is nonetheless vivid and powerful.

The Real Charlotte stands alone as the finest novel written by Somerville and Ross, though the others are not without interest. The best of the uneven remainder is *The Big House of Inver*. This novel was written by Edith Somerville alone and published in 1925. Violet Martin had died in 1915, but the idea for the book had been jointly conceived, and in any case Edith maintained the joint authorship for all her subsequent books, pointing out that 'an established Firm does not change its style and title, when, for any reason, one of its partners may be compelled to leave it'.

The opening chapter of *The Big House of Inver* recalls *Castle Rackrent*. We are told how 'five successive generations of mainly half-bred and wholly profligate Prendevilles rioted out their short lives in the Big House, living with country women, fighting, drinking, gambling'. Christopher Fitzrobert Prendeville fights a fantastic duel, up to his waist in the sea. The seconds, also out in the sea, have just done their duty by acting jointly as godfathers to his infant son:

> A grand sight it was, and a great day altogether for the parish of Ross Inver! Everyone was delighted. Four of the finest young gentlemen in the country walking out to their middles in the water for all the world to see, and they in their Sunday clothes, with their tall hats on them! No four finer young men in the Globe of Ireland! Well, and isn't it a shame for the like o' them to be shooting at one another? Oh pity! Beat on the donkey Mickel Paudyeen! Let ye be hirrying before we'll be late! What call have we coming here at all and we to be late?

Unfortunately Christopher is killed in the duel, and later on his widow leases the Big House to the Rev. Harry D'Arcy, whose Rectory has been burned to the ground in tithe riots:

> The Reverend Harry was not an improving tenant, nor can the company he kept be said to have been of an improving nature. He was a bachelor and a sportsman, and he filled the Big House with his sporting friends, among whom was young Lord Ballyfail, that dashing blade of whom it was said;

'No dog with a tinkettle tied to his tail,
Made half such a racket as Lord Ballyfail!'
The Reverend Harry and his young friends seem to have
made a very considerable racket in the Big House, one of
the party even, with a regrettable lack of originality,
dragging a favourite hunter up the hall-doorsteps, riding
him, slipping and clattering, across the marble-paved hall
into the great dining-room, and there setting him to jump
the dinner-table, with the result that the horse broke
several legs of the table and one of his own, so that he had
to be shot where he fell. The rider, who was drunk, escaped uninjured.

All this is background history to the main story, which
concerns the struggle of Shibby Pindy (Miss Isabella Prendeville), the illegitimate daughter of Capt. James Prendeville,
the feckless master of Inver House, to re-establish the family
name and fortunes through the marriage of her handsome
legitimate brother. Her struggle fails, and at the end the Big
House is burnt down by her hopeless father. The story is told
with considerable skill and force, though it lacks the keen
edge of *The Real Charlotte*.

The most popular of all the writings by Somerville and
Ross are their short stories, several of them hunting stories,
about the Irish R.M. Collections of these stories were published separately as follows: *Some Experiences of an Irish R.M.*
(1899), *Further Experiences of an Irish R.M.* (1908), *In Mr
Knox's Country* (1915). The best of the stories are to be
found in the first two volumes, which are often issued
together as *Experiences of an Irish R.M.*

R.M. stands for Resident Magistrate, an office that no
longer exists in the Republic of Ireland, though it still survives
in Ulster. A Resident Magistrate was frequently an outsider,
appointed to dispense justice in an unfamiliar Irish town, so
that the appointment had a semi-colonial flavour. Major
Yeates, the 'hero' of the R.M. stories, is of Irish extraction,
but he was educated in England and he served in the British
Army in India. He is something of a foreigner in 'the wilds
of Ireland', feeling that 'civilisation seemed a thousand miles
off', and he spends long lonely evenings in his house,
Shreelane, with only the rats for company.

Shreelane, too, has affinities with Castle Rackrent. It is large and dilapidated and draughty, and there is no bath. The neighbouring Aussolas Castle, home of the eccentric Mrs Knox, is even closer to Rackrent in its age and incongruities. The hall, panelled in dark oak, is hung with family portraits. In the venerable dining-room the guests eat a perfect salmon on a chipped kitchen dish.

This background might suggest a sombre set of stories but the prevailing tone is one of hilarious comedy. In 'Trinket's Colt', for example, the Major finds himself inextricably involved in stealing a colt from Mrs Knox, with whom he has just dined. Flurry Knox, her grandson, wishing to procure a horse for the Major, remembers that his grandmother had promised him a colt. Since she does not show any sign of redeeming her promise, Flurry decides to help himself, and he gets Slipper (his kennel man) and the Major to assist him in removing the colt. Mrs Knox calls in the police to search for it, and, to avoid discovery, the ingenious Flurry hides the colt in a small sandpit among furze bushes. Here the Major himself is forced to retreat when Mrs Knox suddenly appears on the scene:

> I writhed deeper into the furze bushes, and thereby discovered a sandy rabbit run, along which I crawled, with my cap well over my eyes, and the furze needles stabbing me through my stockings. The ground shelved a little, promising profounder concealment, but the bushes were very thick, and I laid hold of the bare stem of one to help my progress. It lifted out of the ground in my hand, revealing a freshly cut stump. Something snorted, not a yard away; I glared through the opening, and was confronted by the long, horrified face of Mrs Knox's colt, mysteriously on a level with my own.
>
> Even without the white diamond on his forehead I should have divined the truth; but how in the name of wonder had Flurry persuaded him to couch like a woodcock in the heart of a furze brake? For a full minute I lay as still as death for fear of frightening him, while the voices of Flurry and his grandmother raged on alarmingly close to me. The colt snorted, and blew long breaths through his

wide nostrils, but he did not move. I crawled an inch or two nearer, and after a few seconds of cautious peering I grasped the position. They had buried him.

A brief extract from this tale cannot do justice to the comedy. It is easier to demonstrate wit than humour. The stories need to be read in full to get the proper comic flavour. But I would like to cite one more example, from 'Lisheen Races, Second-hand'. In this story we find Major Yeates unexpectedly entertaining a friend of his student days at Oxford, who arrives in Ireland as private secretary to Lord Waterbury. It is soon clear that the friendship is a thing of the past:

The stout young friend of my youth had changed considerably. His important nose and slightly prominent teeth remained, but his wavy hair had withdrawn intellectually from his temples; his eyes had acquired a statesmanlike absence of expression, and his neck had grown long and birdlike. It was his first visit to Ireland, as he lost no time in telling me, and he and his chief had already collected much valuable information on the subject to which they had dedicated the Easter recess [the liquor question in Ireland]. He further informed me that he thought of popularizing the subject in a novel, and therefore intended to, as he put it, 'master the brogue' before his return.

Finding the company of Leigh Kelway something of a strain, Major Yeates jumps at the suggestion made by Flurry Knox that they should take him to 'some typical country races, got up by the farmers at a place called Lisheen'. But a series of comic misadventures with horses and vehicles prevents the party from ever reaching the races. They do, however, manage to reach a pub where many of the race-goers have gathered on their way home. Here they get a graphic description of one of the races from the lips of the partly drunken Slipper, who had taken a hand in this race by landing a blow with his stick on a horse's backside.

'Well, when I seen them comin' to me, and Driscoll about the length of the plantation behind Clancy, I let a couple of bawls. "Skelp her, ye big brute!" says I. "What good's in ye that ye aren't able to skelp her?"'

The yell and the histrionic flourish of his stick with which Slipper delivered this incident brought down the house. Leigh Kelway was sufficiently moved to ask me in an undertone if 'skelp' was a local term.

'Well, Mr Flurry, and gintlemen,' recommenced Slipper, 'I declare to ye when owld Bocock's mare heard them roars she stretched out her neck like a gandher, and when she passed me out she give a couple of grunts, and looked at me as ugly as a Christian.

"Hah! says I, givin' her a couple o' draws o' th' ash plant across the butt o' the tail, the way I wouldn't blind her; "I'll make ye grunt!" says I, "I'll nourish ye!"

"I knew well she was very frightful of th'ash plant since the winter Tommeen Sullivan had her under a side-car. But now, in place of havin' any obligations to me, ye'd be surprised if ye heard the blaspheemious expressions of that young boy that was ridin' her; and whether it was over-anxious he was, turnin' around the way I'd hear him cursin', or whether it was some slither or slide came to owld Bocock's mare, I dunno, but she was bet up agin the last obstackle but two, and before ye could say "Shnipes," she was standing on her two ears beyond in the' other field! I declare to ye, on the vartue of me oath, she stood that way till she reconnoithered what side would Driscoll fall, an' she turned about then and rolled on him as cosy as if he was meadow grass!'

Slipper stopped short; the people in the doorway groaned appreciatively; Mary Kate murmured: 'The Lord save us!'

'The blood was dhruv out through his nose and ears,' continued Slipper, with a voice that indicated the cream of the narration, 'and you'd hear his bones crackin' on the ground! You'd have pitied the poor boy.'

'Good heavens!' said Leigh Kelway, sitting up very straight in his chair.

'Was he hurt, Slipper?' asked Flurry casually.

'Hurt is it?' echoed Slipper in high scorn; 'killed on the spot!' He paused to relish the *dénouement* on Leigh Kelway. 'Oh, devil so pleasant an afthernoon ever you seen; and, indeed, Mr Flurry, it's what we were all sayin', it was a great pity your honour was not there for the likin' you had for Driscoll.'

As he spoke the last word there was an outburst of singing and cheering from a car-load of people who had just pulled up at the door. Flurry listened, leaned back in his chair, and began to laugh.

'It scarcely strikes one as a comic incident,' said Leigh Kelway, very coldly to me; 'in fact, it seems to me that the police ought —'

'Show me Slipper!' bawled a voice in the shop; 'show me that dirty little undherlooper till I have his blood! Hadn't I the race won only for he souring the mare on me? What's that you say? I tell ye he did! He left seven slaps on her with the handle of a hay-rake — '

There was in the room in which we were sitting a second door, leading to the back yard, a door consecrated to the unobtrusive visits of so-called 'Sunday travellers.' Through it Slipper faded away like a dream, and, simultaneously, a tall young man, with a face like a red hot potato tied up in a bandage, squeezed his way from the shop into the room.

'Well, Driscoll,' said Flurry, 'since it wasn't the teeth of the rake he left on the mare, you needn't be talking!'

Leigh Kelway looked from one to the other with a wilder expression in his eye than I had thought it capable of. I read in it a resolve to abandon Ireland to her fate.

The discomfiture of Leigh Kelway is not yet complete. He is forced to travel home in a crowded outside car with the drunken spectators from the races. His car collides with the Bianconi mail car which carries his chief, the Earl of Waterbury, and under his baleful eye he struggles up from the ditch where he has been thrown, with Driscoll hanging on his neck. In this story, as in the others, there is wit as well as humour, and the writers have a gift for the lively and imaginative phrase.

Lionel Fleming, a cousin of Edith Somerville, who grew up in Co. Cork in the early years of this century, paid her a handsome tribute. 'There are no other works which I can pick up to read in London that can so instantly give me back that feeling of furze-bushes and ragged stone walls; of moisture dripping from tall trees; of flat, slated mansions; and of the sea-mist creeping in from the Atlantic. And the dialogue never puts a foot wrong — the idiom is always true, and one can almost hear the accent.' An even greater tribute was paid by Frank O'Connor, who himself moved in the Gaelic and Republican world that Somerville and Ross ignored. He put the R.M. stories alongside *Dubliners:* 'With Joyce's *Dubliners, The R.M.* is the most closely observed of all Irish story books, but, whereas Joyce observes with cruel detachment, the authors of *The R.M.* observe with love and glee.'

6

George Moore

George Augustus Moore was born at Moore Hall, Muckloon, Lough Carra, Co. Mayo, in 1852. Moore Hall, a fine Big House of cut stone was built in 1785 by his grandfather (also George Moore) who had made something of a fortune in the wine trade with Spain. The house is now a burnt-out shell (it was burnt by Republican guerillas in 1923) but on one blackened wall there is a plaque commemorating John Moore, who was the first President of the Republic of Connaught. This John, son of George Moore the builder of the house, joined General Humbert when he landed in 1798 at Killala Bay and captured Castlebar. But John was soon to find himself in prison, and he languished there until his death a year later. The Moores claimed descent from Sir Thomas More, who was executed for his resistance to King Henry VIII, but in Ireland they seem to have been mainly Protestants. George Moore's father, however, married into the Roman Catholic gentry, when he took Mary Blake of Ballinafad for his wife, and his children were brought up as Catholics.

The young George Moore grew up in a semi-feudal community and he gives us some vivid glimpses of it in his autobiographical work, *Hail and Farewell*. On Sundays the gentry rode to Mass in their carriages along a road where the respectful peasantry walked:

Along this road our tenantry used to come from the villages, the women walking on one side (the married women in dark blue cloaks, the girls hiding their faces behind their shawls, carrying their boots in their hands, which they would put on in the chapel yard), the men walking on the other side, the elderly men in traditional

61

swallow-tail coats, knee-breeches and worsted stockings; the young men in corduroy trousers and frieze coats. As we passed the women curtsied in their red petticoats; the young men lifted their round bowler-hats; but the old men stood by, their tall hats in their hands. At the bottom of every one was a red handkerchief, and I remember wisps of grey hair floating in the wind. Our tenantry met the tenantry of Clogher and Tower Hill, and they all collected round the gateway of the chapel to admire the carriages of their landlords. We were received like royalty as we turned in through the gates and went up the wooden staircase leading to the gallery, frequented by the privileged people of the parish — by us, and by our servants, the postmaster and postmistress from Ballyglass, and a few graziers. In the last pew were the police, and after the landlords these were the most respected.

George Moore soon began to look away from Ireland, to London and Paris. When his father died in 1870 he dropped all pretence of preparing for an army career and became a student of art. He went to Paris in 1873, and, although he soon abandoned the idea of becoming a painter, he stayed on, enjoying the café society of Montmartre and mixing with writers and painters. But the failure of rents on his Irish estates put an end to his Parisian life. This was the time of the Land League in Ireland, when the peasants were combining against the landlords to get their rents reduced. So Moore turned to writing to earn money, and eventually moved to London. At this time he had little interest in Ireland and his attitude to it was largely one of contempt. In 1887 he published a sketch of Ireland and Irish conditions, entitled *Parnell and His Island* (it had appeared in French as *Terre D'Irlande*, the year before). In this book he sees Ireland as 'a primitive country and a barbarous people'. Even in Dublin there is mostly poverty and ignorance. As for the countryside, it is bleak and depressing. He describes the peasant farmers as follows:

In their tiny fields, not divided by luxuriant hedges like the English fields, but by miserable stone walls, which give an unspeakable bleakness to the country, they cultivate oats and potatoes. With the former crop and the pig they pay the landlord, with the latter they live. As Balzac says, 'Les beaux sentiments fleurissent dans l'âme quand la fortune commence de dôrer les meubles;' and never have I observed in these people the slightest aesthetic intention – never was a pot of flowers seen in the cottage window of an Irish Celt.

You want to know what Ireland is like? It is like the smell of paraffin oil! The country exhales the damp, flaccid, evil smell of poverty . . .

With one exception Moore's early novels have English settings and deal with English experience. *A Mummer's Wife* (1884) is set in the pottery town of Hanley in the English 'Black Country', and *Esther Waters* (1894), the most popular of Moore's novels, has its background in Sussex and London. This novel is a deeply-moving human document telling the story of a servant-girl who is seduced and abandoned. Her illegitimate baby is a formidable handicap in her desperate struggle to find work, but she refuses to abandon him, and fights a lonely and ultimately successful battle for survival.

In later life Moore turned to the past for his themes and settings. In the *The Brook Kerith: A Syrian Story* (1916) he tells of a Jesus who survives the ordeal on the cross and is nursed back to health by his friend Joseph of Arimathea. Subsequently he becomes a shepherd in an ascetic community of Essenes. After this Moore told the story of the famous medieval lovers in *Heloise and Abelard* (1921).

Moore wrote a great many books, but only a few of them deal with his Irish experience. Nevertheless he made a significant contribution to Anglo-Irish literature, and for a time he was deeply involved with the Irish literary movement. This was at the turn of the century, when he was drawn into the affairs of the Irish Literary Theatre by Edward Martyn and W. B. Yeats. Long before this he had written a novel of Irish life called *A Drama in Muslin* (1884). He later revised and reissued the book under the changed title of *Muslin* (1915). This novel was largely the result of Moore's spending a winter in Ireland, in 1883–4, when he observed and took part in the social scene at the Vice-Regal Court in Dublin.

The 'muslin' of the book's title refers to the muslin dresses worn by the young ladies attending the Vice-Regal Ball at Dublin Castle. This was the highlight of the Dublin 'Season', to which the wives of the landed gentry brought their daughters in the eager hope of finding suitable husbands for them. These hopes were frequently disappointed, and Moore tells us why in *Parnell and His Island:*

> The girls outnumber the men in the proportion of three to one, the competition is consequently severe; and it is pitiable to see these poor muslin martyrs standing at the door, their eyes liquid with invitation, striving to inveigle, to stay the steps of the men as they pass by. But although these balls are little else for the young girls than a series of heartbreaks, nevertheless the most abject basenesses are committed to secure an invitation.

In the novel Moore brings out the comedy as well as the pathos of the marriage market, and the novel is critical of the dependent position of women. In his preface he tells us that his subject is the same as that of *A Doll's House.* Alice Barton escapes from the traditional feminine role of the period. She achieves a measure of economic independence, and she chooses a husband for herself — not a lord or a squire, but a humble and useful dispensary doctor.

In spite of some lively social comedy, the picture of Ireland that we get from the book is a sombre one, haunted by shadows of poverty and the land war. The contrasts between rich and poor are drawn sharply. When the carriages of the gentry are held up on their way to the Castle Ball the poor gaze in upon the guests:

> Despite the weather the streets were lined with vagrants, patriots, waifs, idlers of all sorts and kinds. Plenty of girls of sixteen and eighteen came out to see the 'finery'. Poor little things in battered bonnets and draggled skirts, who would dream upon ten shillings a week; a drunken mother striving to hush a child that cries beneath a dripping shawl, a harlot embittered by feelings of commercial resentment; troops of labourers; hang-dog faces, thin coats, torn shirts; Irish-Americans, sinister faced and broad brimmed. Never

were poverty and wealth brought into plainer proximity. In the broad glare of the carriage lights the shape of every feature, even the colour of the eyes, every glance, every detail of dress, every stain of misery was revealed to the silken exquisites who, a little frightened, strove to hide themselves within the scented shadows of their broughams; and in like manner the bloom on every aristocratic cheek, the glitter of every diamond, the richness of every plume, was visible to the wondering eyes of those who stood without in the wet and cold.

Mrs Barton remains steadfastly opposed to her daughter's marriage and forbids her husband to attend the wedding. Only two friends are present at the simple ceremony, and the couple drive through the rain to the station on their way to London, where Dr Reed has bought a practice in Notting Hill. Their last images of Ireland are sad ones: 'Through the streaming glass they could see the strip of bog; and the half-naked woman, her soaked petticoat clinging about her red legs, piling the wet peat into the baskets thrown across the meagre back of a starveling ass.'

A little later they pass an eviction scene, 'a dozen policemen grouped round a roadside cottage, out of which furniture had just been thrown'. On an impulse Alice suggests that they should pay the rent for this hapless family. But it turns out that they owe five years' rent – more than the young couple can pay. Their last words have a ring of hopelessness, even though they are seasoned with a little spice of anti-clerical wit, very typical of Moore:

'You believe then that this misery will last for ever?'
'Nothing lasts in Ireland but the priests. And now let us forget Ireland, as many have done before us.'

At the end of this novel Moore is turning his face away from Ireland, but ten years later his interest in the country of his birth was dramatically re-awakened through his contact with some of the leaders of the Irish literary movement. In the overture to *Ave*, the first volume of his partly fictional autobiography, *Hail and Farewell*, he tells us how one night in London Edward Martyn suddenly said to him: 'I wish I knew

enough Irish to write my plays in Irish.' Moore was astonish-
ed. 'You'd like to write your plays in Irish! I exclaimed. I
thought nobody did anything in Irish except bring turf from
the bog and say prayers.'

But Moore's imagination began to play on Ireland, and
before long he was approached by Martyn and Yeats to
help them found a Literary Theatre in Dublin. Moore had
had some experience of the London theatre, and he had
written a play, *The Strike at Arlingford.* Eventually he
became deeply involved in the Irish literary movement, and
for a time he was enthusiastic about the Gaelic League and
the revival of the Irish language. In 1901 he moved to Dublin
to live for some years in Ely Place. The literary results of his
Irish phase, which lasted about ten years, are to be found in
a volume of short stories, *The Untilled Field,* a novel, *The
Lake,* and most substantial of all, the autobiography, *Hail
and Farewell.* These books have a special place in Irish
literary history, but all of them are worth reading for themselves.

The Untilled Field was begun with the intention of providing some literary models for the new writers of Irish that it
was hoped would come forward as a result of the Gaelic
League's enthusiastic propaganda. Moore wrote the stories in
English and they were translated into Irish by Taidgh
O'Donoghue and published in Dublin by Seeley, Bryers &
Co., in 1902, under the title *An T-Ur Gort, Sgealta.* The book
proved to be a dead duck; 'a very pretty book of which
nobody took any notice, and that the Gaelic League could
not be persuaded to put in its window', as Moore wryly
remarks in the preface to the second edition of the book in
English (1904). He published the stories in English in order
to find some readers. Although he began the book in his
enthusiasm to assist the cause of Gaelic, the stories naturally
reflect Moore's interests and obsessions. In writing to his
London publisher, T. Fisher Unwin, he said:

A very flamboyant title for my book has occurred to me
'The Sin Against the Holy Ghost'. I believe religious
minded young men and women have been puzzling their
heads over this sin. I believe the sin to be the sin against

life. All that tends to diminish, to impoverish and to humiliate life is the sin against the Holy Ghost and the theme of my book is that the excessive Catholicism that prevails in Ireland tends to diminish the vitality of the human plant . . .

There is a strong anti-clerical bias in some of the stories but it is less consistent than Moore seems to suggest. Indeed he admits in his preface that 'the somewhat harsh rule of Father Maguire set me thinking of a gentler type of priest, and the pathetic figure of Father MacTurnan tempted me.' The two stories in which Father MacTurnan appears, 'A Letter to Rome' and 'A Playhouse in the Waste', are among the best in the collection. The gentle priest's desire to help his poor parishioners takes bizarre forms, and the comedy and pathos are strangely and effectively mingled.

'Home Sickness' is another moving story, telling of the love-hate relationship of James Bryden with his home district in the west of Ireland. He returns from New York to convalesce in Ireland and almost stays on to marry Margaret Dirken, but he is repelled by the weakness and incompetence and submissive humility of the people. He goes back to his Bowery bar, but he is haunted by memories of Margaret and the past:

> There is an unchanging, silent life within every man that none knows but himself, and his unchanging, silent life was his memory of Margaret Dirken. The bar-room was forgotten and all that concerned it and the things he saw most clearly were the green hill-side, and the bog lake and the rushes about it, and the greater lake in the distance, and behind it the blue line of wandering hills.

As this final paragraph shows, Moore was finding a prose rhythm to suit the reflective mood of his stories.

The Lake was originally planned as part of *The Untilled Field* collection, but it became more than a short story. Its theme is the struggle that takes place in the heart and mind of a priest as he begins to discover his real thoughts and feelings, which are quite out of keeping with the impersonal conscience of the religious tradition he belongs to. The trau-

matic event that causes Father Gogarty to search his heart
occurs before the story begins, and we learn of it from his
thoughts and memories, and later from an exchange of letters.
By his harsh words in a Sunday sermon on chastity he causes
a young school-mistress to leave the parish (Rose Leicester in
the earlier, Nora Glynn in the later, editions of the novel).
She was pregnant and she resolutely declined to tell the priest
the name of the child's father. Later, as the priest paces to
and fro by the lake, he deeply regrets his uncharitable words.
He slowly comes to realise that he loves the girl he had driven
away, and the awareness changes his life. Moore wrote in a
letter to his brother: 'Rose Leicester represents the spring
tide and her breath awakens Gogarty. He gets up and goes in
search of life. The story is no more than a sun myth. The
earth is frozen in dogma and the sun comes and warms it
to life.' At the end of the book the priest escapes to a new
life in America by swimming across the lake at night, leaving
his clerical clothes on the bank so that people will imagine
him drowned, and putting on civilian clothes that he had
previously hidden on the other side. The novel ends as he still
hears the sounds of the lake on the deck of the steamer
leaving Cork for America: 'There is a lake in every man's
heart,' he said, 'and he listens to its monotonous whisper year
by year, more and more attentive till at last he ungirds.'

The lake is partly symbolic of the deep waters of instinc-
tual and emotional life that lie hidden in everyone; but it is
also a real lake that forms the backdrop to the whole novel.
The story unfolds in the priest's mind as he paces by the lake,
and Moore deliberately restricts himself to the method of
imaginative reverie. He tells us in the preface that 'to keep
the story in the key in which it was conceived, it was necessary
to recount the priest's life during the course of his walk by
the shores of a lake, weaving his memories continually,
without losing sight however, of the long, winding, mere-like
lake, wooded to its shores, with hills appearing and disappearing into mist and distance.' The mood of reverie is skilfully
caught in the slow-moving and delicate rhythms of the prose,
and Moore has made apt use of symbol and image. *The Lake*
works in a narrower and more restricted mode than *Esther
Waters,* but it is still a fine novel.

The last work that grew out of Moore's Irish phase is something entirely different. *Hail and Farewell* is a partly fictional autobiographical account of Moore's involvement with the Irish literary world at the turn of the century. He claims in his amusing preface, 'Art without the Artist', that Nature, not he, is the real author of the book:

> . . . for years I believed myself to be the author of *Hail and Farewell,* whereas I was nothing more than the secretary, and though the reader may doubt me in the sentence I am now writing, he will believe that I am telling no more than the truth when the narrative leads him to Coole Park and he meets the hieratic Yeats and Lady Gregory out walking, seeking living speech from cottage to cottage, Yeats remaining seated under the stunted hawthorn usually found growing at the corner of the field, Lady Gregory braving the suffocating interior for the sacred cause of Idiom. And the feeling that there is something providential in the art of *Hail and Farewell* will be strengthened when the reader comes upon Yeats standing lost in meditation before a white congregation of swans assembled on the lake, looking himself in his old cloak like a huge umbrella left behind by some picnic-party; and raising his eyes from the book, the reader will say: This is Nature, not Art!

The book is witty and amusing and essential reading for any one interested in the Irish literary movement. Although Moore is clearly not an impartial witness, and the tone of mockery colours his reminiscences, yet he brings vividly before us many of the significant scenes and occasions in those interesting years. The major figure in the memoirs is, of course, W.B. Yeats, and he is the major target of Moore's mockery. One of the funniest parts of the book is that describing the collaboration of Yeats and Moore in the attempt to write a play for the Irish Literary Theatre. The subject chosen was the legend of Diarmuid and Grania. Lady Gregory had brought the two writers together at Coole Park, but collaboration proved very difficult. Moore found it hard to accept the kind of idiom that Yeats wanted, excluding many simple modern words ('soldier', for instance had to be 'fighting man'), and in a heated moment he exclaimed: 'I'd sooner write the play in French.'

Why not write it in French? Lady Gregory will translate it.

And that night I was awakened by a loud knocking at my door, causing me to start up in bed.

What is it? Who is it? Yeats!

I'm sorry to disturb you, but an idea has just occurred to me.

And sitting on the edge of the bed he explained that the casual suggestion that I preferred to write the play in French rather than in his vocabulary was a better idea than he had thought at the time.

How is that, Yeats? I asked, rubbing my eyes.

Well, you see, through the Irish language we can get a peasant Grania.

But Grania is a King's daughter. I don't know what you mean, Yeats; and my French —

Lady Gregory will translate your text into English. Taidgh O'Donoghue will translate the English text into Irish, and Lady Gregory will translate the Irish text back into English.

And then you'll put style upon it? And it was for that you awoke me?

But don't you think a peasant Grania —

No, Yeats, I don't, but I'll sleep on it and tomorrow morning I may think differently. It is some satisfaction, however, to hear that you can bear my English style at four removes. And as I turned over in the hope of escaping from further literary discussion, I heard the thin, hollow laugh which Yeats uses on such occasions to disguise his disapproval of a joke if it tells ever so little against himself.

Moore often makes us laugh at Yeats. But he makes us laugh at nearly everyone else, including himself. Every age and every literary movement has aspects of absurdity. Moore had a keen nose for absurdity and a gift for exposing it on the printed page. But his intention, as Dr Cave tells us in his excellent introduction to his recent annotated edition of *Hail and Farewell* (1976), is to liberate the Irish imagination: 'Absurdity is an inevitable part of the human condition and, in Moore's opinion, to recognise that fact is a truly civilizing

experience. Thus the theme of the book — liberation for
Ireland, and its method — liberation through laughter, are
perfectly matched.'

7

William Carleton

Patrick Kavanagh once claimed in a BBC talk that William Carleton was one of the two great native writers of Ireland (the other being James Joyce). Yeats also staked a high claim for Carleton. His list of the thirty best Irish books, published in the *Daily Express* (Dublin) on 27 February 1895, contains three by Carleton: *Fardorougha the Miser, The Black Prophet,* and *Traits and Stories of the Irish Peasantry.* At the time Yeats made his list, Carleton's unfinished autobiography had not been published. It was added to, and published, by Frances Cashel-Hoey in 1896. Carleton's own portion of it was published separately in 1968, with a brief preface by Patrick Kavanagh, in which he states that Carleton wrote 'two books and a great deal of melodramatic trash'. His two books 'are the *Traits and Stories* and this unfinished autobiography'.

My own reading of Carleton supports Kavanagh's choice of the two best books. 'Trash' may be too harsh a word for the novels, but their reality, shining through in occasional passages of detailed and authentic description, is destroyed by crude melodrama. Here, for example, is a passage from *Valentine McClutchy, the Irish Agent or Chronicles of the Castle Cumber Property* (1845). 'In truth . . . the diabolical and cowardly crime of Phil McClutchy towards their sweet and unoffending sister, had changed her three brothers from men into so many savage and insatiable Frankensteins, resolved never to cease dogging his guilty steps, until their vengeance had slaked its burning thirst in his caitiff blood.' Similar writing is to be found in *Fardarougha* and *The Black Prophet;* and yet, in these crude and clumsy novels there are passages which, in Brian Cleeve's words, 'are like windows on the dark and secret peasant Ireland of the early nineteenth century.' *(Dictionary of Irish Writers)*. Carleton's strength lies in his knowledge of an Ireland that existed beyond the range of the Big Houses. Yeats, who edited a selection of *Stories from Carleton* (1889), saw him as 'a great Irish historian', for 'the history of a nation is not in parliaments and battlefields, but in what the people say to each other on fair-days and high days, and in how they farm and quarrel and go on pilgrimage. These things Carleton has recorded.'

Carleton was born near Clogher, in Co. Tyrone, in 1794. He tells us that his family was humble but respectable. He was born in a small house in a poor townland, but he objected strongly to a local artist's imaginary illustration of his birthplace (in the 1842 edition of *Traits and Stories*), calling it 'as vile-looking a hovel as ever sheltered a human being'. He goes on to say (in the *Autobiography*): 'I remember the cottage in which I was born. It was a long, low house, with a kitchen as you enter, and two other rooms, one at each side of it.'

Carleton's father had little formal education but his memory was a remarkable storehouse of folk traditions, legends and stories, and he spoke Irish and English with equal fluency. His mother was less fluent in English, 'although she spoke it with sufficient ease for all the purposes of life'. She was a fine singer, especially of folk songs in Irish. All this information is given us in the opening chapter of the *Autobiography*. The book is written in a straightforward style and is free from Carleton's besetting sin of over-writing. At times the book reminds me of William Cobbett's autobiographical writings. Both men have the same ingenuous pride in their own achievements, and both have a strong sense of humour. Carleton's account of his youthful attempt to walk on water is delightfully told. The book is a valuable and entertaining record, not only of Carleton's early life, but of the world he moved in, the hidden Ireland of small farms and fairs, of pilgrimages, hedge-schools, folk music, legends and story telling.

But Carleton's major work is the *Traits and Stories of the Irish Peasantry* (1830-33). Some of the stories in this collection are flawed by the same melodrama that disfigures the novels; this is especially true of the more serious ones, such as 'Wildgoose Lodge'. Carleton is, through no fault of his own, an uneducated and unself-critical writer. Most of his work could be greatly improved by an editor with a blue pencil. He has little sense of form, and he writes too much. But he has what no editor can supply — abundant zest and humour, and keen powers of observation.

One of his best known stories is 'Denis O'Shaughnessy Going to Maynooth', which illustrates both his virtues and his vices. It deals with a basic theme in Irish life, a young man's struggle to become a priest. As Carleton himself tells us:

> The highest object of an Irish peasant's ambition is to see his son a priest. Whenever a farmer happens to have a large family, he usually destines one of them for the Church, if his circumstances are at all such as can enable him to afford the boy a proper education. This youth becomes the centre in which all the affections of the family meet. He is cherished, humoured in all his caprices, indulged in his boyish predilections, and raised over the heads of his brothers, independently of all personal or relative merit in himself. The consequence is that he gradually becomes self-willed, proud, and arrogant, often to an offensive degree; but all this is frequently mixed up with a lofty bombast, and an undercurrent of strong, disguised affection, that render his early life remarkably ludicrous and amusing.

Carleton begins the story in a tone of mockery; Denis' pedantry and self-importance are humorously exposed. Before long he decides that his family must call him 'sir' or 'Dionysius', instead of the familiar 'Dinny', and that he must eat mutton and beef with a knife and fork. 'I'm not the man now to be placed among the other riff-raff of the family over a basket of potatoes, wid a black clerical coat upon me, and a noggin of milk under my arm.' The night that his mother learns of this change in her son's life, she has a dream:

> I thought we were all gother somewhere that I can't rightly remimber; but anyhow, there was a great sight of people in

it, an' high doins goin' on in the atin' way. I looked about me, an' seen ever so many priests dressed all like the Protestant clergy. Our Dinis was at the head of them, wid a three-cocked hat an' a wig upon him: he was cuttin' up beef an' mutton at the rate of a weddin', and dhrinkin' wine in metherfuls.

'*Musha*, Dinis,' says myself, 'what's all this for?'

'Why,' says he, 'it's all for the good of the Church an' the faithful. I'm now archbishop of the country,' says he. 'The Protestants are all banished, an' we are in their place.'

'The sorra one o' myself all this time but thought he was a priest still; so says I, 'Dinny, you're a-wantin' to anoint Paddy Diarmud, who's given over, an' if you don't make haste you won't overtake him.'

'He must wait, then, till morning',' says Dinny; 'or if he chooses to die against my will and the will o' the Church, let him take the quensequences. We're wealthy now.'

'I was so much frightened at the kind of voice that he spoke to me in that I awoke; an' sure enough, the first thing I heard was the fizzin' o' bacon in the pan. I wondered who could be up so early, an' puttin' my head through the door, there was Dinny busy at it, wid an ould knife in one hand, an' an iron skiver in the other, imitatin' a fork.

'What are you doin' so early, Dinny?' says I.

'I'm practisin',' says he.

'What for?', says I.

'Oh, I'm practisin',' says he back again — 'go to bed; I'm practisin' for the Church, an' the station that's to be in Pether Rafferty's to-day.'

The mockery here spreads wider than Denis himself to include the Church as a whole; but Carleton's humour is by no means confined to mockery. There is much sympathy in his account of the people, their habits and customs, joys and sorrows. When Denis is about to depart on his journey to Maynooth, his friends and relations bring him a strange miscellany of leaving presents:

A poor old widow, who was distantly related to them, came upwards of four miles with two or three score of eggs, together with a cock and hen; the eggs for his own use, and the latter for breeding in Maynooth.

'*Avourneen*, Misther O'Shaughnessy,' said she, in broken English, 'when you ate out all the eggs, maybe you could get a sonsy little corner about the collegian that you're goin' to larn to be a priest in, an' put them both into it' — pointing at the same time to the cock and hen — 'an' whishper,' she continued, in a low friendly voice — 'if you could get a *weeshy* wisp o' sthraw, and slip it under your own bed, it would make a nest for them, an' they'd lay an egg for your breakfast all days in the year.'

The scene of the leaving presents is handled delightfully, but Carleton has another scene to bring before us where his handling is confused by his reading of contemporary fiction. Denis loves the daughter of a neighbouring farmer, Susan O'Connor. He has broken off his courtship of her, telling her that he must obey the call of God to service in the Church. But before he departs to Maynooth he seeks a final farewell meeting with her. The meeting is introduced by an elaborate literary build-up, reminiscent of Mrs Radcliffe: 'It was now the hour of twilight; the evening was warm and balmy; the whitethorn under which he sat, and the profusion of wild-flowers that spangled the bosom of the green glen, breathed their fragrance around him, and steeped the emotions and remembrances which crowded thickly on him in deep and exquisite tenderness.' Carleton is sliding into wordy melo-drama, and fourteen pages later Susan swoons in the arms of her lover.

'Susan, my beloved, will you not hear me? Oh, look upon me, my heart's dearest treasure, and tell me that you're living! Gracious God! her heart is broken — she is dead! This — this — is the severest blow of all! I have killed her!'

She opened her eyes as he spoke, and Denis, in stooping to assist her, weeping at the same time like a child, received — a bang from a cudgel that made his head ring.

'Your sowl to the divil, you larned vagabone,' said her father, for it was he; 'is this the way you're preparing your-self for the Church? — coming over that innocent *colleen* of a daughter o' mine before you set out ...'

Carleton is clearly glad to return to comedy. If we only had to consider the passage above it might be possible to argue that the melodrama is just a build-up for the comic anti-climax. But the previous fourteen pages cannot be disposed of in this way. There is confusion of styles and manners in the story, but the energy and reality survive in spite of this.

The various passages I have quoted above give a fair sample of Carleton's use of dialect. Some readers have found it unnatural and phoney, stage-Irish, in fact. This was the reaction of Somerville and Ross. In an essay on 'Stage Irishmen and Others' (*Strayaways*, 1920) they speak of 'the beings who storm and yell through the pages of Carleton. The compatriot . . . asks himself in bewilderment if these extravagances and violences, these (to an Irishman) humiliatingly exaggerated buffooneries, convey any genuine suggestion of the Irish farmers and workmen, who with decent self-respect and sobriety, now walk this lower earth.'

Nor is it only those from the Big House who object to Carleton's idiom. Frank O'Connor, too, found him ponderous and unreadable: 'His English is leaden, his judgement is dull, and he simply has no ear for speech.' On the other hand Patrick Kavanagh and Benedict Kiely both delight in Carleton's dialogue. It is perhaps worth noting that these men both come from the northern half of Ireland to which Carleton himself belongs.

There is undoubtedly extravagance and bombast in Carleton, but at his best his dialogue has an energy and humour that makes us forgive many faults. Here is a concluding example, drawn from 'The Geography of an Irish Oath'. Eilish is trying to persuade her lazy husband, Peter, to take a small farm:

'You're stout and able,' said she, 'an' as I can manage the house widout you, wouldn't it be a good plan to take a bit o' ground — nine or ten acres, suppose — an'thry your hand at it? Sure, you war wanst the greatest man in the parish about a farm. Surely that ud be dacenter nor to be *slungein'* about, invintin' truth and lies for other people whin they're at their work, to make thim laugh, an' you doin' nothin' but standing over thim, wid your hands down to the bottom o' your pockets? Do, Pether, thry it, *avick*, an' you'll see it'll prosper wid us, plase God.'

'Faix, I'm ladin' an asier life, Ellish.'

'But are you ladin' a dacenter or a more becominer life?'

'Why, I think, widout doubt, that it's more becominer to walk about like gintleman nor to be workin' like a slave.'

'Gintleman! *Musha,* is it to the fair you're bringin' yourself? Why, you great big *bosthoon,* isn't it both a sin an' a shame to see you sailin' about among the neighbours, like a shtray turkey, widout a hand's turn to do?'

I do not know if the terms 'slungein' and 'becominer' will be found in the new Anglo-Irish Dictionary, but they are marvellously and comically apt words; and the image of Peter sailing about among the neighbours like a stray turkey is wholly delightful.

8

Frank O'Connor

Carleton wrote mainly of a pre-famine Ireland. With Frank
O'Connor we take a long jump into the twentieth century.
He too came from a humble background and a small house.
He was actually born in Douglas Street, Cork, in 1903, over a
small sweet-and-tobacco shop, but his childhood memories
began in Blarney Street, as he tells us in his autobiography,
An Only Child: 'No 251, where we lived, is one of the
cottages on the right, near the top, though I realize now that
it would more properly be described as a cabin, for it
contained nothing but a tiny kitchen and a tiny bedroom
with a loft above it. For this we paid two and sixpence —
sixty cents — a week.'

In Blarney Street the children gathered to play in the evenings by the warm glow of the shop-windows, or under the
gas-lamps:

> For kids like myself social life was represented by the
> shop-front and the gas-lamp. This was because we could
> rarely bring other kids home in the evenings; the houses
> were too small, and after the fathers came home from
> work, children became a nuisance. Besides, most families
> had something to hide; if it wasn't an old grandmother like
> mine or a father who drank, it was how little they had
> to eat. This was always a matter of extreme delicacy, and
> the ultimate of snobbery was expressed for us by the loud
> woman up the road who was supposed to call her son in
> from play with: 'Tommy, come in to your tea, toast and
> two eggs!'

Frank O'Connor's real name was Michael Francis
O'Donovan, and his father was a bandsman in the British

Army. His mother had been brought up in a Catholic orphanage and before her marriage she worked as a domestic servant in several houses. Apart from the streets of Cork, O'Connor found food for his young imagination in such English boys' weeklies as the *Gem* and the *Magnet*. Then at school he was lucky enough to be taught by Daniel Corkery, who started in him an interest in the Irish language and the Irish past. He left school at the age of fourteen but he continued to improvise an education for himself as best he could:

> By the time I was fourteen it was clear that education was something I would never be able to afford. Not that I had any intention of giving it up even then. I was just looking for a job that would enable me to buy the books from which I could pick up the education myself. So, with the rest of the unemployed, I went to the newsroom of the Carnegie Library where on wet days the steam heating warmed the perished bodies in the broken boots and made the dirty rags steam and smell. I read carefully through the advertisements and applied for every job that demanded 'a smart boy', but what I really hoped for was to find a new issue of the *Times Literary Supplement, The Spectator, The New Statesman,* or *The Studio* free, so that I could read articles about books and pictures I would never see. . .

He did get jobs, first in a 'pious wholesale drapery business' and then as a messenger boy with the Great Southern and Western Railway. But his heart was not in his work, and before long he was sacked. His real interests were literature, languages and the cause of Ireland. Looking backwards in his autobiography he sees the humour and oddity of his position:

> On the Saturday night I was sacked I read my first paper. It was in Irish, and the subject was Goethe. For me, my whole adolescence is summed up in that extraordinary evening — so much that even yet I cannot laugh at it in comfort. I didn't know much about Irish, and I knew practically nothing about Goethe, and that little was wrong. In a truly anthropomorphic spirit I re-created Goethe in my own image and likeness, as a patriotic young

man who wished to revive the German language, which I considered to have been gravely threatened by the use of French. I drew an analogy between the French culture that dominated eighteenth century Germany and the English culture by which we in Ireland were dominated.

Before long O'Connor was caught up in the patriotic currents of the day. He served with the Republican forces in the guerilla war against England. In the civil war that followed the Treaty of 1921 he took the Republican side, and he was interned in Gormanstown Internment camp for nearly a year in 1923. During this period of enforced leisure he read what books he could find, and his ideas about patriotism and religion began to change. When he left the camp at the age of twenty he gradually moved into a world where he could find the education he so passionately sought. He trained as a librarian and worked in Cork and then in Dublin. He became friendly with AE and with Yeats, and eventually he joined the Board of the Abbey Theatre. Meantime he was turning his pen to various kinds of writing.

In the course of his writing life he published translations from Irish poetry, two novels, a great many short stories, a biography of Michael Collins, two travel books, some poems, several books of literary criticism and a number of essays on literary topics, and two volumes of autobiography. He will be remembered chiefly as a short story writer, but his translations are also important, and his two autobiographies illuminate not only his own life but the life of Ireland in the formative years of the early twentieth century.

His anthology of translations from the Irish, *Kings, Lords and Commons* (1959) provides a fascinating entry into the world of Irish literature for those who, like myself, have no grasp of the Irish language. His translations range from the seventh century to the nineteenth, and they include Bryan Merriman's *The Midnight Court,* rendered into vigorous rhyming couplets. This poem is too long to illustrate adequately by a short quotation. I choose instead two shorter poems to give some idea of the book's qualities. Here is a four line poem on jealousy that illustrates the simple forceful clarity of some Irish epigrammatic verse:

Love like heat and cold
  Pierces and then is gone;
Jealousy when it strikes
  Sticks in the marrowbone.

O'Connor tells us in his preface that he had Yeats's help with his translation of 'Kilcash'. This is one of the poems of lament for the woodlands destroyed in the English clearances after 1691. Here are the first two verses:

What shall we do for timber?
  The last of the woods is down.
Kilcash and the house of its glory
  And the bell of the house are gone,
The spot where that lady waited
  Who shamed all women for grace
When earls came sailing to greet her
And Mass was said in the place.

My grief and my affliction
  Your gates are taken away,
Your avenue needs attention,
  Goats in the garden stray.
The courtyard's filled with water
  And the great earls where are they?
The earls, the lady, the people
  Beaten into the clay.

The short story was a form that suited O'Connor's temperament, and he took it seriously. He wrote a critical study of it, and of the writers he admired, entitled *The Lonely Voice*. Long before this, on his release from internment, he had written, in Irish, a prize-winning study of Turgenev. His own first volume of short stories, *Guests of the Nation,* was published in 1931. The title-story is one of the best known of his writings. Brian Cleeve, in his *Dictionary of Irish Writers,* calls it 'the seminal story of modern Irish literature'. The 'guests of the nation' are two English soldiers Belcher and Hawkins, captured by Republican forces in the Anglo-Irish war. They are held as hostages in a lonely country cottage, and they live on friendly terms with their guards, playing cards with them in the evenings. Only much later do the guards learn the real reason why the two men are being held. When some Republican prisoners are executed by the British army, the two men are taken out to the bog to be shot in reprisal. The end is horrifying but convincing, and O'Connor showed courage and originality in dealing with a theme that inevitably raises doubts about Republican methods and enlists the reader's sympathies for the English soldiers.

Patrick Kavanagh (in an article in *The Bell*, vol. xv, 3) found in the story 'the treacle of sentimentality'. For him the Englishmen were 'a pair of cliché sentimental characters . . . dumb, good-natured Englishmen' and he thought that O'Connor was himself too emotionally involved in the story: ' . . . he himself weeps over their deaths and in this he lacks the courage and integrity of the great artist'. This is harsh criticism, and Kavanagh is wrong about Hawkins, who is anything but dumb. But he has a point; the last paragraph certainly trembles on the brink of sentimentality. After the shooting, the narrator, leaving his fellow-guard and the old woman of the house at their prayers, goes out.

> . . . I stood at the door, watching the stars and listening to the shrieking of the birds dying out over the bogs. It is so strange what you feel at times like that that you can't describe it. Noble says he saw everything ten times the size, as though there were nothing in the whole world but that little patch of bog with the two Englishmen stiffening into it, but with me it was as if the patch of bog where the Englishmen were was a million miles away, and even Noble and the old woman, mumbling behind me, and the birds and the bloody stars were all far away, and I was somehow very small and very lost and lonely like a child astray in the snow. And anything that happened to me afterwards, I never felt the same about again.

In the last few lines of this passage I feel that O'Connor has lost his sureness of touch, and is falling into a vague statement of generalised emotion that doesn't quite ring true. But his description of the actual shooting, and the very different reactions of the two victims, is wholly convincing.

O'Connor is a natural entertainer and has the gift of compelling the reader's attention from his opening sentences. This is partly a matter of tone. Although his stories are conscious literary creations, not oral tales, he retains a suggestion of the speaking voice, of a man who has button-holed you and is about to tell of unusual and interesting behaviour. 'Some kids are cissies by nature, but I was a cissy by conviction' is the opening sentence of 'The Genius'; and 'First Confession' begins: 'All the trouble began when my grandfather died . . . and my grandmother came to live with us.'

Many readers find his humorous stories the most appealing, especially the stories about Larry Delaney, a fictitious version of himself as a small boy. *My Oedipus Complex* gives its title to one of his best collections, and the title-story, which he includes in his own selection of *Modern Irish Short Stories*, is neatly and wittily constructed. It tells of a child's jealousy of his soldier-father when he returns from the Great War. Larry can no longer share his mother's bed in the mornings and chat to her about his plans for the day; he can no longer monopolise her attention. He grows to resent and hate the father for whose safe return he had prayed. But when another son is born, Larry and his father are driven together by common resentment of the new intruder who demands all the mother's attention. Finally the father himself is turned out of his wife's bed to join Larry, and there is a reconciliation between father and son.

The ironic device of telling the story in the manner and tone of the grown man is amusing, but at times it becomes too self-conscious and contrived. Here is the five-year old Larry waking in the morning:

> Next morning I woke at my usual hour, feeling like a bottle of champagne. I put out my feet and invented a long conversation in which Mrs Right talked of the trouble she had with her own father till she put him in the Home. I didn't quite know what the Home was but it sounded the right place for Father. Then I got my chair and stuck my head out of the attic window. Dawn was just breaking, with a guilty air that made me feel I had caught it in the act.

Larry now gets into his parents' bed, but when he starts his

usual chat to his mother, he is cautioned not to wake
Daddy:

'Why?' I asked severely.
'Because poor Daddy is tired.'
This seemed to me a quite inadequate reason, and I was
sickened by the sentimentality of her 'poor Daddy'. I
never liked that sort of gush; it always struck me as insin-
cere.

It is impossible not to be amused by the dialogue and the
story, but it has an air of unreality that lowers it in my
esteem. My own favourites among the humorous stories are
'First Confession' and 'The Star that Bids the Shepherd Fold'.
The first of these is again the story of a child and it depends
to some extent on the child adopting adult perceptions, but
Jackie in the confession box, after the hilarious antics he per-
forms to get himself in the right position, is more natural
than Larry:

'And what's a-trouble to you, Jackie?'
'Father,' I said, feeling I might as well get it over while
I had him in good humour, 'I had it all arranged to kill my
grandmother.'
He seemed a bit shaken by that, all right, because he
said nothing for quite a while.
'My goodness', he said at last, 'that'd be a shocking
thing to do. What put that into your head?'
'Father,' I said, feeling very sorry for myself, 'she's an
awful woman.'
'Is she?' he asked. 'What way is she awful?'
'She takes porter, father,' I said, knowing well from the
way Mother talked of it that this was a mortal sin, and
hoping it would make the priest take a more favourable
view of my case.
'Oh, my!' he said, and I could see he was impressed.
'And snuff, father,' said I.
'That's a bad case, sure enough, Jackie,' he said.

The second story is wholly different in tone and manner; it
has a sharp satiric edge and is a wry comedy of incongruity.
The parish priest, learning that two girls from his parish are

nightly visiting a French boat in the local docks, goes with his curate, who can speak French, to retrieve the girls, and they have an interview with the captain of the boat. The two priests are strangely incongruous; the elderly parish priest who is fond of Zane Grey, has 'the rosy, innocent, good-natured face of a pious old countrywoman who made a living by selling eggs.' His curate is a lonely intellectual, 'pale and worn-looking, with a gentle, dreamy face', and a keen malicious wit. The captain thinks one of the girls is the parish priest's mistress, and he can see no difference between the Irish and the English. When the curate reminds him that France and Ireland fought together against England at the Boyne, and at Fontenoy and Ramillies, it makes no difference: 'You call yourselves Irish, the others call themselves Scotch, but you are all English. It is always the same: always women, always hypocrisy, always excuses. *Toujours des excuses!* Who is this girl? The *curé's* daughter?'

The misunderstandings are not resolved but the girls leave the boat, and there is a final irony in the image of the shepherds folding their sheep.

In *The Lonely Voice* O'Connor explains his title by saying that we find 'in the short story at its most characteristic something we do not often find in the novel — an intense awareness of human loneliness'. This loneliness is certainly found in many of his own most serious and moving stories, in 'Uprooted', for example, and in 'The Bridal Night', 'In the Train' and 'Michael's Wife'.

'Uprooted' brings out poignantly the sense of loss and loneliness that strikes home to two brothers, Tom and Ned Keating, when they return for a week-end to their parental home in the west. Tom is a priest in Wicklow and Ned a teacher in Dublin. They have chosen to leave their country home for new ways of life, but a visit to an island and some friends of their father's, including the beautiful Cait Deignan, stirs memories of the past that they have turned their backs on, and makes them aware of the frustrations that they face, each in his own way. Tom, acutely conscious of the loneliness of the celibate priesthood, thinks that his brother, at least, could marry Cait: 'Like all men with frustration in their hearts, he was full of schemes for others. "You could marry her and get a school down here. That's what I'd do if I was in your place." "No", said Ned gravely, "We made our choice a long time ago. We can't go back on it now."'

I have indicated only the bare bones of the story. What gives it a compelling poignancy is the rich and subtle detail of the landscape and life and people of their home, and of Carriganassa, the island.

'In the Train' is perhaps the finest of all O'Connor's stories. He makes skilful use of contrasted groups of people and contrasted conversations. A murder trial has been held in a town in the west of Ireland, and a woman accused of poisoning her husband has just been acquitted. Now the woman, Helena, and her neighbours, are returning to their remote village by the sea, Farranchreesht. We gather the story in bits and pieces, from the conversations, which are broken and interrupted. It seems that the villagers, even though critical of Helena, have told lies to prevent her conviction, out of loyalty to their village and an instinctive taking of sides against the police. The story, however, is not O'Connor's main concern, but rather the moods and feelings of the people, the attitude of the returning travellers to their village and to Helena; and Helena's own feelings about her release, her reluctance to join her neighbours on the train. The story reaches an unexpected point of illumination at the end as Helena suddenly realises that she has no further interest in the man for whose sake, it seems, she murdered her husband: 'He's no more to me now than the salt sea.'

The intensity of the story is not diminished by the inclusion of much that is comic and bizarre. A lonely drunkard wanders through the train looking for the carriage he first entered. The confusion and mystery of life find an analogue in the lonely train travelling through the dark and the rain, but there are moments of insight:

> 'Listen to the rain' said one of the women. 'E'll have a wet walk home.'
>
> ''Twill be midnight before we're in,' said another.
>
> 'Ah, what matter sure when the whole country will be up? There'll be a lot of talking done in Farranchreesht tonight.'

'A lot of talking and no sleep.'

'Oh, Farranchreesht! Farranchreesht!' cried the young, woman with the haggard face, the ravaged lineaments of which were suddenly transfigured. 'Farranchreesht and the sky over you, I wouldn't change places with the Queen of England tonight!'

And suddenly Farranchreesht, the bare bogland with the hump-backed mountain behind, the little white houses and the dark fortifications of turf that made it seem like the flame-blackened ruin of some mighty city, all was lit up in their minds.

9

Patrick Kavanagh

Patrick Kavanagh was only a year younger than Frank O'Connor and he lived through the same period of national fervour, but his background and experiences were very different. He too was born in a small house, but it was in a remote country district of Co. Monaghan. At his local village school there was no Daniel Corkery to inspire him with an enthusiasm for things Irish, only a formidable Miss Cassidy, who carried a bundle of yellow canes, and Miss Moore who 'could cut cowld iron with her tongue.' He tells us that he once tried to join the IRA but was turned down because he was too young. He learnt a lot of patriotic songs but took little part in any political movement, and he writes in *The Green Fool:* 'In spite of all the loud glory and movement of those years I count them among the lost years of my life.'

He was born on 21 October 1904, in the townland of Mucker in the parish of Inniskeen, about eight miles from the town of Carrickmacross. His father was a shoemaker, an intelligent, thrifty man who managed to save a little money and buy some land. After leaving school at the age of thirteen Kavanagh worked on the family farm. He tried his father's trade of shoemaking but never developed any real skill at it or interest in it. But he did take up the trade of versing. Beginning with useful and topical ballads about local football matches and celebrations, he graduated to the verse corner of a Sunday newspaper, and finally AE published some of his poems in *The Irish Statesman.*

In 1936 his first volume appeared, *Ploughman and Other Poems,* but he still remained at home working on the farm. He went through a period of indecision, reluctant to leave the world he knew, but finally he went, first to London and then

to Dublin, where he settled in a bed-sitter with his brother
Peter in 1939. From then onwards he was committed to the
streets of cities and to life as a writer. He returned often to
Inniskeen but never for very long. He scraped a living by
journalism for many years. Only towards the end of his life
was he free from poverty, when increasing success as a writer
and a special part-time post at University College, Dublin,
brought him a measure of comfort.

Although he settled in Dublin, his subject as a writer was
still for many years the world of Monaghan and the life of
the little tillage fields, but his approach to it changed. The
thin lyricism of his first volume gave way to the much deeper
and more powerful note that is sounded in *The Great Hunger*.
'Ploughman' is the first poem of the early collection, and it
presents a charming graceful picture of the poet-ploughman.

> I turn the lea-green down
> Gaily now,
> And paint the meadow brown
> With my plough.
>
> I dream with silvery gull
> And brazen crow.
> A thing that is beautiful
> I may know.
>
> Tranquillity walks with me
> And no care.
> O, the quiet ecstasy
> Like a prayer.
>
> I find a star-lovely art
> In a dark sod.
> Joy that is timeless! O heart
> That knows God.

Even at the time of writing this Kavanagh was aware that
it was not the whole truth about ploughing. Commenting on
it in *The Green Fool* he said: 'I could not help smiling when
I thought of the origin of my ploughman ecstasy. A kicking
mare in a rusty old plough tilling a rood of land for turnips.'

When he describes Patrick Maguire ploughing in *The Great Hunger* a few years later, the tone and movement of the verse are very different.

> The pull is on the traces, it is March
> And a cold black wind is blowing from Dundalk.
> The twisting sod rolls over on her back —
> The virgin screams before the irresistible sock.
> No worry on Maguire's mind this day
> Except that he forgot to bring his matches.
> 'Hop back there, Polly, hoy back, woa, wae,'
> From every second hill a neighbour watches
> With all the sharpened interest of rivalry.

Those more complex and powerful lines reveal the literary picturesqueness of the earlier poem. Kavanagh has found a voice of his own, and *The Great Hunger* is a major achievement.

The central figure in the poem is Patrick Maguire, whose hunger for life and love is frustrated by a narrow prudence. At the age of sixty-five he remains unmarried, tied to his old mother and his little fields, 'a man who made a field his bride'. The poem opens with a sombre picture of the monotonous toil of the potato gatherers:

> Clay is the word and clay is the flesh
> Where the potato gatherers like mechanized scarecrows
>   move
> Along the side-fall of the hill — Maguire and his men.
> If we watch them is there anything we can prove
> Of life as it is broken-backed over the Book of Death.

The worst thing about Maguire's life is not the fourteen hour day that he works for years but the mixture of narrow morality and caution that keeps him away from the girls until it is too late:

> Who bent the coin of my destiny
> That it stuck in the slot?

There is nothing for him to look forward to but death, when 'he will hardly remember that life happened to him':

Patrick Maguire, the old peasant, can neither be damned
    nor glorified,
The grave-yard where he will lie will just be a deep-drilled
    potato field
Where the seed gets no chance to come through
To the fun of the sun.
The tongue in his mouth is the root of a yew.
Silence, silence. The story is done.

Although Maguire is a small peasant farmer in an Irish
parish he takes on a universal significance. He is typical of
many men who lead lives of quiet desperation. He has some
awareness of his own condition, but he lacks the insight and
the courage to act from the promptings of his own deepest
feelings. In spite of this he is not insignificant or contemp-
tible, and Kavanagh does not despise him or condescend to
him. There is pity for his fate, but it is saved from sentimentality by irony. He writes with profound sympathy because
he himself has been in Maguire's situation, but also with
detachment because he writes as a poet.

Kavanagh wrote prose as well as poetry. Several years
before *The Great Hunger,* which first appeared in an Irish
number of *Horizon* in 1942, he had published *The Green
Fool* (1938). This is written in the form of an autobiography
but Kavanagh always spoke of it as fiction. In the *Irish
Farmers' Journal,* to which he contributed a personal column
for many years, he spoke of it as 'a novel I wrote twenty
years ago . . . in which I tried hard to be entertainingly
"Irish"'. Later on, in *Self-Portrait,* he spoke of it more harsh-
ly: 'a dreadful stage-Irish so-called autobiography . . . '.

Kavanagh, like Dr Johnson, is always forthright and down-
right. His likes and dislikes are plain for all to see. He never
damns with faint praise or assents with civil leer. He condemns much of his own work as vigorously as he condemns
that of other writers. I think he is wrong about *The Green
Fool,* as he is about *The Great Hunger,* which he also condemned. The book is occasionally sentimental and romantic,
and it perhaps simplifies the life of a country boy growing up
to be a poet. The humiliating sexual tensions that he described
in *Tarry Flynn* are omitted, but in spite of this the book has

both vigour and truth, and there is much vivid observation of country life. The authentic tones of country conversation are heard, without any leprechauns or Abbey Theatre bog-talk: 'She'll run the life outa him. Why, man, he won't be worth a second-hand chew of tobacco when he's after sleepin' a week with that one.' This is the malicious comment of a bystander at a wedding, when a bridegroom of sixty is marrying a young girl of twenty-one. Throughout the book the talk of ass-dealers, cattle-dealers and small farmers, of women gossiping about a neighbour's illness or a neighbour's sick cow, is shrewdly recorded.

Tarry Flynn (1948) deals with the same rural world as *The Green Fool*. Although it is a novel, it is in some ways more autobiographical, more subjective than the earlier book. It ploughs a narrower and deeper furrow, and the conversation has a sharper and racier edge. Kavanagh, who was not afraid to praise as well as damn his own work, said it was 'not only the best but the only authentic account of life as it was lived in Ireland this century' (*Self-Portrait*). The book has little plot and it is in essence a portrait of the artist as a young man, though very different from the work of Joyce. We see Tarry, caught in the toils of the little tillage fields, ploughing and ditching, dreaming and writing poems, planning to seduce a neighbour's daughter, humbly adoring and clumsily repulsing the more distant Mary Reilly, daughter of a prosperous farmer. The book ends with Tarry leaving his native parish with his uncle, who is improvident and fond of drink but has vitality and imagination.

One of the best features of the book is the portrayal of Mrs Flynn, who is based on Kavanagh's own mother. She loves her son, Tarry, in spite of his queer and unsatisfactory ways and his 'curse-o'-God rhyming', but her tongue has a sharp and racy edge. She nags at him when he is reluctant to set off to Mass: 'Lord O Lord! Aggie left here to go to Mass at five minutes to eight and there's that man still steaming away at the fag like a railway engine.... Oh look at him there with his big nose on him and the oul'cod of a face like his uncle that — that a Protestant wouldn't be worse than him....'

She tries to encourage Tarry to ambition and independence, and when there is a chance that a neighbour's farm may come into the market, she says:

> And mind you that's as dry and warm a farm of land as there is in the parish. There's a couple of fields there and do you know what it is you could plough them with a pair of asses, they're that free. It's a terrible pity you wouldn't take a better interest in your work and you could be the independentest man in Ireland. You could tell all the beggars to kiss your arse . . .

Much of the comedy and flavour of the book is derived from the contrast between mother and son. She is a peasant and her feet are firmly planted on the earth, so that she is a kind of Sancho Panza to Tarry's Don Quixote. Tarry, dreaming, filled with wonder at the beauty of the fields, comes in from moulding the potatoes to tell his mother that 'The Holy Spirit is in the fields.' But his mother is more concerned with a corn that is troubling her. 'There's a curse o' God corn on that wee toe and it's starting to bother me again. I think we'll have a slash of rain. Get the razor blade and pare it for me.'

The year before *Tarry Flynn* appeared Kavanagh had published another volume of poems, *A Soul for Sale*. This contained some of his best known and best loved 'Monaghan' poems, such as 'A Christmas Childhood', 'Stony Grey Soil', 'Art McCooey' and 'Spraying the Potatoes.' Then there was a long gap until the appearance in 1960 of *Come Dance with Kitty Stobling*, which was the summer choice of the Poetry Book Society. Meantime Kavanagh had achieved some notoriety in Dublin. With Peter's help and financial support he published his own newspaper, *Kavanagh's Weekly*, which ran for thirteen issues and attacked almost every aspect of the Irish establishment for its worship of mediocrity. Kavanagh was himself attacked in an anonymous profile in the *Leader*, an Irish weekly magazine. He sued the *Leader* for libel in a famous Dublin court case lasting seven days in February, 1954. Kavanagh lost the case and next year he entered hospital with lung cancer. He had a lung removed and made a remarkable recovery. During his convalescence that summer he felt himself reborn into the world of sunshine and grass and water, and there was a new outpouring of poetry expressing this mood. We find it in the 'Canal Bank' sonnets and other poems in this last volume.

Kavanagh was an uneven and at times a careless poet. When he died in 1967 he left a good deal of unfinished work, and some of his finished work is weak. But he left enough poems in his middle and later periods to entitle him to a distinctive place in Anglo-Irish poetry. He has almost nothing in common with Yeats, and he moved out entirely from the shadow of Ben Bulben. Two main qualities are apparent in his best work: his ability to illuminate the commonplace, and his religious vision.

He takes his stand firmly on the lowest common denominator of beauty: not for him romantic scenery, the tall rock, the mountain and the deep and gloomy wood, the rainbow or the nightingale. He stands in the laneway or, as in 'Spraying the Potatoes', in the potato fields and looks at the dry clay, the nettles, the rushes and the weeds:

Dandelions growing on headlands, showing
Their unloved hearts to everyone.

He speaks out of an Irish world that is older and more enduring than the world of the literary revival and the 'troubles'. It is less exciting, perhaps, more monotonously bound to clay and bog, but it reaches back to Carleton and the times before the Famine, and it still lives on in the back parts of the bourgeois economy of modern Ireland. It is the world of hens and donkeys in the backyard, of the broken straw-stuffed straddle and the old plough upside down on a weedy ridge.

In many of the Monaghan poems Kavanagh succeeds in conveying to the reader the beauty and wonder of common sights — the frost on the potato-pits, the tracks of cattle to a drinking place, a green stone lying sideways in a ditch. He writes with affection of the landscape of memory as one who has been inside the world he describes, intimately engaged in the country tasks of carting dung, spraying the potatoes or cleaning the ditches. In most of these poems there is a relaxed easy acceptance of the country world, without any straining or standing on tiptoe to catch a glimpse of wonder. 'Peace' is a good example:

And sometimes I am sorry when the grass
Is growing over the stones in quiet hollows
And the cocksfoot leans across the rutted cart-pass
That I am not the voice of country fellows
Who now are standing by some headland talking
Of turnips and potatoes or young corn
Or turf banks stripped for victory.
Here peace is still hawking
His coloured combs and scarves and beads of horn.

Upon a headland by a whinny hedge
A hare sits looking down a leaf-lapped furrow
There's an old plough upside-down on a weedy ridge
And someone is shouldering home a saddle-harrow.
Out of that childhood country what fools climb
To fight with tyrants Love and Life and Time?

The mode of this is neither Horation nor Wordsworthian
but plain Kavanagh. He remembers not the primrose or the
daffodil but the cocksfoot and the grass growing over the
stones. The detail, deliberately commonplace, is sharply
focussed and remembered with affection. The tone and
movement of the verse is relaxed; the words seem casual and
yet the lines fall with a quiet force in a firm pattern of
rhyme, so that we can accept the rhetorical lift of the last
couplet.

From time to time Kavanagh's love of the commonplace
intensifies to become a religious vision. Like Tarry Flynn
he finds the Holy Spirit in the fields: 'God is in the bits and
pieces of everyday.' He wrote in *Kavanagh's Weekly:* 'What
transmutes the commonplace of a man's life into something
that is of exciting importance for all of us is a mystery. Two
men walk down a road and one man's walk is half in the
eternal.' When he himself walked the lanes of Monaghan,
they often became 'eternal lanes of joy'. 'Standing on the
side of a hill in Monaghan,' he wrote in the journal *X*, 'an
indifferent landscape of crooked lanes and little humpy hills
covered with whins, I found love, the kind of love that
purifies, a sort of Divine love.' He experienced again this kind
of love when he walked the canal bank after his operation.
It finds expression in the sonnet 'Canal Bank Walk':

Leafy-with-love banks and the green waters of the canal
Pouring redemption for me, that I do
The will of God, wallow in the habitual, the banal,
Grow with nature again as before I grew.

The rhythm and language of the sonnet suggest an out-flowing, indeed an overflowing, of love and praise for the ordinary world on the bank of the canal. It is not simply a matter of the convalescent's delight in returning health; the note of blessing and praise is sounded *before* his sojourn in hospital as well as after. In 'Prelude' for example, he admonished himself to count his blessings and recall his past moments of vision and joy:

Gather the bits of road that were
Not gravel to the traveller
But eternal lanes of joy
On which no man who walks can die.

Kavanagh never became, like Yeats, 'a sixty-year old smiling public man'. He remained an outsider, 'a queer one' as he called himself in his witty ballad, 'If ever you go to Dublin Town'. But he shared Yeats's belief that there is no good literature without praise. In the last number of *Kavanagh's Weekly* he stated that the purpose of the poet is to give people an enthusiasm for life. In spite of unevenness and occasional sourness, in spite of sometimes shouting praise and beauty, instead of revealing and presenting them, he does kindle once more the reader's enthusiasm for life. He does, in Wordsworth's phrase, 're-invest with spirituality the material universe', and lead us back to 'The placeless heaven that's under all our noses'.

Supplement to Part Two

Notes on some other nineteenth century writers: poetry, prose, drama.

Poetry

Thomas Kinsella, surveying the poets of Ireland in the nineteenth century (in the Tower Series of Anglo-Irish Studies II) found little joy in them: 'Judging the poems themselves as best I could — asking myself only were they good or bad, not did they represent anything or contribute to anything — my main finding in the nineteenth century was dullness, a huge supply of bad verse.' My own view is not quite so dismissive, but I must agree that there is plenty of dullness, and no major poet until Yeats appears on the scene.

Thomas Moore (1779–1852) was thought by many people to be Ireland's first national poet. His *Irish Melodies* (1820) proved immensely popular. They were written to Irish airs and they were intended for singing, and it is as songs that they are chiefly remembered. Much of Moore's verse, including the songs, is vapid and thin, facile and pretty. As Hazlitt put it: 'Mr Moore converts the wild harp of Erin into a musical snuff-box.' But his biographer, Terence de Vere White, asks us: 'Who has not got the first lines, at least, of half a dozen of his *Melodies* by heart? How many poets have written better *first* lines?' Certainly some of his first lines stick in my mind: 'At the mid-hour of night, when stars are weeping, I fly,' 'Silent O Moyle be the roar of thy waters', 'The harp that once through Tara's halls.' Moore is not a poet whom we are likely to re-read, or even to read once, but some of his lines will not be forgotten.

James Clarence Mangan (1803–49) is a haunting, mysterious figure, an early version of the *poète maudit*, a near drop-out, taking to drugs and drink, hopeless, self-destroying, dying young. His poetry is uneven, much of it bad, but he has qualities that Moore lacked, intensity and passion. This gives a nervous tension and excitement to his best poems, to 'My Dark Rosaleen' for example:

> I could scale the blue air
> I could plough the high hills
> O I could kneel all night in prayer
> To heal your many ills.

The tension is felt here in the rhythm, with its sudden lengthening in the third line. 'Siberia', 'The Nameless One' and 'Twenty Golden Years Ago' all have intensity. In a different vein his translation from the Irish of 'The Woman of Three Cows', is lively, jaunty and amusing.

Sir Samuel Ferguson (1810—1886) lived a life at the other end of the scale from Mangan. He was born of upper middle class parents in Belfast and educated at the Belfast Academical Institution and Trinity College, Dublin. He had a distinguished career as a lawyer in Dublin. He was also a fine scholar and he did a great deal to encourage Irish studies. In 1878 he was knighted for his public services and a little later he was made President of the Royal Irish Academy. Malcolm Brown sees him as a cultural agent of the Protestant Ascendancy, trying to claim the Gaelic inheritance of Ireland for the ruling classes. He calls him 'laureate of Belfast ship-building and inventor of the Celtic Twilight'. He had a bourgeois, sectarian side, but it faded as he grew older, and his love of Ireland is stronger than party sympathies. He tried to popularise Gaelic legend and saga by writing 'Lays of the Western Gael', 'Congal' and 'Conary'. Yeats had a passionate admiration for him, which it is easy to understand but hard to share. In spite of his commendable zeal and energy his long poems are tedious to read. But there is a fine ballad vigour in 'The Vengeance of the Welshmen of Tirawley', and some of the shorter lyrics from the Irish are appealing. 'Cashel of Munster', 'The Fair Hills of Ireland', 'The Lapful of Nuts', 'Dear Dark Head (Cean Dubh Deelish)' which begins:

Put your head, darling darling darling,
　Your darling black head my heart above;
Oh, mouth of honey, with the thyme for fragrance,
　Who, with heart in breast, could deny you love?

In 'The Fairy Thorn' a ballad based on a rural Ulster tale, he succeeds in evoking an eerie sense of the supernatural. This poem is certainly a forerunner of the Celtic Twilight, and it appealed to all those who had a romantic interest in the fairies.

One of these was William Allingham (1824–1889) who has the misfortune of being chiefly remembered for two pretty minor poems, 'The Fairies' and 'Four Ducks on a Pond'. He deserves a better fate, for he had considerable gifts and a sensitivity to the life around him. In many ways he is a better poet than Mangan but he lacks a central passion, and he wrote too much pretty verse in the shadow of Tennyson. His long poem, *Laurence Bloomfield in Ireland* (1864), reveals a keen observing eye and an incisive pen. It is a narrative poem in heroic couplets about the conditions of Ireland in the eighteen-sixties and the land troubles. There are some memorable portraits. He also wrote a few good ballads and some of his lyrics have a haunting quality, such as 'The Dead' 'The Boy from his Bedroom Window' and 'The Ruined Chapel'. His late collection 'Blackberries' (1884) shows that he could turn a neat epigram:

Is idleness indeed so black a crime
What are the Busy doing, half their time?

In 1842 *The Nation* newspaper was founded by Thomas Davis, Charles Gavan Duffy and John Blake Dillon, who became known as the Young Ireland group. They supported Daniel O'Connell in his movement for the repeal of the Union with England, but later they parted ways with him. Davis (1814–45) was young, romantic, intensely patriotic. His poems were propaganda for the national cause. One of them is entitled 'A Nation Once Again' and it begins:

When boyhood's fire was in my blood,
　I read of ancient freemen,
For Greece and Rome who bravely stood,
　THREE HUNDRED MEN and THREE MEN.

And then I prayed I yet might see
  Our fetters rent in twain,
And Ireland, long a province, be
  A NATION ONCE AGAIN.

This is a fair sample of Davis's work, which is simple and rhetorical, though his 'Lament for the Death of Owen Roe O'Neill' is a finer poem.

There were many other minor poets in the nineteenth century but in this brief outline I can only mention a few more names. I recommend, for further information, Geoffrey Taylor's *Irish Poets of the Nineteenth Century*. In addition to those I have already mentioned he picks out J. J. Callanan, Aubrey de Vere, T. C. Irwin and J. F. O'Donnell. He compares the last named, in status and significance, to Ebeneezer Elliot, known only to those who travel the byways of English poetry, and goes on:

> Irish poetry of the nineteenth century is but a network of such byways — bohreens we should call them — though we try sometimes to mark some of them on the map as main thoroughfares. Between Tom Moore and Yeats, then, if we would travel at all, it is down these small roads we must go. And anyhow, there are times when a lane has charms that many a main road lacks.

Callanan (1795–1829) is remembered for his translations, or derivations, from Irish sources, and for the way he caught a Gaelic rhythm in the movement of his verse. 'The Outlaw of Loch Lene' begins:

> O many a day have I made good ale in the glen,
> That came not of stream, or malt, like the brewing of men.
> My bed was the ground, my roof, the greenwood above,
> And the wealth that I sought — one far kind glance from
>   my love.

Aubrey de Vere (1814–1902) was famous in his day, a friend of Wordsworth, Landor, Tennyson and others. He was devoted to Ireland and became a Roman Catholic in middle life. He wrote prolifically, and with skill, but little of his verse is memorable.

Irwin (1823–1892) resembled Tennyson in his close observation of nature and in the limpid music of his verse:

> I walk of grey noons by the old canal
>   Where rain-drops patter on the autumn leaves,
> Now watching from some ivied orchard wall
>   In slopes of stubble figures pile the sheaves . . .

Finally we must not forget the unnamed poets. The oral tradition was always strong in Ireland, and throughout the eighteenth and nineteenth centuries there were a number of ballads and popular songs that survived because they were sung or recited, and handed down to posterity, preserved by their wit or style, or maybe by the beauty of the tune that went with the words. 'She moved through the fair', 'I know where I'm going' are still sung, and so are 'The night before Larry was stretched' and 'The rakes of Mallow'.

Prose

Lady Morgan (1785–1859), born Sydney Owenson, daughter of an actor, was a very different kind of writer from Maria Edgeworth. Her romantic and melodramatic first novel, *The Wild Irish Girl* (1806) won her immediate fame. Brian Cleeve has aptly summed it up:

> It contained everything which polite England wished to hear about Ireland; a beautiful, windswept heroine playing a harp on the ruined battlements of a romantic castle; a dispossessed Gaelic nobleman, and an even more noble Englishman. The thing is ridiculous, but powerfully ridiculous, and had the same effect that *Ossian* had had for an earlier generation. Sydney 'Glorvina' Owenson became the social rage.

She espoused the cause of the Catholic gentry of Ireland in *O'Donnel* (1814) and *Florence Macarthy* (1819). In spite of her ornate and high-flown style, there is some vivid detail of Irish life in her books, especially in *The O'Briens and the O'Flahertys, A National Tale* (1827).

Gerald Griffin (1803–40) came from a middle class Catholic background in Limerick. At the age of twenty he went to London, hoping to have his plays produced in the

London theatres, but he was unsuccessful and had to struggle for a living by journalism. He returned to Ireland and after publishing some tales and novels gave up literature and joined the Christian Brothers. *The Collegians* (1829) has been called 'the first and most famous of Irish romantic novels'. Based on an actual murder, it tells the story of two college friends, Kyrle Daly and Hardress Cregan. Cregan is responsible for the murder of the lovely, pathetic heroine, Eily O'Connor, the girl he has secretly married, but the murder is done by his faithful boatman and servant, Danny Mann. Discerning critics such as John Cronin and Thomas Flanagan have given high praise to the book. I was disappointed when I read it. Although it reveals aspects of Irish life, and there are some well drawn characters, the melodramatic tone and style give it an air of unreality.

John Banim (1798–1842) and Michael Banim, his brother (1796–1874) were sons of a Catholic shopkeeper in Kilkenny. Together they produced *Tales of the O'Hara Family,* stories of Irish life in pre-famine days. Stephen Gwynn says they give 'the picture of a country where transitions are violent, and contrast savagely accumulated; where life is held cheap, yet where affections are of passionate intensity; where the tragic and ludicrous jostle each other. Yet the darker strain predominates.' *The Nowlans* (1827) is a lurid and melodramatic story set against vivid and convincing pictures of various Irish households and different social groups. John Banim also wrote an historical novel, *The Boyne Water* (1826).

Charles Lever (1806–1872) was a prolific novelist and in the Victorian period he enjoyed esteem and popularity. But now his reputation is at a low ebb and his work is out of print. The adjective commonly used to describe his novels is 'rollicking', though this only applies to his earlier ones. He is accused of exploiting Irish scenes and characters to amuse English readers, and there is some truth in this charge. He was influenced by his friend, W. H. Maxwell (1792–1850), whose *Wild Sports of the West* describes Connemara in the days of hard riding, hard drinking, duelling and extravagantly hospitable landed gentry. *Charles O'Malley* (1841) describes a high spirited young Irish gentleman who loves hunting and practical jokes. After a frolicsome career at Trinity College, he joins the army and fights in Wellington's Peninsular campaign against Napoleon. Although some of the humour in the book is crude and tasteless, there is a certain vitality. On the whole the later novels are more interesting, *The Martins of Cro'Martin, The Knight of Gwynne,* and *Lord Kilgobbin.* In general Lever sees Ireland and Irish people from an Ascendancy, 'Big House' viewpoint, but *Lord Kilgobbin* shows some real understanding of Irish nationalism, and there is an edge to his dialogue at times: 'those English puppies with their soft voices and their sneers about Ireland'.

The name of Samuel Lover (1797—1868) is often coupled with that of Lever, especially in adverse comments. *Handy Andy* (1842), his best known work, is seen as another picture of Irish buffoonery. Handy Andy is a simple minded blundering servant. When given a jug of cold water by his master and told to throw it out, he throws jug and all out the window. Lover can write with an edge of irony at times, but he lacks any serious guiding intention, and so the book becomes something of a rag-bag of anecdote and incident, with songs thrown in for good measure. At the same time it does reveal amusingly some aspects of Irish life. Lover was keenly interested in folk-lore, legend and ballad, and he published a collection, *Legends and Stories of Ireland,* which he also illustrated.

Charles Joseph Kickham (1828—1882), from a Catholic middle-class family in Co. Tipperary, belongs to an Ireland little known to Lever and Lover. Involved first in the Young Ireland movement, he later joined the Fenians and spent four years in prison where he wrote *Sally Cavanagh* (1869). His best work, *Knocknagow or The Homes of Tipperary* (1879), appealed to a wide middle class Catholic Irish readership in England, Ireland and America. R. V. Comerford points out that Kickham was anxious to establish the respectability of the Catholic Irish, so he gives a selective view of Irish life, with no wakes, fairs or faction fights. Stephen Gwynn thought that *Knocknagow* could not 'be seriously regarded as literature', and Yeats, in *Plays and Controversies*, tells how a village shoe-maker he knew as a boy raged against Kickham because he sentimentalised the people. 'The sentimental mind', Yeats wrote, 'is found among the middle classes, and it was this mind which came into Irish literature with Gerald Griffin and later on with Kickham.'

There is sentimentality in *Knocknagow* and it is rather shapeless as a novel, so that its value is perhaps less literary than social and historical, but it does certainly reveal sides of Irish life neglected by many other novelists.

In addition to the novelists I would like to mention two other prose writers, each of whom wrote a book of considerable interest. Sir Jonah Barrington (1760–1834) gave a fascinating account of Irish life in his day in his *Personal Sketches* (vols. i, ii, 1827, vol. iii, 1832). Various editions of these memoirs were published later, one in Every Irishman's Library under the title: *Recollections of Jonah Barrington.* Barrington sees Ireland from a Big House and Ascendancy viewpoint but his recollections are vivid and racy. I thought the drunkenness of the Rackrent squires must be grossly exaggerated until I read Barrington's chapter on 'Irish Dissipation in 1778'.

A very different book is the *Jail Journal* (1854) written by John Mitchel (1815–1875). Son of a Presbyterian minister in Dungiven, Mitchel joined forces with Davis in *The Nation.* In 1848 he founded *The United Irishman,* and in the same year he was sentenced to fourteen years transportation for writing seditious articles. Sent to Bermuda, then to Van Dieman's Land, he finally escaped to America. The journal tells the story of his prison voyages and his years in the penal colony, and not surprisingly he makes some bitter attacks on the British Government. Yeats, writing in *New Ireland* in 1915, deplored in Mitchel 'the harsh Ulster nature, made harsher still by the tragedy of the famine, and the rhetoric of Carlyle'. There is certainly harshness in the journal, but it shows other sides of Mitchel's nature besides his passionate political faith. He was interested in many things outside politics, and he is a keen observer of men and nature. Under the blazing sun of Bermuda he recalls the soft Irish landscape, vividly expressing the nostalgia of the exile.

Drama

There is really no Anglo-Irish drama to consider until we come to the literary theatre movement at the end of the nineteenth century. There were many famous Irish-born dramatists and actors, and theatres flourished in Dublin in the late eighteenth century, but there was no indigenous drama. Even the folk drama of Mummers and Christmas Rhymers which became traditional in several rural parts of Ireland, was imported from England, though it gathered to itself some Irish characters and flavours.

There is only one dramatist to mention in the nineteenth century, Dionysius Boucicault (1820–1890). Born in Dublin he tried his luck as entertainer in England, France and America. He started as an actor but had an early success with his play *London Assurance* (1841), which combined comedy of manners with farce. Later, learning from French sentimental melodrama, he combined elements of comedy, melodrama and sensational spectacle to entertain his audiences. He once remarked: 'Art is not a church. It is the philosophy of pleasure.'

He wrote three Irish plays: *The Colleen Bawn* (1860), adapted from Griffin's novel *The Collegians, Arrah na Pogue* (1864), and *The Shaughraun* (1875). The last is the best, with a good deal of lively wit and humour, as well as melodrama. Boucicault did something to transform the traditional stage-Irish comic servant. Conn, the tramp-figure in *The Shaughraun*, became the hero of the play. Boucicault's plays were very popular in Ireland, and both Synge and O'Casey, who saw his plays in Dublin, learned a good deal from him.

I have not mentioned Oscar Wilde because his plays have no Irish dimension. Shaw will be briefly discussed later.

PART THREE

A Group of Dubliners

10

James Joyce

James Joyce is the greatest Dubliner of them all, in at least two senses. He is the most important writer ever to come out of Dublin, and he is more concerned with Dublin than any other writer. From his first collection of short stories, *Dubliners*, to his last labyrinthine creation, *Finnegans Wake*, Dublin is at the centre of his consciousness. Although he left the city in 1904, and lived and wrote in Trieste, Zurich and Paris, he turned to Dublin again and again for his settings and his characters.

James Augustine Joyce (1882–1941) was born in Dublin into the family of John Stanislaus Joyce, an improvident official in the Tax Office, who lost his job and found it difficult to support his family. Joyce attended Clongowes Wood College as a boarder from the age of six, but left when his father could no longer pay the fees and went to Belvedere College, and later to UCD, where he studied languages and read Aristotle and Thomas Aquinas. Before leaving college in 1902 he had determined to become a writer, but he had great difficulty in earning a living. His other great difficulty, in later life, was the condition of his eyes, which troubled him from 1917 onwards. He had twenty-five operations and was blind for short periods. In 1902 he borrowed money to go to Paris but returned to Ireland the next year when his mother died. In 1904 he fell in love with a Galway girl, Nora Barnacle. He left Ireland with her for Zurich, but the couple were not married until 1931 when their daughter insisted on it. Joyce paid two further visits to Ireland, in 1909 and 1912, but the rest of his life was lived in Europe, the latter part of it mostly in Paris. He died in Zurich and is buried there.

Joyce not only removed himself physically from Dublin

and Ireland; he preserved a strict artistic distance from his subjects as a matter of critical principle. In one of his earliest writings he remarks: 'No man, said the Nolan, can be a lover of the true and the good unless he abhors the multitude; and the artist, though he may employ the crowd, is very careful to isolate himself.' 'The Nolan' is Giordano Bruno, philosopher and heretic, who was burnt at Rome in 1600, and it is characteristic of Joyce that he should quote from such a source. This strong assertion of critical distance comes from his student essay, 'The Day of the Rabblement', a fierce attack on the Irish Literary Theatre, which Joyce thought had begun as a 'movement of protest against the sterility and falsehood of the modern stage' but 'must now be considered the property of the rabblement of the most belated race in Europe'.

Joyce was an uncompromising, indeed an arrogant, individualist, but he also felt strongly that the Celtic Twilight vision of Ireland promoted by Yeats and his friends was false and misleading, 'an Ireland peopled only by Anglo-Irish aristocrats like Lady Gregory and the Syngean peasants of *Riders to the Sea'*, as Kenneth Grose puts it, in his excellent introductory study of Joyce. Joyce wanted to express the Ireland he knew at first hand in the streets and homes of Dublin, and his stories in *Dubliners* deal with stagnation, corruption and frustration in a mainly lower middle class urban world, that remained outside the scope of the Irish Literary Movement. Joyce told his publisher that he had written the book 'for the most part in a style of scrupulous meanness, and with the conviction that he is a very bold man who dares to alter in the presentment, still more to deform, whatever he has seen and heard'.

Dubliners owes something to *The Untilled Field*. Although Joyce despised Moore's stories he learned from them, and they helped to shape his own vision of an Ireland suffering from moral paralysis. When he wrote in 1905 to his brother Stanislaus about his short stories, *The Untilled Field* was in his mind.

When you remember that Dublin has been a capital for thousands of years, that it is the 'second city' of the British Empire, that it is nearly three times as big as

Venice, it seems strange that no artist has given it to the world. I read that silly, wretched book of Moore's 'The Untilled Field' which the Americans found so remarkable for its 'craftsmanship'. O, dear me! It is very dull and flat, indeed; and ill written.

There are several detailed critical studies of *Dubliners* one of which is listed in the bibliography. I must content myself with a brief look at three of the stories. It should be remembered that the book is not simply a collection of individual stories; they are carefully planned to build up a total picture of Dublin as Joyce saw it at the time. They move from childhood, through adolescence to studies of ineffective and frustrated adults, and the later ones take in the wider life of Dublin, including politics.

'A Painful Case' is a powerful and moving study of a man locked into a deliberate and methodical self-sufficiency. Mr Duffy 'lived at a little distance from his body, regarding his own acts with doubtful side-glances. . . . He had neither companions nor friends, church nor creed'. Through a chance meeting with a married woman at a concert Mr Duffy finds himself almost involved in a human relationship, but when a passionate gesture from Mrs Sinico disturbs his conviction of the soul's incurable loneliness, he breaks off his friendship with her. Four years later, as he is eating his evening meal of corned beef and cabbage, he sees a paragraph in the local paper, sub-titled 'A Painful Case', describing an inquest. Mrs Sinico, who had turned to drink for solace, was knocked down and killed by a train. After Mr Duffy has read through the full report he wanders out into the Dublin night, and the story reaches a finely controlled peak of painful intensity. Mr Duffy faces a bleak moment of truth. 'He gnawed the rectitude of his life; he felt that he had been outcast from life's feast. One human being had seemed to love him and he had denied her love and happiness: he had sentenced her to ignominy, a death of shame.' Joyce preserves scrupulously his artistic distance, but the impact of the story releases springs of compassion in the reader, both for Mrs Sinico and for Mr Duffy.

'Ivy Day in the Committee Room' throws a sharp side-light on a municipal election campaign in Dublin. It is the sixth of

October, the anniversary of the death of Parnell, and Mr O'Connor, wearing an ivy-leaf in commemoration, is sitting in the dark, bare committee room, where a meagre fire is coaxed to give heat and light by an elderly caretaker. O'Connor is working as a canvasser for Mr Richard J. Tierney, P.L.G. Other people come in and there is some discussion of the candidate, 'Tricky Dicky Tierney'. He is running on a Nationalist ticket, but his canvassers suspect that he will support the move to present an address of welcome to the visiting King Edward VII. They are chiefly concerned with whether or not he will pay them for their work. At the end of the story, Joe Hynes, who also wears an ivy-leaf, reads a poem he has written on the death of Parnell. I quote the penultimate verse, which gives a fair sample of its quality:

They had their way: they laid him low.
    But Erin, list, his spirit may
 Rise, like the Phoenix from the flames,
    When breaks the dawning of the day . . .

It may be a trite and sentimental poem, but there is something genuine in the feeling that it arouses in Hynes and O'Connor. The shadow of a great man is cast over the shabby committee room.

The details of scene, conversation and character in the story are finely observed and controlled to build up a sense of the meanness and pettiness of Dublin politics. The brief appearance of Father Keon, apparently an unfrocked priest, the mystery of whose life remains unexplained, adds to the total effect of spiritual squalor. The story is not as painful as that of Mr Duffy, but it brings out strongly the sense of moral paralysis that Joyce meant to convey.

'The Dead', the last and longest story in *Dubliners,* is rightly the most admired. It is more subtle and varied, and wider in its range than the preceding stories; it also includes a strong autobiographical element and Joyce's obsession with sexual jealousy. At the same time Joyce maintains artistic control of the story. At the end we recognise that he is writing prose with much of the delicacy and rhythmic power of poetry. The last paragraph, describing the snow falling over Ireland, is justly famous. The reader is caught up with

Gabriel Conroy, brooding over the vast host of the dead: 'His soul swooned slowly as he heard the snow falling faintly through the universe and faintly falling, like the descent of their last end, upon all the living and the dead.'

Stephen Hero was a first draft of what later became *A Portrait of the Artist as a Young Man*. Joyce never published it. In fact he threw the manuscript on the fire in a fit of temper, but his sister rescued most of it from the flames. After Joyce's death a part of the manuscript was edited by Theodore Spencer, an American professor, and it was published in 1944.

The book covers only two years of Stephen's life as student, whereas the more compressed and distanced *A Portrait of the Artist* takes Stephen from babyhood to the time of his leaving college. There is more detail in *Stephen Hero* about Stephen's college friends, and there are long passages of dialogue. The girl whom Stephen desires, the shadowy E.C. of *A Portrait of the Artist*, is fleshed out as Emma Clery, and there is more about Stephen's pursuit of her. Some passages re-appear unchanged in *A Portrait of the Artist*, and naturally the two books make an interesting comparison. But apart from this, *Stephen Hero* is worth reading on its own account. Even though it is somewhat shapeless and incomplete in comparison with the later book, it presents a fascinating and closely observed account of the development of a young man's mind and feelings.

Joyce's habit of noting 'epiphanies' is clearly revealed in this book. As Stephen passes through Eccles Street one misty evening he observes a young lady 'standing on the steps of one of those brown brick houses which seem the very incarnation of Irish paralysis. A young gentleman was leaning on the rusty railings of the area.' Stephen overhears a fragment of their conversation, the lady alluringly and temptingly resisting the young man's advances and telling him he is very wicked:

The triviality made him think of collecting many such moments together in a book of epiphanies. By an epiphany he meant a sudden spiritual manifestation, whether in the vulgarity of speech or of gesture or in a memorable phase of the mind itself. He believed that it was for the man of letters to record these epiphanies with extreme care, seeing that they themselves are the most delicate and evanescent of moments.

A Portrait of the Artist as a Young Man itself is surely one of the seminal books of the early twentieth century. It was certainly seminal for me when I read it as a sixth-form boy at school. For this reason I find it hard to write about. Both Stephen's daring *non serviam* — 'I will not serve that in which I no longer believe, whether it call itself my home, my father-land or my church' — and the exultant call of life that he hears on the seashore, after rejecting the idea of becoming a priest — 'On and on and on and on he strode, far out over the sands, singing wildly to the sea, crying to greet the advent of the life that had cried to him' — both these moods must have found a passionate echo in thousands of young hearts and minds; and many lips must have repeated Stephen's prayer at the end of the book as he prepares to leave home: 'Amen. So be it. Welcome, O life! I go to encounter for the millionth time the reality of experience . . . '.

The theme of *A Portrait* has been deftly summarised by Richard Ellmann, in the eighteenth chapter of his fine biography, as 'the gestation of a soul':

In the first chapter the foetal soul is for a few pages only slightly individualized, the organism responds only to the most primitive sensory impressions, then the heart forms and musters its affections, the being struggles towards some unspecified, uncomprehended culmination, it is flooded in ways it cannot understand or control, it gropes wordlessly towards sexual differentiation. In the third chapter shame floods Stephen's whole body as conscience develops; the lower bestial nature is put by. Then at the end of the fourth chapter the soul discovers the goal towards which it has been mysteriously proceeding — the goal of life. It must swim no more but emerge into air, the new metaphor being flight.

Judged as a novel — for it is fiction not autobiography, in spite of the close kinship between Stephen Dedalus and James Joyce — the book is highly original in form and manner, extending and deepening the exploration of the inward consciousness that is one of the main features of the novel in the early twentieth century. The use of the interior monologue and the stream-of-consciousness techniques Joyce carried further in *Ulysses,* but already he was making effective use of them. He continued to develop also the use of such poetic devices as rhythm and repetition to deepen and intensify the force of his prose. We find this, for example, in the passage describing the young girl whom Stephen sees on the seashore; and again when Stephen and Cranly, walking in the suburbs one evening, hear a servant girl singing:

Cranly stopped to listen, saying:
—*Mulier cantat*
The soft beauty of the Latin word touched with an enchanting touch the dark of the evening, with a touch fainter and more persuading than the touch of music or of a woman's hand. The strife of their minds was quelled. The figure of a woman as she appears in the liturgy of the church passed silently through the darkness: a white-robed figure, small and slender as a boy, and with a falling girdle. Her voice, frail and high as a boy's, was heard intoning from a distant choir the first words of a woman which pierce the gloom and clamour of the first chanting of the passion:
—*Et tu cum Jesu Galilaeo eras.*
And all hearts were touched and turned to her voice, shining like a young star, shining clearer as the voice intoned the proparoxytone and more faintly as the cadence died.

This passage illustrates another significant aspect of the book, the great importance for Stephen, and Joyce, of the shape and sound and colour of words. The young Stephen had reflected on the word 'wine': 'The word was beautiful; wine. It made you think of dark purple because the grapes were dark purple that grew in Greece outside houses like white temples.' Grown older Stephen reflects on the power of the words that he is beginning to handle as an artist:

He drew forth a phrase from his treasure and spoke it softly to himself:

— A day of dappled seaborne clouds.

The phrase and the day and the scene harmonized in a chord. Words. Was it their colours? He allowed them to glow and fade, hue after hue: sunrise gold, the russet and green of apple orchards, azure of waves, the grey-fringed fleece of clouds. No, it was not their colours: it was the poise and balance of the period itself.

In the history of the novel in the twentieth century *Ulysses* towers like a giant over all other books. Walter Allen called it 'the most stupendous attempt to see life whole in fiction in our century', and he claimed that Bloom is the 'most universal character in modern fiction, a creation of Shakespearean amplitude, comparable in achievement with Falstaff.' Is it possible for any writer to see life whole? Certainly Joyce attempts it. He devotes over nine hundred pages to one day (16 June, 1904) in the lives of a group of people in Dublin. He has built up an elaborate structure of correspondences for each chapter of the book. Apart from the Homeric parallels with the *Odyssey*, each chapter has its own time and place, its different art, technique and symbol. A full account of the structure may be found in Stuart Gilbert's *James Joyce's Ulysses* (1930), and there is illuminating discussion of it in Richard Ellmann's *Ulysses on the Liffey* (1972).

Joyce was deeply drawn to the theme of Ulysses. In his biography Richard Ellman quotes from a journal kept by one of Joyce's language pupils. He records what Joyce said to him at a café one summer evening in 1917.

The most beautiful, all embracing theme is that of the Odyssey. It is greater, more human than that of *Hamlet, Don Quixote,* Dante, *Faust.* The rejuvenation of old Faust has an unpleasant effect upon me. Dante tires one quickly; it is like looking at the sun. The most beautiful, most human traits are contained in the Odyssey. I was twelve years old when we took up the Trojan War at school; only the Odyssey stuck in my memory. I want to be frank: at twelve I liked the supernaturalism in Ulysses. When I was writing *Dubliners,* I intended at first to choose the title *Ulysses in Dublin* but gave up the idea. In Rome, when I had finished about half the *Portrait,* I realized that the Odyssey had to be the sequel, and I began to write *Ulysses.*

Leopold Bloom, the twentieth century shade of Ulysses, is a deliberately unheroic and unromantic figure, though he is deeply human. Aged thirty-eight, he is an Irish-born Jew of Hungarian extraction, and he earns his living by canvassing advertisements for a local newspaper. He wanders the streets of Dublin, meeting many different people, thinking his own thoughts and indulging fragmentary daydreams and fantasies. We are drawn deeply and minutely into his consciousness. Joyce evolves a style and manner finely tuned to reveal the stream of human consciousness. It is difficult to illustrate this in a short quotation, because one of the things Joyce is doing is building up a sense of the multiplicity and variety of the impressions that impinge on a man in his daily experience of the world inside and outside. But the following passage will give some idea of Joyce's achievement. Bloom is on his way to lunch, passing up Grafton Street. Looking in the shop windows at the gleaming silks and petticoats, he feels a stirring of sexual desire at the thought of yielding, perfumed bodies:

A warm human plumpness settled down on his brain. His brain yielded. Perfume of embraces all him assailed. With hungered flesh obscurely, he mutely craved to adore.

Duke Street. Here we are. Must eat. The Burton. Feel better then.

He turned Combridge's corner, still pursued. Jingling hoofthuds. Perfumed bodies, warm, full. All kissed, yielded: in deep summer fields, tangled pressed grass, in trickling hallways of tenements, along sofas, creaking beds.

— Jack, love!
— Darling!
— Kiss me, Reggy!
— My boy!
— Love!

His heart astir he pushed in the door of the Burton restaurant. Stink gripped his trembling breath: pungent meatjuice, slop of greens. See the animals feed.

Men, men, men.

Perched on high stools by the bar, hats shoved back, at the tables calling for more bread no charge, swilling, wolfing gobfuls of sloppy food, their eyes bulging, wiping wetted moustaches.

We know from Joyce's friend, Frank Budgen, that he spent a whole day simply adjusting the *order* of the words in the sentence: 'Perfume of embraces all him assailed: with hungered flesh obscurely he mutely craved to adore.' This is just a pointer to the scrupulous care which Joyce devoted to his task. It took him seven years to write *Ulysses*. Not surprisingly the book repays many readings. The significances, the correspondences and contrasts, the cross-references grow with each reading. It is a great bedside book; one can dip into most of the chapters and be caught up in the fascinating detail of the scenes and impressions.

Yet the book is not without its longeurs and dull stretches. Joyce's faithfulness to his choice of style for a particular episode forces him to try the reader's patience sorely. For instance, in chapter sixteen (Eumaeus) where the narrative is 'old', he is imitating a flabby, pseudo-literary, feebly prolix style of journalism. The fourth sentence reads: 'For the nonce he was rather nonplussed but inasmuch as the duty plainly devolved upon him to take some measures on the subject he pondered suitable ways and means during which Stephen repeatedly yawned.' This is not a chapter that encourages re-reading. And although I recognise the brilliance of Joyce's imitative skill in chapter fourteen (The Oxen of the Sun), where he runs through a gamut of literary styles from Anglo-Saxon to the nineteenth century, I don't find myself drawn to re-read this chapter. But most of the chapters can be read and re-read with increasing understanding and pleasure. *Ulysses* is surely the ideal choice of reading for a desert island.

I must be quite frank about *Finnegans Wake*. I have not read my way through it, and I don't think I ever shall. I have only nibbled at bits and pieces of it. The first part I read — it was then only part of 'Work in Progress' — was 'Anna Livia Plurabelle'. This is still the part I like best and find easiest to assimilate. I was fortunate enough to hear an early recording of Joyce himself reading the closing paragraphs. His reading certainly helped a great deal to establish the sense and movement of the passage.

Anna Livia Plurabelle is the female principle in the book, appearing variously as woman and river, and representing all women and all rivers. In this section she is a Dublin girl and also the river Liffey. Two washerwomen, washing their clothes in the water of the river, are gossiping about her: 'Tuck up your sleeves and loosen your talk-tapes.' At the end the women are tired, night falls and the sound of the running water drowns their voices. Here is the closing paragraph:

Can't hear with the waters of. The chittering waters of. Flittering bats, fieldmice bawk talk. Ho! Are you not gone ahome? What Thom Malone? Can't hear with bawk of bats, all thim liffeying waters of. Ho, talk save us! My foos wont moos. I feel as old as yonder elm. A tale told of Shaun or Shem? All Livia's daughtersons. Dark hawks hear us. Night! Night! My ho head halls. I feel as heavy as yonder stone. Tell me of John or Shaun? Who were Shem and Shaun the living sons or daughters of? Night now! Tell me, tell me, tell me, elm! Night night! Tellmetale of stem or stone. Beside the rivering waters of, hitherandthithering waters of. Night!

Although the language and sentence formation in this passage are unusual, the general drift is clear. It contains within itself, to use Coleridge's critical touchstone, the reason why it is so and not otherwise. It is rightly a famous passage and probably the best known piece in the whole book.

At the beginning of *Finnegans Wake* we are faced with a much more formidable prospect. Here is a packed, encoded language containing references that need working out. We find ourselves solving puzzles rather than reading. The short opening paragraph is not difficult, but here is the second.

Sir Tristram, violer d'amores, fr'over the short sea, had passencore rearrived from North Armorica on this side the scraggy isthmus of Europe Minor to wielderfight his penisolate war; nor had topsawyer's rocks by the stream Oconee exaggerated themselse to Laurens County's gorgios while they went doublin their mumper all the time; nor avoice from afire bellowsed mishe mishe to tauf-tauf thuart peatrick; not yet, though venissoon after, had a kidscad buttended a bland old isaac; not yet, though all's fair in vanessy, were sosie sesthers wroth with twone nathandjoe. Rot a peck of pa's malt had Jhem or Shen brewed by arclight and rory end to the regginbrow was to be seen ringsome on the aquaface.

Kenneth Grose, in his little book on Joyce, offers a helpful commentary on this passage. After four pages of explanation he goes on: 'So far only the more obvious allusions in only fourteen lines have been looked at. To deal with the whole book at this length would take sixteen hundred times as long.... Only people who are able to devote years of study to the book can hope to disentangle its verbal complexities. . . . 15,000 words have been written on one sentence.'

'The writer expresses. He does not communicate. The plain reader be damned.' These are not Joyce's words but they could well serve as an epigraph for *Finnegans Wake*. They come from a manifesto written by Eugene Jolas. Eugene and Maria Jolas edited an avant-garde journal in Paris, *Transition*, which published sections of Joyce's 'Work in Progress'. Their intransigent attitude to the plain reader encouraged Joyce in his 'wilful obscurity'. These latter words are used, not by a frustrated plain reader, but by a patient scholar. Adaline Glasheen, in her *Census of Finnegans Wake* (1956), writes: '*Finnegans Wake* is wilfully obscure. It was conceived as obscurity; it was executed as obscurity; it is about obscurity.'

The language of the book has been defended by Richard Ellmann in his biography. Since Joyce is presenting the world of night and dream, where the rational daylight order and control no longer apply, it was necessary for him to use a broken polyglot language: 'To imitate the sophistication of word- and image-formation in the unconscious mind . . . he took settled words and images, then dismembered and reconstituted them.'

Finnegans Wake remains a remarkable, if largely unreadable, work. Joyce may not be the greatest writer of his century but he is certainly the most daring and original.

11

James Stephens

James Joyce once referred to James Stephens as 'my rival, the latest Irish genius', and in his later years he seriously thought of asking Stephens to carry on with *Finnegans Wake* in the event of his own untimely death. But Stephens' first encounter with Joyce was hardly promising. He described it in a broadcast talk for the BBC in 1946:

I was walking up Dawson Street, thinking of nothing, which was and is my favourite form of thinking, when I noticed that two men were coming towards me, and that one of them was deliberating upon me as if I were a life-buoy spotted suddenly in a sea of trouble. Suddenly they stopped, and that one said, 'Stephens, this is Joyce,' and then, turning to his companion, he said, 'I've got to run' — and he ran.

There stood Joyce and I, he stuck with me, and I stuck with him, and the other drowning man was swimming to a reef two streets off. Joyce looked at me without a word in his mouth, and I looked at him with nothing in my mouth except vocabularies. We halted upon each other. We were very different-looking people. Joyce was tall, which I wasn't; he wore specs, which I didn't; he looked down at me, which I couldn't; he rubbed his chin at me, which I wouldn't . . .

[Stephens finally ended this embarrasing pause by inviting Joyce for a drink in a nearby tavern.]

The barman brought the refreshment that I ordered — it was called a 'Tailor of Malt'. It was larger than a single, and it only escaped being a double by the breadth of a tram-ticket, and it cost me three pence. When Joyce had silently dispatched one-third of a tailor into his system he became more human. He looked at me through the spectacles that made his blue eyes look nearly as big as the eyes of a cow — very magnifying they were.

'It takes,' said I brightly, 'seven tailors to make a man, but two of these tailors make twins. Seven of them,' I went on, 'make a clan.'

Here Joyce woke up: he exploded moderately into conversation. He turned his chin and his specs at me, and away down at me, and confided the secret to me that he had read my two books; that, grammatically, I did not know the difference between a semi-colon and a colon: that my knowledge of Irish life was non-Catholic and, so nonexistent, and that I should give up writing and take to a good job like shoe-shining as a more promising profession.

I confided back to him that I had never read a word of his, and that, if Heaven preserved to me my protective wits, I never would read a word of his, unless I was asked to destructively review it.

We stalked out of Pat Kinsella's; that is, he stalked, I trotted.

James Stephens (1880–1950) was born in obscurity. Even the date of his birth is uncertain, but it seems likely to have been 9 February 1880. His father, a Dublin vanman, died when James was only two years old. He was sent to an orphanage but ran away, and was later committed to the Meath Protestant Industrial School for Boys because he was found wandering, and perhaps begging, in the streets. After various odd jobs he found a post in a solicitor's office. He wrote, secretly at first, and then for the paper *Sinn Fein,* edited by Arthur Griffith. He was encouraged by AE and began to move in literary circles. He sat one day in the Bailey tavern with Arthur Griffith, Tom Kettle, Oliver Gogarty, Seamus O'Sullivan and others, and later he remarked. 'I had my first adventure in that air, oxygen and gin, which we call wit.'

His first volume of poems, *Insurrections,* was published in 1909, but it was the year 1912 that brought him fame, when the 'two books' referred to by Joyce in the passage above, were published. These were *A Charwoman's Daughter* and

The Crock of Gold. In 1915 Stephens was appointed to a post as Registrar at the National Gallery. In 1924, finding the atmosphere of the newly established Free State uncongenial, he resigned, and the next year moved to London. He had a high reputation as a talker as well as a writer, and in the last years of his life he gave talks and readings for the BBC.

Stephens published some seven volumes of poetry; but, with a few exceptions his poems, fashioned in the somewhat worn literary mould of the Georgian poets, lack the vigour and vitality of his prose. The energy in the poems often seems adventitious. At other times the verse is thin and facile, and it can become sentimental. He is too fond of the word 'little'. In 'Lovers' the moon and the sea face each other in loneliness and longing,

> The pretty, timid moon, and the
> Poor, unhappy, little sea.

His best work is in his vigorous, free translations from the Irish, mostly appearing in *Re-incarnations* (1918). A good and popular example is 'A Glass of Beer', where the poet puts his curse on a publican's wife who refuses to draw him a glass of beer:

> The lanky hank of a she in the inn over there
> Nearly killed me for asking the loan of a glass of beer.
> May the devil grip the whey-faced slut by the hair
> And beat bad manners out of her skin for a year.
>
> That parboiled ape with the toughest jaw you will see
> On virtue's path, and a voice that would rasp the dead,
> Came roaring and raging the minute she looked at me,
> And threw me out of the house on the back of me head!
>
> If I asked her husband he'd give me a cask a day,
> But she, with the beer at hand, not a gill would arrange!
> May she marry a ghost and bear him a kitten, and may
> The High King of Glory permit her to get the mange.

In prose, Stephens had more than one kind of writing at his command. He wrote an admirable eye-witness account of the Easter Rising, entitled *The Insurrection in Dublin* (1916).

Day by day he recorded, in simple but telling words, exactly what he saw and heard in the streets of Dublin. At the end of the book he made a moving plea to the English government for understanding and clemency:

> A peace that will last for ever can be made with Ireland if you wish to make it, but you must take her hand at once, for in a few months' time she will not open it to you; the old bad relations will recommence, the rancour will be born and grow, and another memory will be stored away in Ireland's capacious and retentive brain.

Unfortunately this plea fell on deaf ears, and the rancour has not yet ceased.

Stephens employs a similar plain and telling prose in one or two stark stories of unemployment and poverty. The best example is 'Hunger', a story first published in booklet form in 1918, and later reprinted in *Etched in Moonlight* (1928). This is a stark account of crushing poverty and ruthless hunger in Dublin in the year 1914. A housepainter becomes unemployed, and he and his wife and three children go down deep beyond the bread line. Other families could retrench and economise in times of hardship, but the housepainter's wife had nothing to give up:

> What could she eliminate, who had come to the bare bone and shank of life? The necessity for the loaf comes daily, recurs pitilessly from digestion to digestion, and with the inexorable promptitude of the moon the rent collector wanes and waxes.
>
> They managed . . .
> A bone in a world of bones! And they gnawed these bones until it seemed that nothing moved in the world except their teeth.

In a last desperate effort to beat starvation the husband goes to find work at a munitions factory in Scotland. The morning after he begins work he is found dead in a laneway, from hunger and exposure. Meantime his wife, waiting in Dublin for news and money, gets in touch with a relief organisation. A gentleman calls at their home, but one child has already died of hunger. It is hard to look at the prose of this story with critical detachment. It should certainly be compulsory reading for the wealthy nations of the world.

A keen awareness of the meaning of poverty also underlies *The Charwoman's Daughter*, but here Stephens is moving into the world of fantasy that is to be his special preserve. The name of the principal character, Mary Makebelieve, suggests the fairy-tale element in this short novel. At the end of the story Mary and her mother are rescued from poverty by a fairy uncle in America who dies and leaves them money. But the opening paragraph reveals the harsh details of poverty that are relentlessly present in the story:

> Mary Makebelieve lived with her mother in a small room at the very top of a big, dingy house in a Dublin back street. As long as she could remember she had lived in that top back room. She knew every crack in the ceiling, and they were numerous and of strange shapes. Every spot of mildew on the ancient wallpaper was familiar. She had, indeed, watched the growth of most from a greyish shade to a dark stain, from a spot to a great blob, and the holes in the skirting of the walls, out of which at night time the cockroaches came rattling, she knew also . . .

Apart from the proper name, this opening suggests a technique of detailed realism, but even in the first chapter we are introduced to Mrs Makebelieve's daydreams. She and her daughter would play at imagining that someone had died and left them a great fortune:

> They were to move the first thing in the morning to a big house with a garden behind it full of fruit trees and flowers and birds. There would be a wide lawn in front of the house to play lawn-tennis on, and to walk with delicately fine young men with fair faces and white hands, who would speak in the French language and bow often with their hats almost touching the ground . . .

Apart from the daydreams, the element of fantasy soon appears in the style. Stephens' imagination quickly leaps from fact to fancy. Mrs Makebelieve is suddenly called to work by the steps of the labouring man next door:

... she bounded from her bed; three wide twists put up her hair; eight strange, billow-like movements put on her clothes; as each article of clothing reached a definite point on her person Mary stabbed it swiftly with a pin ...

The mundane details of dressing have been transformed into a bizarre and fantastic ritual.

When Stephens describes the respectable middle-class house of Mrs O'Connor, where Mary takes her mother's place as charwoman, it begins to take on a muted life of its own:

It was a dark house. The windows were all withered away behind stiff curtains, and the light that laboured between these was chastened to the last degree of respectability. The doors skulked behind heavy plush hangings. The floors hid themselves decently under thick red and black carpets, and the margins which were uncarpeted were disguised by beeswax, so that no one knew they were there at all. The narrow hall was steeped in shadow, for there two black velvet portieres, at distances of six feet apart, depended from rods in the ceiling. Similar palls flopped on each landing of the staircase, and no sound was heard in the house at all, except dim voices that droned from somewhere, muffled and sepulchral and bodiless.

This passage reminds me of Dickens' description of Mr Dombey's house in *Dombey and Son*:

Mr. Dombey's house was a large one, on the shady side of a tall, dark, dreadfully genteel street in the region between Portland Place and Bryanstone Square. It was a corner house, with great wide areas containing cellars frowned upon by barred windows, and leered at by crooked-eyed doors leading to dustbins. It was a house of dismal state, with a circular back to it, containing a whole suite of drawing-rooms looking upon a gravelled yard, where two gaunt trees, with blackened trunks and branches, rattled rather than rustled, their leaves were so smoke-dried.

At first sight one would not associate Stephens with Dickens but their imaginations sometimes work in similar ways. Both have a leaning to the grotesque and the bizarre, though Dickens of course has a far more voluminous imaginative inventiveness. George Orwell pointed out, in his stimulating essay on Charles Dickens, that 'the outstanding, unmistakable mark of Dickens' writing is the unnecessary detail.' He goes on to quote from Jack Hopkins' story in *The Pickwick Papers,* where the family's dinner is mentioned '—baked shoulder of mutton and potatoes under it—' which has no real relevance in the story of the child who swallowed a bead necklace. I was reminded of this when I read Stephens' short story 'Three Lovers Who Lost.' The story is about a timid and respectful young man who seeks the hand of Julia Elizabeth O'Reilly, and calls on her parents. A pot of jam makes its way into the story for no apparent reason. It was sent by Mrs O'Reilly to the young man's Aunt Jane, an invalid, but her children got at it before her and cleaned the pot. It is sometimes the irrelevant episodes in Stephens' stories that are the liveliest and most amusing, like the conversation between the cow and the fly in Book VI of *The Crock of Gold.* I think Dickens would have approved of the touches of exaggeration and fantasy that frequently give a comic vitality to Stephens' writing.

The Crock of Gold is perhaps the best known of Stephens' works, though it is not as flawless as *The Charwoman's Daughter,* which is almost perfect in its delicate blend of reality and fantasy. In his first book Stephens restricts himself to the streets of Dublin, but in *The Crock of Gold* he moves from the pine forest of the two Philosophers, Coilla Doraca, to the realm of Pan and Angus Og. He has a wide range of unusual characters, including the Leprechauns of Gort na Cloca Mora. He also has a wide range of styles, and at times he falls into tedious abstractions and moralizing. His Gods are occasionally a little boring; but his two Philosophers and their thin wives, his policeman and leprechauns and rural people are full of comic vitality. Even his insects and animals have entertaining conversations. A tinker's ass, who has just received three kicks on the nose from his master, has the following exchange with a spider:

There was a spider sitting on a hot stone in the grass. He had a small body and wide legs and he wasn't doing anything.

'Does anybody ever kick you in the nose?' said the ass to him.

'Ay does there,' said the spider; 'you and your like that are always walking on me, or running over me with the wheels of a cart.'

'Well, why don't you stay on the wall?' said the ass.

'Sure, my wife is there,' replied the spider.

'What's the harm in that?' said the ass.

'She'd eat me,' said the spider, 'and, anyhow, the competition on the wall is dreadful, and the flies are getting wiser and timider every season. Have you got a wife yourself, now?'

'I have not,' said the ass; 'I wish I had.'

'You like your wife for the first while,' said the spider, 'and after that you hate her.'

'If I had the first while I'd chance the second while,' replied the ass.

'It's bachelor's talk,' said the spider; 'all the same, we can't keep away from them' and so saying he began to move all his legs at once in the direction of the wall. 'You can only die once,' said he.

'If your wife was an ass she wouldn't eat you,' said the ass.

'She'd be doing something else then,' replied the spider, and he climbed up the wall.

The substance of this discussion may be neither original nor profound, but the fact that it is carried on between an ass and a spider gives it a twist of comic surprise that seems to me delightful. It is all part of the zest and energy with which Stephens tackles his multi-layered world. When the children meet a leprechaun he reels off a delightful list of the games he can teach them:

'Did you ever play Jackstones?' said the Leprechaun.

'No, sir,' replied Seamus.

'I'll teach you how to play Jackstones,' said the Leprechaun, and he picked up some pine cones and taught the children that game.

'Did you ever play Ball in the Decker?'

'No, sir,' said Seamus.

'Did you ever play 'I can make a nail with my ree-ro-raddy-O, I can make a nail with my ree-ro-ray?'

'No, sir,' replied Seamus.

'It's a nice game,' said the Leprechaun, 'and so is Cap-on-the-Back, and Twenty-four yards on the billy-goat's tail, and Towns and Relievo, and Leap-frog. I'll teach you all those games,' said the Leprechaun, 'and I'll teach you how to play Knifey, and Hole-and-taw, and Horneys and Robbers.'

For those who have never read any James Stephens a good starting point might be his story 'A Rhinoceros, Some Ladies and a Horse'. This may be found in Frank O'Connor's collection of *Modern Irish Short Stories* (Oxford: World's Classics, 1942). This piece seems to have begun as a fragment of autobiography, but it turned into a short story. It deals with the experiences of a small errand-boy, in his first job, with the animals and humans of the title. The boy has two bosses, one very thin, the other very fat. The fat one

was composed entirely of stomachs. He had three baby-stomachs under his chin; then he had three more descending in even larger englobings entirely to the ground: but, just before reaching the ground, the final stomach bifurcated into a pair of boots. He was very light on these and could bounce about in the neatest way.

The rhinoceros, which the small boy encounters in the zoo when he is pushed through the bars of its cage by two other boys, is also very fat, 'but it wasn't fat like stomachs, it was fat like barrels of cement.'

The title of the story suggests its rich and extravagant comedy, which is reflected in the style. The first lady encountered by the boy is a famous music-hall singer, who calls on the theatrical agents for whom he is working: 'She was very wide, and deep, and magnificent. She was dressed in camels and zebras and goats . . . '. When she finally noticed the boy she sank to her knees and spread out both arms to him:

'Come to my Boozalum, angel,' said she in a tender kind of way.

I knew what she meant, and I knew she didn't know how to pronounce that word. I took a rapid glance at the area indicated. The lady had a boozalum you could graze a cow on. I didn't wait one second, but slid, in one swift, silent slide, under the table.

Whimsy is out of fashion in contemporary literature and contemporary taste is hostile to it. It must be frankly admitted that there is an element of whimsy in the humour of James Stephens, as indeed there is in the humour of Dickens. But the whimsical imagination expresses itself with such splendid vitality and dexterity that it carries most readers with it.

When the small boy of the story goes out to post letters he is suddenly landed with a horse to hold. The horse falls in love with him: 'He started to lean against me and woo me with small whinneys.' So the boy pinches an apple from a nearby barrow (he distinguishes nicely between 'pinching' an apple for the horse, and taking one for himself which would be 'stealing'), and feeds it to the horse:

The good nag had watched every move I made, and when I got back his eyes were wide open, his mouth was wide open, and he had his legs all splayed out so that he couldn't possibly slip. I broke the apple in halves and popped one half into his mouth. He ate it in slow crunches, and then he looked diligently at the other half. I gave him the other half, and, as he ate it, he gurgled with cidery gargles of pure joy.

The English genius for understatement is sometimes set against the Irish genius for overstatement, and I have already argued (in chapter 3) that many Irish writers take a delight in extravagance and flamboyance. Certainly one can feel in his prose the zest with which Stephens embarks on his comic extravagance. Here is a passage from another story, 'Three Happy Places' in *Here Are Ladies*, describing a sullen and pugnacious schoolboy:

He was densely packed with pugnacity. He lived for ever on the extreme slope of a fight, down which he slid at a word, a nod, a wink, into strenuous and bloodthirsty warfare. He was never seen without a black eye, a bruised

lip, or something wrong with his ear. He had the most mis-
cellaneous collection of hurts that one could imagine, and
he was always prepared to exhibit his latest injury in
exchange for a piece of toffee. If this method of barter was
not relished he would hit the proprietor of the toffee and
confiscate the goods to his own use.

It would be wrong to assume that the energy and vitality
of James Stephens springs solely from extravagance. He is a
master of many modes. He can suggest a great deal in a brief
phrase. He speaks of the Gaelic hero Fionn, 'new come from
leaves and shadows and the dipple and dapple of a wood',
and the forest background is flashed into our minds. His
retelling of Gaelic stories in his later books is often stark and
simple, but our attention is fully, and dramatically, engaged.
His version of the Deirdre legend (in prose) is the finest that I
know, far more powerful than the Deirdre plays of either
Yeats or Synge. It begins with Conachur, lonely and restless
at the house of his story-teller, Felimid. He claps his hands
for a servant.

'Is Felimid mac Dall married?'
'He is, master.'
'Give my compliments to Felimid,' said Conachur,
'and tell him that his wife is to sleep with me tonight.'

Felimid's wife cannot come because she is in childbed, and
that night the ill-fated Deirdre is born:

'A child has just been born in this house. She will bring
evil to Ireland, and she will work destruction in Ulster as a
ferret works destruction in a rabbit's burrow.'

James Stephens is not without faults; he is sometimes too
arch and sometimes too abstract. He is rarely good when he
preaches to his readers. But as a story-teller he can delight
and surprise us, and his lively prose contains much less than is
commonly supposed of what Joyce called 'cultic twalette'.

12

Sean O'Casey

In the *Who's Who* entry for Sean O'Casey we read: 'Education: in the streets of Dublin.' This gives a fair enough picture of his background and upbringing. He was not exactly born in the slums, as is sometimes stated, but he knew the facts of poverty in Victorian Dublin and was familiar with the lives and manners of the working class.

He was born John Casey in 1880, the last of thirteen children, eight of whom died in infancy. His father Michael Casey, a Protestant, worked as a clerk in the Society for Church Missions. He died when John was only six, leaving the family to manage as best they could. John was not a strong child and he had a good deal of eye trouble, so that he had little formal education. He took a number of humble jobs and as he grew up he became a socialist and a nationalist, learning Irish and changing his name to Sean O'Casey. He came under the influence of Jim Larkin and for a time he was secretary of the Council of the Irish Citizen Army.

But O'Casey, never a conformist, soon found himself at odds with the Citizen Army. He disapproved of uniforms and of the Army's cooperation with the Irish Volunteers. So he took no part in the Easter Rising, though he was arrested by the British as a suspect. His sympathies were with the non-combatants whose lives were endangered, like his own mother, and the man he admired most was the pacifist Francis Sheehy-Skeffington, who tried to prevent looting and was wrongfully shot.

The young O'Casey was an ardent reader. The first book that influenced him was the Bible, and its rhythms and imagery stayed with him all his life, finding many echoes in his plays. His brother organised a small acting group and Sean took part in plays by Shakespeare and Boucicault. To his passionate reading of Shakespeare, he later added Darwin, Shaw and Marx. His first attempts at writing were mainly political and topical, but later he turned to drama and about 1919 he submitted a play to the Abbey Theatre. His first attempts were rejected but *The Shadow of a Gunman* was accepted and performed in 1923. The next year *Juno and the Paycock* met with such success that he was encouraged to give up his current job as a builder's labourer and become a full-time writer.

His next play, *The Plough and the Stars* (1926), caused riots in the theatre. There had been murmurs and cries of disapproval during the first performances, and on the fourth night the play was stopped altogether in the third act. Yeats called in the police and went on to the stage to make a speech to the turbulent audience, a speech that he had carefully prepared. Here is a piece of it:

You have disgraced yourselves again. Is this to be an ever-recurring celebration of the arrival of Irish genius? Synge first and then O'Casey. The news of the happenings of the past few minutes will go from country to country. Ireland has once more rocked the cradle of genius. From such a scene in this theatre went forth the fame of Synge. Equally the fame of O'Casey is born here to-night. This is his apotheosis.

I recall that O'Casey, when discussing this famous occasion in a TV interview, remarked: 'I went home and looked up "apotheosis" in the dictionary.'

In 1927 he married a young Irish actress Eileen Carey, who had played Nora Clitheroe in *The Plough and the Stars* in London, and he took up residence in England for the rest of his life. This was largely the result of a bitter quarrel with the Abbey Theatre, first over the rejection of his next play, *The Silver Tassie*, and then over the performing rights of *Juno* and *The Plough*. *The Silver Tassie* is a play about the first World War and it has an Expressionist second act, where numbered but nameless soldiers crouch round a huge field gun and chant their weariness and disillusion with the war. The play is not wholly successful, but it has considerable dramatic power, and the Abbey should certainly have performed it. But Yeats took a dislike to it and insisted on rejecting it. So O'Casey became an exile, living mostly in Torquay in Devon, and without a theatre to work closely with. He continued to write plays, and to experiment with new techniques, but none of his later plays achieved the popularity and success of his early ones.

In my view the early plays set in Dublin — *The Shadow, Juno* and *The Plough* — are not only the most popular but also the best. They have the strength of close contact with Dublin idiom and Dublin people. All three deal with the 'Troubles' that accompanied Ireland's struggle for independence between 1916 and 1923. But it is not true, as is sometimes suggested, that the plays are simply photographic impressions of Dublin working-class life during the time of the Troubles. A close look at the texts reveals, not reportage, but a creative adjustment of reality. There is a strong element of caricature, of the grotesque, in his plays. His evident delight in oddity and diversity of character reminds us at times of Dickens. Consider, for example, the way he introduces some of the characters in the stage-directions. Captain Boyle's head 'looks like a stone ball that one sometimes sees on the top of a gate-post' and his walk is a slow consequential strut'. Joxer's face is 'like a bundle of crinkled paper . . . he has a habit of constantly shrugging his shoulders with a peculiar twitching movement, meant to be ingratiating. His face is invariably ornamented with a grin'. Peter Flynn in *The Plough and the Stars,* is described as 'a little thin bit of a man, with a face shaped like a lozenge; on his cheeks and under his chin is a straggling wiry beard of a dirty-white and lemon hue. His face invariably wears a look of animated anguish, mixed with irritated defiance, as if everybody was at war with him, and he at war with everybody.' Mrs Gogan 'is a doleful-looking little woman of forty, insinuating manner and sallow complexion. She is fidgety and nervous, terribly talkative, has a habit of taking up things that may be near her and fiddling with them while she is speaking. Her heart is aflame with curiosity, and a fly could not come into nor go out of the house without her knowing.'

The method of O'Casey's early plays is naturalistic, not

symbolic and abstract as in some of the later plays, but characters such as those just described do not belong to a tradition of social realism. Their affinity is rather with the tradition of popular comedy and music-hall. They are nearer to Boucicault than to Ibsen. As with Synge, though in a different manner and setting, there is a note of extravagance, of comic exaggeration, that should not be underplayed.

The Shadow of a Gunman is set in 1920, when the British authorities, with the help of auxiliary troops (the so-called 'Black-and-Tans'), were fighting a sporadic war with Republican guerillas and gunmen. O'Casey called the play 'a tragedy in two acts', but it would be truer to call it tragi-comedy with an edge of satire, the special O'Casey mix that we find in all three Dublin plays. It has roots in O'Casey's own experiences in 1920. When he moved to live with a friend in 35 Mountjoy Square, some of the neighbours thought that he was a gunman on the run. Sometime afterwards the house was raided and bombs were discovered. The action of the play is similar. Its main theme, however, is human selfishness. Donal Davoren, a poet, and Seamus Shields, a lapsed patriot, who share a tenement room, are exposed as egocentric and cowardly by the dauntless Minnie Powell, who hides the bombs in her own room, is arrested by the Black and Tans and then shot in an ambush. Davoren, at least, acknowledges his shame — 'Oh, Davoren . . . poet and poltroon . . . !' — but Shields remains selfish and superstitious, and has the last line, a characteristic comic-ironic ending: 'I knew something ud come of the tappin' on the wall!'

Other characters, preoccupied with their own concerns, contribute to the comedy and to the main theme, and O'Casey puts into the mouth of Shields a jeremiad on the violent state of the country, in which the rhythm gives force to the words:

The country is gone mad. Instead of counting their beads now they're countin' bullets; their Hail Marys and paternosters are burstin' bombs — burstin' bombs, and the rattle of machine-guns; petrol is their holy water; their Mass is a burnin' buildin'; their de Profundis is 'The Soldiers' Song', and their creed is, I believe in the gun almighty, maker of heaven an' earth — an' it's all for 'the glory o' God and the honour o' Ireland'.

In his next two plays O'Casey develops the qualities he has already revealed. The comedy and irony are richer and deeper, the tragic-satiric overtones more powerful, and he has created some unforgettable characters. Of the two plays I prefer *Juno and the Paycock,* because I think the characters are more successfully realised, and the dialogue is more convincing and natural. In *The Plough and the Stars*, which some critics have judged to be O'Casey's finest play, there is alliterative colouring that sometimes calls attention to itself in a way that makes the speech less natural: 'Is a man fermentin' with fear to stick th' showin' off to him of a thing that looks like a shinin' shroud?' says Fluther Good; and Peter Flynn, in a rage, rounds on his tormentor, The Covey: 'I'll not stick any longer these tittherin' taunts of yours, rovin' around to sing your slights and slanders, reddenin' th' mind of a man to th' thinkin' an' sayin' of things that sicken his soul with sin!'

Juno is free from the tendency to over-write that mars much of O'Casey's later work, including the autobiographies. It is easier to accept Joxer's repetition of the word 'darlin' than Fluther's repetition of 'derogatory' and 'vice versa'. In spite of these small faults *The Plough* still has great vigour and gusto in the dialogue, and there is a splendid shouting match between Mrs Gogan and Bessie Burgess in the pub scene, but *Juno* still has the edge. There is strength of line as well as colour in the dialogue, a neat balancing of phrases that gives them shape and style. Juno says: 'If that's the way you go on when you get the money it'll be the grave for you, an asylum for me and the poorhouse for Johnny.' This is wholly natural speech, but it takes the shape of a neat triad.

When Boyle is pretending he has news of a job and is talking of taking his shovel, Juno, who knows only too well that this is only pretence, bursts out in natural indignation, but her speech has balance and wit: 'Shovel! Ah then me boyo, you'd do far more work with a knife an' fork than you'll ever do with a shovel! If there was e'er a genuine job goin' you'd be dh'other way about — not able to lift your arms with the pains in your legs! Your poor wife slavin' to keep the bit in your mouth, and you gallivantin' about all the day like a paycock!'

A little later Juno says to Boyle: 'Don't be actin' as if you couldn't pull a wing out of a dead bee.' The simile is natural, not carefully contrived. It might well be a common Dublin expression picked up by O'Casey, and not an original coinage of his own. This is probably true of a good deal of the dialogue in the play. That it is not newly-minted does not matter. The dialogue is wholly convincing, in keeping with character and it gives pleasure to the ear. Another memorable example is Jerry Devine's outburst against the rival who has ousted him in Mary's affections — 'a thin, lanky strip of a Micky Dazzler with a walkin' stick an' gloves.'

With the possible exception of Charlie Bentham, the rival just referred to, who is necessary to the plot but not fully realised as a character, the people in *Juno* are vivid and distinctive dramatic personalities. The speeches of Juno, already cited, reveal her firm grip on mundane reality. Boyle dreams up a rich fantasy life of the times when he was 'sailin from the Gulf o' Mexico to the Antanartic Ocean.' In times of storm he was 'fixed to the wheel with a marlinspike, an' the winds blowin' fierce an' the waves lashin' an' lashin' . . .' At times Juno punctures his dreams with sharp reminders of the real facts: 'Everybody callin' you "Captain", an' you only wanst on the wather, in an oul' collier from here to Liverpool, when anybody to listen or look at you, ud take you for a second Christo For Columbus!'

Juno and the 'paycock' make a fine dramatic contrast, but the most famous pair in the play are himself and his butty, Joxer. They are something of an archetypal pair, belonging to a theatrical tradition that goes back to the 'miles gloriosus', the braggart captain, and his parasite or hanger-on. One of the funniest scenes in the whole repertoire of the Abbey Theatre occurs in the second part of Act I when Boyle, encouraged by Joxer, indulges the daydream of his sailing days referred to above, his boasting ironically punctuated by the voice of the coal vendor peddling coal blocks:

> *Boyle.* An', as it blowed an' blowed, I often looked up at the sky an' assed meself the question — what is the stars, what is the stars?

Voice of Coal Block Vendor. Any blocks, coal-blocks; blocks, coal-blocks!

Joxer. Ah, that's the question, that's the question — what is the stars?

Boyle. An' then, I'd have another look, an' I'd ass meself — what is the moon?

Joxer. Ah, that's the question — what is the moon, what is the moon?

At this point the dreaming is interrupted by the actual appearance of the coal vendor, and shortly afterwards by the unexpected return of Juno. Joxer, to avoid Juno's fury (she has already chased him out once), jumps out of the window on the roof of the return room and has to wait out there until Juno introduces Bentham to the family. Boyle, apparently turning over a new leaf and renouncing Joxer, is interrupted by Joxer climbing angrily through the window:

Joxer. . . . . You're done with Joxer, are you? Maybe you thought I'd stop on the roof all the night for you! Joxer out on the roof with the win' blowin' through him was nothin' to you and your friend with the collar an' tie!

Mrs Boyle. What in the name O' God brought you out on the roof: what were you doin' there?

Joxer (ironically). I was dreamin' I was standin' on the bridge of a ship, an' she sailin' the Antartic Ocean, an' it blowed, an' blowed, an' I lookin' up at the sky an' sayin', what is the stars, what is the stars?

In looking at the dialogue and the comedy, I have so far neglected the main theme of the play, which makes it ultimately a tragedy, or perhaps more correctly, a tragi-comedy. The theme, which is common to all three plays about the 'troubles', could be summed up as 'man's inhumanity to man'. The phrase from Burns is quoted, with comic irony, by Joxer, who has just lifted one of Boyle's last two bottles of stout. The theme is most clearly presented in *Juno* and it finds expression in what might be called the 'theme speech', spoken by Mrs Tancred as she goes to the funeral of her son, Robbie, shot in an ambush. It is repeated by Mrs Boyle, when her son, Johnny, responsible for Robbie's death, is shot as an informer by his fellow Republicans. At the end of the play, before she leaves with the police to identify the body of her son, Juno laments:

> ... What was the pain I suffered, Johnny, bringin' you into the world to carry you to your cradle, to the pains I'll suffer carryin' you out o' the world to bring you to your grave! Mother o' God, Mother o' God, have pity on us all! Blessed Virgin, where were you when me darlin' son was riddled with bullets, when me darlin' son was riddled with bullets? Sacred Heart o' Jesus, take away our hearts o' stone, and give us hearts o' flesh! Take away this murdherin' hate, an' give us Thine own eternal love!

There has been some argument over this famous speech, where O'Casey uses the poetic devices of rhythm and repetition to heighten the emotion. Some critics have seen in it a 'phoney lyricism', and they have been dismissive of the tragic poetry that others have found in the play. This view is put sharply by Patrick Kavanagh, who remarked in his *Self-Portrait*: 'The English reviewers went crazy about the poetry of O'Casey's *Juno*, whereas in fact we only endure that embarrassment for the laughs in Captain Boyle.' Is Juno's speech sentimental or tragic, embarrassing or moving? It is an important question for the success of the play. I think O'Casey himself was aware of the danger of sentimentality because he has introduced a note of harsh comedy just before the speech when Maisie Madigan has a brief exchange with the impatient police: 'Take your hour, there, take your hour! If yous are in such a hurry, skip off, then, for nobody wants you here — if they did yous wouldn't be found ... As far as I can see, the Polis as Polis, in this city, is Null an' Void!'

The speech is followed by an ironic and comic anti-climax when the drunken Boyle and Joxer stumble into the empty room. Many producers have baulked at this final scene and cut it out, so that the play ends on the high tragic note of Juno's prayer for humanity. But it seems to me that O'Casey's dramatic instinct was right. The final scene not only prevents Juno's speech from becoming a sentimental end-piece, but it actually reinforces the tragic hopelessness of Irish civil strife by ironical resonances. The hopeless, drunken Boyle boasts of his patriotic services to Ireland, and says: 'If the worst comes... to the worse ... I can join a ... flyin' ... column.' The dream fantasy is tragic as well as comic. Juno prays God to take away our hearts of stone but we are left with the maudlin mutterings of two hopeless, selfish, irresponsible men, and a world that is '... in a terr ... ble state o' ... chassis!' O'Casey's ending contains a pungent mixture of comedy, tragedy and irony, though it is admittedly a difficult scene to present on the stage.

As a creative playwright O'Casey rightly refused to confine himself to the limits of his three Dublin plays. He went on to experiment, first in *The Silver Tassie*, then with a series of other plays, all of which have originality and dramatic imagination, though not all are convincing and successful. Among the later plays I would select as the most rewarding to read or see, *The Silver Tassie, Red Roses for Me* and *Cock-a-Doodle-Dandy*. O'Casey considered the last to be his best written play. It certainly has an élan and a gaiety of its own, combining the symbolic and supernatural in a way that makes it difficult to stage. But the old attack on Irish puritanism and repression seems somewhat trite and repetitive.

It is for his plays that O'Casey will be best remembered, but he also wrote essays, short stories, autobiographies and a great many letters. The autobiographies are vivid and full of interest, though he sometimes tries for effects that do not come off, and he sometimes gets high on the potent influence of Joyce. He published six volumes of autobiography between 1939 and 1954, beginning with *I Knock at the Door*. His dramatic imagination, and dramatic method, is evident from the first sentence of this book:

In Dublin, sometime in the early eighties, on the last day of the month of March, a mother in child-pain clenched her teeth, dug her knees home into the bed, sweated and panted and grunted, became a tense living mass of agony and effort, groaned and pressed and groaned and pressed, and pressed a little boy out of her womb into a world where white horses and black horses and brown horses and white-and-black horses and brown-and-white hores trotted

tap-tap-tap tap-tap-tappety-tap over cobble stones, con-
ceitedly, in front of landau, brougham, or vis-à-vis; lumber-
ingly in front of tramcar; pantingly and patiently in front
of laden lorry, dray, or float; and gaily in front of the
merry and irresponsible jaunting-car:

This first paragraph is in fact only part of the first enor-
mous sentence that goes on for two pages, with paragraphs
coloned off. In it O'Casey tries, and largely succeeds, in
presenting a sense of the late Victorian background by an
accumulation of colourful and humorous detail.

Later in this chapter we find him marking the contrast
between the mother returning from hospital with her dead
baby and the excitement of a Parnell procession that holds
up the taxi she is travelling in. O'Casey writes of himself in
the third person as Johnny Casside so that there is an element
of fiction in his presentment of himself. This device enables
him also to present dramatically the historical and social
background. He does this partly by the method of the first
paragraph, and partly by describing characters who come
alive in his sketches. Here is the scene where Mrs Casside
takes Johnny to see the illuminations and flags on the
occasion of Queen Victoria's Jubilee. In the pushing crowd
struggling to get on a tram, Mrs Casside pleads priority for
Johnny's sore eyes:

The conductor leaned forward from the porch of the tram,
stretched out a sudden hand, and pulled Johnny and his
mother on, pushing them up the narrow stairs to the top,
as he planked himself in front of the others, perspiring and
pushing their way on to the platform.
— A man 'ud want St Pathrick's crozier to knock a little
decency into yous, he said viciously as he tried to turn the
pushing into an orderly parade. A nice way the whole of
yous musta been reared, with your pushin' an' shovin', like
a horde of uncivilised savages that has never seen anything
beyond the rim o' their own land! I don't know th'hell
why Parnell's wastin' his time thryin' to shape yous into
something recognizable as men an' women. Honest to
Jasus, I'm gettin' ashamed of me life to mention I'm Irish
in front of anyone showing the meanest sign or vestige of

dickorum. And all of yous risking the breakage of your bodies to see a few twinklin' lights set over your heads to do honour to a famine queen rollin' about in a vis-à-vis at a time the Irish were gettin' shovelled, ten at a time, into deep and desperate graves.

— You mind your own business be pullin' the bell for decent people to get on the thram, and decent people to get off the thram, said a man, having a wide watery mouth with a moustache hanging over it like a weeping willow . . .

Like Carleton before him O'Casey has a tendency to over-write, but the energy and vitality comes through. He does give us insights into Victorian Dublin and he reveals vividly the background of his own childhood.

13

Austin Clarke

Austin Clarke was born in Dublin in 1896, and he went to Belvedere College and University College, where Joyce had been before him. He had a very strict puritan Catholic upbringing. In his autobiography, *Twice Round the Black Church*, he tells of an occasion when, shortly after going to confession, in a fit of childish temper, he had said 'Damn you' to his mother:

> Fearful that I might drop down in that state of sin, she hurried me back to confession at once. Along Dorset Street that winter's evening I struggled, overwhelmed with horror of myself and conscious that, from the sky, the angered Man Above, to use my father's constant phrase, was watching me. One moment I was Cain fleeing through the wilderness; the next, I was the Boy Who had Cursed His Own Mother. . . . It was not the flames of Purgatory but those of Hell itself which threatened me and I could hear their dull roar. I made the sign of the cross at the font as I dashed into the church for I knew that in a few minutes more all the priests would have left. My only chance was Father O'Hara. He had confessed me only a short time before but his meekness and gentleness would save me again. I was just in time and I trembled as I awaited the familiar question.
> 'How long is it, my child, since your last confession?'
> 'Twenty minutes, Father.'
> Perhaps he did not quite hear my mumbled explanation; perhaps he was weary. Certainly he showed no sign of consternation when I mentioned my dreadful offence against the third commandment. Once more he repeated the little homily on the sufferings which Jesus had endured

for my sake. I scarcely listened to those sentiments which I knew so well for, wild with superstition, I only wanted to hear the unintelligible words in Latin for they alone could save me. To my own astonishment, my dread and pain disappeared as soon as I left the church . . . Once more I was a good boy.

He was still to suffer a great deal of mental anguish in his struggles with a narrow puritan concept of religion. He was haunted by hell fire: 'I heard in the school chapel the celebrated sermon on Hell which James Joyce has described. Constantly I listened for the ticking of the great clock below. Religious instruction and retreats made us all aware of the millions of human beings condemned to eternal torture.' When he reached the age of puberty he was frightened by the signs of developing sex and tried to arrest the growth of his pubic hair by cutting it off: 'Ignorant and confused by physical development and the change in scrotal sensation, I became convinced that the devil entirely possessed me and, startled by the first bristles below, I seized a scissors and in an agony of alarm shore myself.'

I have quoted at some length to illustrate this aspect of Clarke's youth because I think it helps to explain both his understanding of the asceticism of early Irish Christians, and his later criticism of the Church in Ireland for its hostility to natural instinct and the delight of the senses.

At University College, Clarke's reading of English literature widened his spiritual horizons and released him from his preoccupation with the fires of hell. At the same time he was influenced by the literary revival and the re-discovery of the Gaelic past. His teacher of Irish was Douglas Hyde, and he also came under the influence of George Sigerson and Thomas MacDonagh. He recalls the powerful effect that Hyde's words had upon him:

On the morning of our first term, he spoke of the aims and ideals of the language revival; we were all equal, all united in the Gaelic movement. There was no vulgar competition, no showing off, no twopence-halfpenny looking down on two-pence. Those plain words changed me in a few seconds. The hands of our lost despised centuries were laid on me.

Clarke learnt Irish, made friends with the Irish poet, Padraic O Connaire, and read deeply in early Irish legend and saga. His first published work was a narrative poem entitled *The Vengeance of Fionn* (1917).

In 1917 Clarke was made an assistant lecturer in English at UCD to take the place of Thomas MacDonagh, who was executed after the Easter Rising. He held this post for a few years, but after he entered into a civil marriage in 1921, his contract was not renewed. So he went to London to look for literary work and he did reviewing for a number of news-papers and magazines. He also continued with his own writing — poetry, verse-plays and prose romances.

In 1937 he returned to Dublin and spent the rest of his life there, living at Bridge House, Templeogue, and gradually becoming accepted as the senior Irish poet. He took a special interest in verse drama and together with Robert Farren he founded the Dublin Verse Speaking Society. Out of this grew the Lyric Theatre Company which produced his own verse plays. He died, in Dublin in 1974.

Clarke began by writing narrative poems based on Irish mythology. *The Vengeance of Fionn*, dealing with the legend of Diarmuid and Grainne, was followed by *The Sword of the West* (1921) and *The Cattledrive in Connaught* (1925). There is considerable poetic fluency and descriptive skill in these poems but I prefer the lyrics that preface the latter poem. One of these in particular, 'The Lost Heifer', shows the influence of Gaelic poetry on Clarke's English style, and has a delicate and intricate verbal music:

When the black herds of the rain were grazing
In the gap of the pure cold wind
And the watery hazes of the hazel
Brought her into my mind,
I thought of the last honey by the water
That no hive can find.

Brightness was drenching through the branches
When she wandered again,
Turning the silver out of dark grasses
Where the skylark had lain,
And her voice coming softly over the meadow
Was the mist becoming rain.

The lost heifer, appropriate in a poem about cattle, is related to the Gaelic *aisling* or vision poems, where the 'silk of the kine' is an image for the lost queen or leader who will restore the defeated kingdom. But the patriotic motif is blended with a love motif. In this poem the use of assonance and the echoing of sounds owes much to Clarke's familiarity with Gaelic verse, but he is not imitating a specific Gaelic verse pattern. He tells us in his booklet on *Poetry in Modern Ireland* (1951) that he has followed Gaelic prosody in some of his poems. In 'The Scholar' he uses one of the simplest forms, where 'the tonic word at the end of the line is supported by an assonance in the middle of the next line':

> Summer delights the scholar
> With knowledge and reason.
> Who is happy in hedgerow
> Or meadow as he is?

In the following verse from 'Aisling' he uses stopped rhyme '(e.g. ring — kingdom; breath — method)':

> Coil of her hair, in cluster and ringlet,
> Had brightened round her forehead and those curls —
> Closer than she could bind them on a finger —
> Were changing gleam and glitter. O she turned
> So gracefully aside, I thought her clothes
> Were flame and shadow while she slowly walked,
> Or that each breast was proud because it rode
> The cold air as the wave stayed by the swan.

Here, in addition to the stopped rhyme, there is a chiming and echoing of sounds that suits the idealistic, love-worshipping mood of a vision poem.

Both these poems are from the volume *Pilgrimage* (1929) where Clarke's special qualities as a lyric poet are first fully revealed. The first verse of the title-poem has these lines:

> There by dim wells the women tied
> A wish on thorn, while rainfall
> Was quiet as the turning of books
> In the holy schools at dawn.

The hushed music of these lines and the image of the holy

schools is characteristic, and wholly in tune with the pilgrimage, made to Clonmacnoise in monastic days, when the 'cloistered scholars . . . were all rejoicing daily'.

The second poem in the collection, 'Celibacy', gives a vivid picture of the holy monk or hermit desperately wrestling with visions of seductive womanhood. The spare hard lines of the opening, with water 'thorned/By colder days', suggest powerfully the nature of the ascetic ideal:

> On a brown isle of Lough Corrib,
> When clouds were bare as branch
> And water had been thorned
> By colder days, I sank
> In torment of her side;
> But still that woman stayed,
> For eye obeys the mind.
>
> Bedraggled in the briar
> And grey fire of the nettle,
> Three nights, I fell, I groaned
> On the flagstone of help
> To pluck her from my body;
> For servant ribbed with hunger
> May climb his rungs to God.

These early lyrics reveal another aspect of Clarke's poetry, his ability to suggest the nuances of Irish weather. Arland Ussher called attention to this aspect when Clarke was awarded the Gregory Medal for literature by the Irish Academy in 1968: 'More than in any other poet I know — one feels the constant presence of the *weather*, of the Irish light and the Irish air.' This is strongly felt in such poems as 'The Lost Heifer' and 'Pilgrimage'.

It was a long time before Clarke moved away from the Gaelic past, and from medieval Christian Ireland, into the present. He himself comments on this a little ruefully in the second volume of his autobiography, *A Penny in the Clouds:* 'It took me many years before I was able to write about the present age, and when I did so, I found that other poets had retired to the campus and the quadrangle, having rejected the belief that writers should be concerned with social reform.'

But his picture of medieval Ireland sometimes had clear implications for the present. In 1932 he published a prose romance, *The Bright Temptation*, which he sent to Yeats. Yeats wrote to Olivia Shakespeare about it: 'It is like one of William Morris's romances — 12th Century — on the surface, but turns out when you read it to be a charming and humorous defiance of the censorship and its ideals. It is the falling into temptation of a clerical student and all set in a fantastic and extravagant world.'

Aidan, a scholar from the abbey of Cluanmore, becomes through various mishaps, a straying student wandering the woods with Ethna. One night this beautiful girl, trying to wind up the falling ringlets of her hair, lets slip her cloak and reveals 'the lost treasure of Ireland':

> In the pure cold ray of light, remote and clear, was the naked girl. The gold falls of her curls had half hidden her throat and shoulders; they had tried to reach her breasts, but they had not been entirely freed, and being challenged by themselves had failed. Untouchable and firm, her two small breasts had escaped; they were pale and glimmering but for the winestain of each nipple. He saw the slender curve of her side as she turned in bewilderment to the light, the delicate grace of her naked body filled him with wonder. Its fair ivoried curves were simple and idle but for a glint of curls a little way below her navel, so tiny that her hand might hide them all — and brighter than lost gold in the fords of Ireland.

Compared with erotic passages from contemporary fiction, this description seems strangely innocent and old-fashioned, but the book was nevertheless banned in Ireland.

In his later verse, from *Ancient Lights* (1955) onwards, Clarke attacks with satire and astringent comment many aspects of the Irish Church and State. But long before this his attitude to a repressive, puritanical church is made clear. 'Penal Law' from *Night and Morning* (1938) is short and sharp:

> Burn Ovid with the rest. Lovers will find
> A hedge-school for themselves and learn by heart

All that the clergy banish from the mind,
When hands are joined and head bows in the dark.

The word play and ambiguities in this epigram are characteristic. Penal law recalls the days when the Catholic Church
was repressed, but it also recalls 'penis'. Hands may be joined
in prayer, and in love, and 'learn by heart' has two meanings.
'Penal Law' is echoed many years later by 'The Envy of
Poor Lovers':

Pity poor lovers who may not do what they please
With their kisses under a hedge, before a raindrop
Unhouses it; and astir from wretched centuries,
Bramble and briar remind them of the saints.

Her envy is the curtain seen at night-time,
Happy position that could change her name.
His envy—clasp of the married whose thoughts can be alike,
Whose nature flows without the blame or shame.

Many of Clarke's later poems are topical and deal with the
social problems of his time in Ireland, such as the controver-
sial Mother and Child bill, unmarried mothers, the shipping
of horses for meat, corporal punishment in schools, the Pill
and official Catholic attitudes to birth control. Less direct,
but still deeply critical of Catholic piety, is 'Martha Blake at
Fifty-One'. This is a narrative poem telling the story of a
pious spinster who falls victim to severe abdominal pains and
palpitations of the heart. Before her relations can come to
her help, her 'kind neighbours', wishing to be rid of her, call
the ambulance and send her to a Nuns' hospital. Here, instead
of the quiet sick ward that she had dreamed of, she finds
noise, inside and out: 'The Nuns had let the field in front/As
an Amusement Park.' Regulations forbid her the daily
sacrament, which was her chief comfort before entering
hospital, and she lies in misery, unable to eat:

Unpitied, wasting with diarrhea
    And the constant strain,
Poor Child of Mary with one idea,
    She ruptured a small vein,
Bled inwardly to jazz. No priest

> Came. She had been anointed
> Two days before, yet knew no peace:
>   Her last breath, disappointed.

The poem should be read alongside the earlier poem, 'Martha Blake', in *Night and Morning*, where the younger Martha is rapt in the miracle of Mass every morning:

> Yet ignorant of all the rest,
> The hidden grace that people
> Hurrying to business
> Look after in the street.

Now, in her illness and middle age, the neglected body of Martha takes its revenge.

> Cunning in body had come to hate
>   All this and stirred by mischief
> Haled Martha from Heaven. Heart palpitates
>   And terror in her stiffens.

The poem is a kind of stark social document, plain and bleak in style, very different from Clarke's early romantic verse. There is close attention to factual detail:

> Then, slowly walking after Mass
>   Down Rathgar Road, she took out
> Her Yale key, put a match to gas-ring,
>   Half-filled a saucepan, cooked
> A fresh egg lightly, with tea, brown bread . . .

The poem as a whole combines a telling exposure of the limitations of traditional piety with a deep compassion for the narrow life and lonely death of Martha Blake.

In his later years Clarke extended the range of his poetry to include many different styles and themes. In 1966 he wrote a fairly long narrative poem about mental breakdown, *Mnemosyne Lay in Dust*. Maurice Devane is taken to St. Patrick's Hospital in Dublin, the institution that Swift left money to found:

> He gave the little wealth he had
> To build a house for fools and mad.

The poem vividly and dramatically evokes the nightmare horror of lost memory and lost identity. Maurice is put in a padded cell and then fed forcibly. The memory of one word leads to his removal from his cell to a dormitory:

> Midnight follies. Shriek after shriek
> From the female ward. No terror
> Of clanking chains, poor ghost in sheet,
> Vampire of bloodless corpse, unearthed,
> In Gothic tale but only blankness.
> Storm flashed. Dr. Rutherford spoke.
> Maurice whispered from the blanket
> The one word: 'Claustrophobia'.
> That remnant of his memory
> Carried him to the dormitory.
>
>   . . . .
>
> *Timor Mortis* was beside him.
> In the next bed lolled an old man
> Called Mr. Prunty, smallish, white-haired
> Respectable. If anyone went past,
> He sat up, rigid, with pointed finger
> And shrieked: 'Stop, Captain, don't pass
> The dead body!' All day, eyes starting,
> Spectral, he shrieked, his finger darting.

The narrative moves with speed and force and the reader is drawn in compulsively to Maurice's world of madness. The effect is cumulative, and it is difficult to suggest by quoting two isolated stanzas; but the verses above will give some idea of the mood and manner of the poem.

There is a surprisingly wide range of theme and style in Clarke's later poetry. In a mood and manner totally different from *Mnemosyne* he wrote a poem on one of his early meetings with Yeats, 'In the Saville Club'. He had undertaken to write a book about Yeats and his publisher had asked him to try to find out more about the real woman who had inspired the love poetry of *The Wind Among the Reeds*. So he went to see Yeats at the Saville Club in London:

> I met him at four o'clock in the Saville Club
> Within the Lounge, chairs waiting for artist, savant,

> Bohemian. Smiling, all savoir faire,
> Yeats rose to greet me, stately, cloud-grey-tweeded,
> White-haired.

Yeats was in London to see about the publication of his book *A Vision*. The mystical, occult-probing side of the elder poet held no appeal for Clarke, but Yeats, pleased with himself, felt that he had 'solved the Arcane Problem':

>   Head
> Bowed low, he stood, respectful, for a few
> Moments before himself.

Later in the meeting the two poets sit down together at a small table:

> Soon, speaking of his plays, we leaned so close
> That I could see a tiny brown eye peeping
> Behind his left lens cutely from the Celtic
> Twilight at mine.

There is clearly a touch of malice in Clarke's wit, though we must smile at the skill with which he pin-points some of the less attractive aspects of Yeats. It is not surprising that Clarke failed to get the information he was seeking (he would have been wiser not to seek it at all, in spite of his publisher) and that his book on Yeats remained unwritten.

Clarke wrote about many other poets — Frost, Pound, Lorca, Neruda, Hopkins, James Stephens and F.R. Higgins. He wrote 'A Sermon on Swift', and poems on Irish political figures, and in his last years he was re-telling erotic tales from Ovid. Not all his poems are good; he can be cryptic and baffling, and some of his topical poems demand inside knowledge. But he has left a considerable body of good poetry that deserves to be more widely known than it is.

14

Flann O'Brien

'Born Paris 1891. Widely troubled. A connoisseur of potheen
and stirabout. Took part in 1898 insurrection. Member of
Seanad Eireann, 1925—7. Minister for Justice, May-August
1931. Regius Professor of Potheen, TCD. President of Ireland
1945.' This biographical note about himself was supplied by
Myles na gCopaleen (another pseudonym, which he adopted
in *The Irish Times*) and it strikes the right note of fantasy for
a writer whose imagination had more than one universe to
play with.

Brian O'Nolan, to give him his real name, was actually
born in Strabane, Co. Tyrone, where his father was an officer
in the Customs and Excise. He soon became a Dubliner, however, for he was educated there, and he subsequently lived
and worked and wrote in Dublin. He studied languages — Irish
in particular — at University College, and wrote an M.A.
thesis on nature in Irish poetry. He joined the Civil Service
and worked in the Department of Local Government, but
continued the writing that he had begun at college. His first
book, *At Swim-Two-Birds,* was published in March, 1939,
and six months later only 244 copies had been sold. But
when the book was re-issued in 1960 it soon achieved fame
and recognition.

At first approach a reader who is unfamiliar with Flann
O'Brien is likely to find it a puzzling book. First there is the
odd title. It turns out to be the translation of an Irish place
name 'Snamh-dá-én', a small place on the river Shannon,
which was visited by mad Sweeny, a character who appears in
a twelfth century Irish tale, and also in the novel. On the first
page of the book are three separate openings, and before long
the reader finds himself involved with three separate worlds,

each of them bizarre, not to mention the seemingly irrelevant extracts from other books, such as a school Literary Reader and a multi-volumed reference work of 1854 entitled *A Conspectus of the Arts and Natural Sciences*. The cure for puzzlement is to read on, and when the book is finished, to read it again. The kind of response the book demands will be clear on the first page. It is not only an odd book, it is clearly a very funny book. The Pooka MacPhellimey, 'seated at his diptych or ancient two-leaved hinged writing table with inner sides waxed'; John Furriskey, who has the rare distinction of being born at the age of twenty-five, thus entering the world 'with a memory but without a personal experience to account for it'; and Finn Mac Cool, 'not mentally robust' but 'a man of superb physique', are obviously characters designed to amuse. Even a reader who has no acquaintance with Irish myth and legend must smile at the description of Finn's massive frame: 'Each of his thighs was as thick as a horse's belly, narrowing to a calf as thick as the belly of a foal. Three fifties of fosterlings could engage with handball against the wideness of his backside, which was large enough to halt the march of men through a mountain-pass.'

There are three main levels in the book, which partly overlap, but are chiefly used for effects of ironic and comic contrast. The frame story concerns the narrator himself, a student at University college, who lives with his uncle but spends most of his time locked in his bedroom. Much of his energy goes into his 'spare-time literary activities'. He is writing a book about Dermot Trellis of the Red Swan Hotel, who is himself writing a salutary book on the dire consequences that follow wrong-doing. Trellis assembles a motley group of characters, including the Pooka 'a species of human Irish devil' and Finn Mac Cool. He brings his characters to his hotel where he can keep an eye on them, but when he is asleep they live their own independent lives. They finally take their revenge on him by getting his own son, conceived when he assaulted Sheila Lamont, one of his own characters, to write about *him*, and compel him to undergo punishment.

It will be clear from this brief sketch of the plot that one of O'Brien's aims is to blur the distinction between imagination and reality and to mock the assumptions of literary creation. Early in the book the narrator proclaims that a 'satisfactory novel should be a self-evident sham'. He goes on to argue that 'Characters should be interchangeable as between one book and another. The entire corpus of existing literature should be regarded as a limbo from which discerning authors could draw their characters as required, creating only when they failed to find a suitable existing puppet. The modern novel should be largely a work of reference. Most authors spend their time saying what has been said before — usually said much better.' A few lines later the narrator's ingenious theorising is somewhat undermined by his friend Brinsley's comment: 'That is all my bum.'

The narrator's theories need not be pressed too hard but they give O'Brien scope to play with levels of reality, to mingle past and present and to enjoy a good deal of comic anarchy. Above all this method allows him to play with contrasting styles. Anne Clissman, in her book on Flann O'Brien, points out that he 'often sees reality in terms of the way it is expressed and he is hyperconscious of the way in which language and style condition perception'. She has counted no less than thirty-six different styles in the book. Like Joyce, O'Brien is a skilful parodist, and he can expose a style by using a deliberately unsuitable word. When Furriskey, the villain, came home, he was anxious not to wake the sleeping Trellis: 'He crept up the stairs with the noiseless cat-tread of his good-quality woollen socks.' The unexpected 'good-quality', belonging to a different order of discourse, makes us aware of the hackneyed adventure-story style of the rest.

The saga-style of the Sweeny story is played off against the talk of the other mixed characters, including the Dublin cowboys, Shorty and Slug (borrowed from the 'western' novels of William Tracy). The travellers have observed movement in the branches of a tree and Shorty pulls his gun. Just before this point there has been some discussion, typical of O'Brien's keen interest in words, of the distinction between 'marsupial' and 'kangaroo':

> Come down out of that tree, roared Shorty, come down out of that, you bloody ruffian!
> Keep your dander down, said Slug, you can't shoot anything that's sitting.

Whatever it is, observed the poet, it's not a man. It hasn't got a trousers on it. It's likely a marsupial.

I still fail to see the distinction, said the Pooka quietly, or why marsupial should be preferred to the more homely word.

If you don't come down out of that tree in two seconds, bellowed Shorty with a cock of his two hammers, you'll come out a corpse in three! I'll count to ten. One, two . . .

I'm glad I have no body, said the Good Fairy. With that demented bully flourishing his irons every time he gets the sight of something he can shoot, nobody is safe. The term kangaroo, being the lesser, is *contained* in marsupial, which is a broader and more comprehensive word.

Five, six, seven . . .

I see, said the Pooka, you mean that the marsupial carries a kangaroo in its pouch?

TEN, said Shorty in decision. For the last time are you coming down?

There was a gentle rustle in the thick of the green branches, a slow caress like the visit of a summer breeze in a field of oats, a faint lifeless movement; and a voice descended on the travellers, querulous and saddened with an infinite weariness, a thin voice that was occupied with the recital of these staves:

> Sweeny the thin-groined it is
> in the middle of the yew;
> life is very bare here,
> piteous Christ it is cheerless.
>
> Grey branches have hurt me
> they have pierced my calves,
> I hang here in the yew-tree above,
> with chessmen, no womantryst.
>
> I can put no faith in humans
> in the place they are;
> watercress at evening is my lot,
> I will not come down.

Lord save us! said Slug.

Shorty waved his guns about him in the air, swallowing at his spittle.

You won't come down?

I think I know the gentleman, said the Pooka courteously interposing, I fancy (it is possible that I may be wrong) that it is a party by the name of Sweeny. He is not all in it.

In spite of some mockery and parody in the old Irish story-telling style of Finn Mac Cool, the epic tale of the persecution of Sweeny appeals to the imagination, and the lyrics recited by Sweeny in his distress are genuinely moving. This is made clearer when they are set off against the banal verses of the Dublin poet, Jem Casey, author of A PINT OF PLAIN IS YOUR ONLY MAN.

Bernard Benstock, writing in *Eire-Ireland* (vol.III, no.3), sees O'Brien's wit as finally anarchic and destructive: 'It is the serious lack of commitment in any direction that limits Brian O'Nolan and ensnares him within the second rank, below Joyce and Yeats and Sean O'Casey — nor does the reader find the sort of sincere despair to which Samuel Beckett is so vitally committed that he can find no other commitment.' This seems to me a doubtful statement about O'Brien's work in general, and it is certainly not applicable to *At Swim-Two-Birds*. J.C.C. Mays is nearer the truth in his essay on 'Brian O'Nolan: Literalist of the Imagination', when he writes: 'The real subject of the book is vigorous ingenuity, wildness and sweetness, those qualities of the legendary Brother Barnabas and other *personae* which Brian O'Nolan's friends remember at their most unrestrained in his College years and in the years immediately following . . . the book writes out at large the same ever-renewing energy delighted in for itself that has passed into legend.'

O'Brien's next book was *The Third Policeman*. He finished this in 1940, but the publishers declined it because they thought it altogether too fantastic. He was very disappointed, put away the manuscript and said that it had been lost. Later he re-wrote it, or rather used portions of it in *The Dalkey Archive*. Only after his death was the original manuscript published, in 1967. The publishers added a note at the end of the novel, consisting mainly of an extract from a letter written by O'Brien to William Saroyan. This reveals that the narrator, who admits to committing a murder in the opening sentence of the book, 'has been dead throughout the book and . . . all the queer ghastly things that have been happening to him are happening in a sort of hell which he earned for the killing.' A further note from the author states: 'Hell goes round and round [at one point he used this as the title of the novel]. In shape it is circular and by nature it is interminable, repetitive and very nearly unbearable.'

In his letter to Saroyan, O'Brien goes on to say: 'It is supposed to be very funny but I don't know about that either . . . I think the idea of a man being dead all the time is pretty new. When you are writing about the world of the dead — and the damned — where none of the rules and laws (not even the law of gravity) holds good, there is any amount of scope for back-chat and funny cracks.' The overall impression of the book is perhaps nightmarish rather than comic, but it is built up on comic distortions and dislocations of reality. The narrator is an admirer of an absurd philosopher, de Selby, and he joins in a planned robbery and murder chiefly in order to get money to publish his 'De Selby Index'. De Selby, who regards human existence as an hallucination, reverses the generally accepted views of the universe. Night is 'an insanitary condition of the atmosphere due to accretions of black air.' The earth is not spherical but sausage-shaped. After investigating time and eternity by a system of mirrors, he became so obsessed by mirrors that: 'As time went on he refused to countenance a direct view of anything and had a small mirror permanently suspended at a certain angle in front of his eyes by a wired mechanism of his own manufacture. After he had resorted to this fantastic arrangement, he interviewed visitors with his back to them and with his head inclined towards the ceiling; he was even credited with long walks backwards in crowded thoroughfares.' We are reminded of the professors at the Grand Academy of Lagado in *Gulliver's Travels*.

De Selby's absurdities and the remarks of his learned commentators, cited in lengthy footnotes, constitute a satiric attack on pedantry. But J.C.P. Mays points out that there is also an attack on self-absorption: 'The book's method is its theme; the dizzying indulgence in the abyss of selfhood (der selbe), the regardless pursuit of omniscience.'

Whatever we make of the theme of the book and its vision of hell, it certainly gave O'Brien scope for 'backchat and funny cracks'. Even if the ultimate effect is horrific, the style and manner of the book is comic. The reader is constantly surprised by the narrator's encounters and conversations with the people he meets. The 'funny-peculiar' and the 'funny-ha, ha', blend into each other. When the narrator wakes from a short sleep he finds himself being watched by a tricky little man smoking a tricky pipe. He tries unsuccessfully to find out the man's occupation:

> 'Tricky-looking man, you are hard to place and it is not easy to guess your station. You seem very contented in one way but then again you do not seem to be satisfied. What is your objection to life?'

> 'Is it life?' he answered. 'I would rather be without it,' he said, 'for there is a queer small utility in it. You cannot eat it or drink it or smoke it in your pipe, it does not keep the rain out and it is a poor armful in the dark if you strip it and take it to bed with you after a night of porter when you are shivering with the red passion. It is a great mistake and a thing better done without, like bed-jars and foreign bacon.'

A little later, at the police-station, the narrator has a conversation with Serjeant Pluck, who is obsessed with bicycles:

> 'Five years ago we had a case of loose handlebars. Now there is a rarity for you. It took the three of us a week to frame the charge.'
> 'Loose handlebars,' I muttered. I could not clearly see the reason for such talk about bicycles.
> 'And then there is the question of bad brakes. The country is honeycombed with bad brakes, half of the accidents are due to it, it runs in families.'
> I thought it would be better to try to change the conversation from bicycles.
> 'You told me what the first rule of wisdom is,' I said. 'What is the second rule?'
> 'That can be answered', he said. 'There are five in all. Always ask any questions that are to be asked and never

answer any. Turn everything you hear to your own advantage. Always carry a repair outfit. Take left turns as much as possible. Never apply your front brake first.'

'These are interesting rules,' I said dryly.

'If you follow them,' said the Serjeant, 'you will save your soul and you will never get a fall on a slippy road.'

'I would be obliged to you,' I said, 'if you would explain to me which of these rules covers the difficulty I have come here today to put before you.'

'This is not today, this is yesterday,' he said, 'but which of the difficulties is it? What is the *crux rei*?'

An additional ingredient in the bizarre comic flavour is the curiously mixed and at times convoluted style of the Serjeant's speech. When Gilhaney rides off on his bicycle the narrator ventures the comment that he is 'a droll man.' The Serjeant then describes him as 'a constituent man . . . largely instrumental but volubly fervous.'

From 1939 until his death in 1966 Flann O'Brien wrote a humorous column in *The Irish Times* under the heading of 'Cruiskeen Lawn' (the full little jug). He used the pseudonym Myles na gCopaleen ('Myles of the Ponies') from Gerald Griffin's novel *The Collegians*. The column began in Irish, then English was used on alternate days, but eventually it was written mainly in English. An amusing series was devoted to Keats and Chapman. He brought these characters together to explode an outrageous and ingenious pun. Chapman calls at Keats's lodging with a highly trained but disabled pigeon. Keats opens its beak, inspects it, and then extracts a piece of champagne cork: 'Immediately thereafter the poet sat down (essential literary preliminary even for those already seated) and wrote a sonnet entitled "On First Looking into Chapman's Homer".'

Following this a number of stories were invented leading up to puns or word-play of some kind. Keats and Chapman frequently appear in unlikely situations, as when Keats, tracking a horse escaped from its stable, meets Chapman on a solitary walking tour in a remote mountainy place. Chapman calls out:

'What are you doing, old man?
'Dogging a fled horse,' Keats said as he passed by.

The 'Cruiskeen Lawn' columns included a witty and skilful catechism of cliché, a series about 'the Brother' and another about 'The Plain People of Ireland'. There is mockery of all kinds aimed in many different directions, including literature and the arts. Here he is mocking Synge:

A lifetime of cogitation has convinced me that in this Anglo-Irish literature of ours (which for the most part is neither Anglo, Irish, nor literature) (as the man said) nothing in the whole galaxy of fake is comparable with Synge. That comic ghoul should be destroyed finally and forever by having a drama festival at which all his plays should be revived for the benefit of the younger people of today. The younger people should be shown what their fathers and grand-daddies went through for Ireland, and at a time when it was neither profitable nor popular. . . . It is not that Synge made people less worthy or nastier, or even better than they are, but he brought forward with the utmost solemnity amusing clowns talking a sub-language of their own and bade us take them very seriously. There was no harm done there, because we have long had the name of having heads on us. But when the counterfeit bauble began to be admired outside Ireland by reason of its oddity and 'charm', it soon became part of the literary credo here that Synge was a poet and a wild celtic god, a bit of a genius, indeed, like the brother. We, who knew the whole inside-outs of it, preferred to accept the ignorant valuations of outsiders on things Irish. And now the curse has come upon us, because I have personally met in the streets of Ireland persons who are clearly out of Synge's plays. They talk and dress like that and damn the drink they'll swally but the mug of porter in the long nights after Samhain.

In 1941 O'Brien published a satirical work in Irish, *An Béal Bocht*. This was translated into English by Patrick Power as *The Poor Mouth*. In his preface he comments on the difficulties of translating the book because the writer is 'parodying the style of certain Gaelic authors'. Bernard Share, writing in *Hibernia* (30 November, 1973) expressed the view that translation was really an impossible task. 'The whole raison d'etre of the book was that it was written in Irish. Half the jokes are linguistic . . . The ironies have all gone up in smoke.' Even so, I found the English translation amusing. One can partly guess at the original idiom; but since I don't know Irish I had better say no more.

The Hard Life (1961) is a much simpler book than *At Swim-Two-Birds* or *The Third Policeman,* but O'Brien's delight in word-play is evident from the first sentence: 'It is not that I half knew my mother. I knew half of her; the lower half — her lap, legs, feet, her hands and wrists as she bent forward.' This sets the tone for the hilariously absurd story of Mr Collopy, whose mission in life, never directly stated, is to relieve the long-suffering women of Dublin by erecting public lavatories for them. With his friend, Fr Kurt Fahrt, S.J., he finally visits Rome to plead his cause in a special audience with the Pope, but this ends in disaster.

I find the first half of the book the most entertaining; the comedy of the situation begins to wear a little thin as time goes on. There is an entertaining sideline in the ingenious and audacious confidence tricks practised by 'the brother', but perhaps the liveliest aspect of the book is Mr Collopy's Dublin idiom. When Fr Fahrt mildly suggests that a hint might be dropped to the Dublin Corporation he explodes:

> If a hint were dropped, my hat and parsley! Right well you know that I have the trotters wore off me going up the stairs of the filthy Corporation begging them, telling them, ordering them to do something. I have shown you copies of the letters I have sent to that booby the Lord Mayor . . . What result have I got? Nothing at all but abuse from cornerboys and jacks in office.

Mr Collopy refers to Cervantes as 'the Aubrey de Vere of Spain'. When he discovers that the young Finbarr cannot yet read he exclaims:

> Well, may the sweet Almighty God look down on us with compassion! Do you realise that at your age Mose Art had written four symphonies and any God's amount of lovely songs? Pagan Neeny had given a recital on the fiddle before the King of Prussia and John the Baptist was stranded in the desert with damn the thing to eat only locusts and wild honey. Have you no shame man?

Mr Collopy has his fine moments; but 'an exegesis of squalor' (the sub-title of the book) has its limitations, and it ends with 'a tidal surge of vomit'. *The Dalkey Archive* ends with the prospect of marriage and a family. It is a richer and saner book, and the humour has a wider range. In spite of the wild fantasies — an underwater interview with St Augustine, a secret formula that will destroy the world, James Joyce alive and well and writing pamphlets for the Catholic Truth Society while indignantly repudiating that dirty book, *Ulysses* — the balance of the familiar world returns. Mick's determination to end his relationship with Mary and enter a Trappist monastery is suddenly abandoned as they travel home together on a tram.

The spirit of the book is clearly indicated in the dedication:

I dedicate these pages
to my Guardian Angel,
impressing upon him
that I'm only fooling
and warning him
to see to it that
there is no misunderstanding
when I go home.

O'Brien may be only fooling, but when a writer of his wit and originality is doing this the result is a brilliant and heady entertainment. The story, carefully controlled and very compelling, is full of surprises. In the second chapter Mick and his friend Hackett are eating wheaten farls and drinking whiskey with the hospitable and urbane de Selby. He has been discussing Descartes, and explaining his own views on time, which he considers not as something that passes but as 'a condition of absolute stasis'. He goes on:

—Call me a theologian or a physicist as you will, he said at last rather earnestly, but I am serious and truthful. My discoveries concerning the nature of time were in fact quite accidental. The objective of my research was altogether different. My aim was utterly unconnected with the essence of time.
—Indeed? Hackett said rather coarsely as he coarsely munched. And what was the main aim?

—To destroy the whole world.

Feeling it his duty to prevent the destruction of the world by de Selby, who has discovered a chemical compound that can eliminate all the oxygen from the world's atmosphere, Mick seeks the assistance of Serjeant Fottrell. The Serjeant believes in what he calls the 'Mollycule' theory. It is dangerous for a man to ride a bicycle because the molecules of man and bicycle are interpenetrable, and a man may finally end up as a bicycle. Even walking too much is perilous:

> But shure walking too far too often too quickly isn't safe at all either. The cracking of your feet on the road makes a certain amount of road come up into you. When a man dies they say he returns to clay funereally but too much walking fills you up with clay far sooner (or buries bits of you along the road) and brings your death halfway to meet you. It is not easy to know fastidiously what is the best way to move yourself from one place to another.

Serjeant Fottrell's language has the same extraordinary convolutions as that of Serjeant Pluck, his prototype in *The Third Policeman*. He sympathises with any creature 'who is troublous in the stomach enpitments', and sagely remarks that 'not everyone understands the far from scrutable periculums of the intricate world'.

Although some characters and ideas, and even passages of text, from *The Third Policeman* are used in the making of *The Dalkey Archive*, it is a very different book. From the start it is anchored in the physical reality of Dalkey, 'a little town maybe twelve miles south of Dublin'. Mick moves through familiar Dublin streets and sits in the park at St Stephen's Green, whereas in *The Third Policeman* we find ourselves in an unlocalised nightmare world.

There are puns and jokes and witticisms on the side that give a sparkle to *The Dalkey Archive*, but what many people consider to be the cream of the book is Mick's discovery of, and conversations with, James Joyce. It is not possible to illustrate this by a short passage, but we have a surprising picture of a devout and humble James Joyce who wishes to join the Jesuits in order 'to clear the Holy Ghost out of the Godhead and out of the Catholic Church.' O'Brien's opinion of Joyce was ambivalent. He admired him but thought him conceited and arrogant, and he disapproved of *Finnegans Wake*. There is perhaps a touch of malice in his portrait of Joyce, but this does not distort the delightful fantasy of his return to Ireland.

Although *The Dalkey Archive* has not the ebullience and effervescence of *At Swim-Two-Birds* that 'magnificent piece of ludic bravura', to borrow Bernard Bergonzi's apt phrase, in its own controlled and quiet way it is a fine comic novel.

O'Brien's total output was not large, but he occupies an assured and special niche in Anglo-Irish writing. He could never be mistaken for an English or an American novelist. Some of the characteristics of Anglo-Irish writing that I mentioned in chapter three, such as love of fantasy and delight in word-play, are found in their purest state in his work. At the same time his knowledge of Irish, and his extensive reading in the older literature of Ireland, gave a Gaelic dimension to his fantasy and humour. As Anne Clissman reminds us: 'In pursuing the world of imagination, and eschewing the realistic, mundane and moralistic tradition of English novelists, O'Nolan was returning to the Celtic models he admired.' She also rightly emphasises his acute perception of the spoken word. 'One of his greatest talents was an ear for dialogue, especially for the Dubliner's conversations — repetitive, opinionated, boring, misinformed and brilliant. He loved the weight and colour of words and linguistic games of all kinds.' (Hogan (ed.) *A Dictionary of Irish Literature*.)

At all levels, whether in his daily newspaper column or in his novels, O'Brien is lively, witty and funny. But at his best he offers us more than witty anarchy and 'ludic bravura'. Pedantry, intellectual pretensions and fanaticisms of all kinds are reduced to size by his laughter, and the energy that is eternal delight is exalted.

PART FOUR

Yeats and Synge

15

William Butler Yeats

W. B. Yeats was born at Sandymount in Dublin on 13 June, 1865. His father, the son of a Church of Ireland clergyman, was a painter who followed the Pre-Raphaelite school. A man of lively and original mind, he set his face against contemporary 'bourgeois' civilisation, with its narrow commercialism and piety, and encouraged his son's artistic and poetic tastes.

Soon after his birth, the Yeats family moved to London and Yeats went to school in Hammersmith. But he spent holidays with his grandparents in Sligo, and became deeply attached to the Sligo countryside. The family returned to Dublin in 1880, and Yeats continued his schooling there, and later went to the Metropolitan School of Art. He made friends with AE. The family moved to London again in 1887, and Yeats became acquainted with Theosophists (including Madame Blavatsky) and poets. He was an active member of the Rhymers Club. So there are three main centres of influence in his formative years — London, Sligo and Dublin.

In London he came under the influence of the aesthetic movement that saw the poet as a dedicated worshipper of beauty, set apart from the vulgar world of business, politics and the newspapers. A passage he wrote about Oscar Wilde reveals his own outlook, except that he did not imitate Rossetti's verse, but rather that of Shelley and Spenser:

> In London he took to the aesthetic movement, in verse to the style of Rossetti, and in prose to that of Pater, and the slow-moving elegance — born of toil and sedentary — became all the more marvellous in his eyes because it was not his natural expression. He was fascinated by it, as I was fascinated as a boy of fourteen when I stood motionless on the street wondering if it was possible to ask my

way in what would be recognised at once as fine prose. It was so hard to believe, after I had heard somebody read out let us say Pater's description of the Mona Lisa, that 'Can you direct me to St. Peter's Square, Hammersmith' was under the circumstances the best possible prose.

The influence of Pater on Yeats's own highly-wrought prose was lasting, and when, years later, he came to edit the *Oxford Book of Modern Verse*, he put in Pater's description of the Mona Lisa (from his essay on Leonardo da Vinci), arranged in lines like free verse, as the first poem in the book.
In Sligo it was the landscape that attracted him, and the people, too, with their stories and folk-lore. In *Estrangement* he wrote: 'I remember when I was nine or ten years old walking along Kensington High Street so full of love for the fields and roads of Sligo that I longed — a strange sentiment for a child — for earth from a road there that I might kiss it.' He wrote from Sligo to Katharine Tynan in August 1887:

It is a wonderfully beautiful day. The air is full of trembling light. The very feel of the familiar Sligo earth puts me in good spirits. I should like to live here always, not so much out of liking for the people as for the earth and the sky here, though I like the people too. I went to see yesterday a certain cobbler of my acquaintance and he discoursed over his cat as though he had walked out of one of Kickham's novels.

In Dublin he came into contact with Irish national aspirations, first through John O'Leary and then through Maude Gonne, for whom he long cherished an unrequited passion. Under her influence he engaged in political activities for a time, but his main energies went into promoting a national literature and theatre in Ireland. He met Lady Gregory in 1897 and she became a firm friend and ally. He spent many summers at her beautiful home, Coole Park in Galway, which he celebrates in his verse. Much of his energy went into founding, and helping to run, the Abbey Theatre, for which he wrote many plays. In his plays, as in his verse, he turned to the Irish myths and legends of the past, made available to him by scholars, many of them, like Douglas Hyde and Standish O'Grady, his Dublin friends and acquaintances.

Speaking in the Senate in 1923 Yeats said: 'The greater proportion of my own writings have been founded upon the old literature of Ireland. I have had to read it in translations, but it has been the chief illumination of my imagination all my life.'

In 1916, after Maud Gonne's husband, Major John MacBride, had been executed for his part in the Easter Rising, Yeats again proposed to her and was refused. He also approached her daughter, Iseult, with the same result. The following year he married George Hyde-Lees, and for her he restored and refurnished a derelict tower, Thoor Ballylee, that he had bought in East Galway, not far from Coole Park.

Yeats's fame as a poet grew steadily, and in the twenties he received recognition and honours. In 1922 President Cosgrave appointed him to the newly formed Senate of the Irish Free State, and in 1923 he was awarded the Nobel Prize for literature. But his greatest poetry was still to come, and he continued writing into his seventies. He died on 28 January, 1939, in the south of France and was buried there, but in 1948 his remains were brought to Ireland and re-buried in Drumcliff churchyard, Co. Sligo, under a headstone inscribed with the famous epitaph that he had written himself.

To this brief sketch of Yeats's life I would like to add two contemporary accounts of Yeats in action as a poet in his earlier years. The first comes from Douglas Goldring's book of literary reminiscences, *South Lodge* (1943). He is writing of one of Yeats's literary Monday evenings at 18, Woburn Buildings, in London. On this occasion Ezra Pound took charge of the proceedings. Pound, much influenced by Yeats's poetry in his youth, became his lifelong friend and he influenced Yeats in his turn, helping to move him away from aesthetic langour and Celtic Twilight towards more forceful and athletic rhythms in his verse:

> I shall never forget my surprise, when Ezra took me to one of Yeats's Mondays, at the way in which he dominated the room, distributed Yeats's cigarettes and Chianti, and laid down the law about poetry. Poor golden-bearded Sturge Moore, who sat in a corner with a large musical instrument by his side (on which he was never given a chance of performing) endeavoured to join in the discussion on

prosody, a subject on which he believed himself not entirely ignorant, but Ezra promptly reduced him to a glum silence. My own emotions on this particular evening, since I did not possess Ezra's transatlantic *brio*, were an equal blend of reverence and a desire to giggle. I was sitting next to Yeats on a settle when a young Indian woman in a *sari* came and squatted at his feet and asked him to sing 'Innisfree', saying that she was certain he had composed it to an Irish air. Yeats was anxious to comply with this request but, unfortunately, like so many poets, he was completely unmusical, indeed almost tone deaf. He compromised by a sort of dirge-like incantation, calculated to send any unhappy giggler into hysterics. I bore it as long as I could, but at last the back of the settle began to shake and I received the impact of one of the poet's nasty glances from behind his pince-nez. Mercifully I recovered, but it was an awful experience.

There was, at times, a comic and ridiculous side to Yeats's performance as a bard, but it was not, of course, the only side. Oliver St John Gogarty gives another account, in a letter to G.K.A. Bell (1904) of Yeats at a literary evening in George Moore's Dublin house:

Yeats was at Moore's the other Saturday, and drank whiskeys and sodas, and recited a passage from a play he is composing, 'Deirdre'. The effects of his reciting this are not to be transmitted to you. He forgot himself and his face seemed tremulous as if in an image of impalpable fire. His lips are dark cherry red, and his cheeks too, take colour, and his eyes actually glow black and then the voice sets all vibrating as he sways like a Druid with his whole soul chanting. No wonder the mechanics in America are mesmerized. I know no more beautiful face than Yeats's when lit with song. Moore of course talked Bawdy.

Before discussing Yeats's poems I would like to take a brief glance at his plays. In reaction from the commercial theatre of his day, with its thin language and vulgar display, he wanted a theatre that would be simple in gesture and scenery, restoring primacy to the spoken word. In 'An Introduction for my Plays' (1937) he wrote: 'When I follow back my stream to its source I find two dominant desires: I wanted to get rid of irrelevant movement – the stage must become still that words might keep all their vividness – and I wanted vivid words.' Yeats mostly sought vivid words in verse, though with Lady Gregory's help, he tried folk speech in *Kathleen ni Houlihan* and *The Pot of Broth.*

In his early plays, *The Countess Cathleen* and *The Land of Heart's Desire,* there is a certain dreamy lyricism, but the verse of *On Baile's Strand* has become firmer and more controlled. The play, one of the first to be based on heroic legend, dramatises the conflict between Cuchulain and Conchubar, freedom versus control, wild courage against the caution of ordered government. Cuchulain speaks in a verse that is resonant but at the same time it suggests something of the movement of speech. Drawing his sword before the assembled kings he says:

> How many of you would meet
> This mutterer, this old whistler, this sand-piper,
> This edge that's greyer than the tide, this mouse
> That's gnawing at the timbers of the world,
> This, this – Boy, I would meet them all in arms
> If I'd a son like you.

It could be said that both ritual and reality are necessary for good drama, but in Yeats the balance swings towards ritual. It is difficult, sometimes impossible, to identify with his characters, and the human interest is reduced. In reaction from the drama of middle class drawingrooms, Yeats dreamed of plays that would be 'remote, spiritual, ideal', and as he grew older he moved further from the folk and the people, until he found himself writing for an aristocratic drawingroom. *At The Hawk's Well* was, in fact, performed in Lady Cunard's drawingroom. In 1919 we find him writing: 'I want to create for myself an unpopular theatre and an audience like a secret society where admission is by favour and never to many' ('A People's Theatre').

Perhaps my own limited experience of seeing Yeats's plays on the stage has been unfortunate, but I have always been disappointed. There may have been vivid words, but somehow they have not been kindled into dramatic life on the stage. For me, the most successful productions have been radio productions, where there was nothing to distract the attention from the vivid words. The BBC Third Programme production of *Purgatory* had a dark resonance that made me think it more effective than any of the stage performances I had seen.

There are poetic merits in most of Yeats's verse plays, but ultimately his greatness depends on his poems, especially the later ones. For more years than I care to recall I found myself teaching and examining university students on this poetry. One of my favourite examination questions, which I must have set many times in varied forms, was: 'What makes Yeats a great poet?' I never got a clear and satisfactory answer. My students told me *ad nauseam* about Yeats's love for Maud Gonne and how he reacted to the Easter Rising, but they found it hard to isolate the qualities of greatness. My question is, in fact, very difficult to answer, and it is perhaps a stupid question to set in a three-hour examination paper. Now I must face it squarely myself; at least I shall have more than an hour to come up with an answer.

A full and detailed account of Yeats's poetry would go far beyond the limits of this book. I offer here only a few brief points based on my own reading of Yeats. I would like to begin by recalling Auden's definition of poetry as 'memorable speech'. Yeats's words, like Shakespeare's, remain ringing in one's head. As with Shakespeare's, some of them have already become clichés, like the chorus line from 'Easter 1916' — 'A terrible beauty is born.' When Yeats first brought beauty and terror together into one phrase to describe his response to the Easter Rising he was wholly original and wholly right, but repetition has staled the phrase. The same qualities of originality and rightness, giving a slight shock of surprise, followed by a delighted acceptance of the aptness of the words, may be found frequently in Yeats, especially in his later work. Here are some examples that spring to my mind at once: 'a lonely impulse of delight', 'all that delirium of the brave', 'the ignominy of boyhood', 'out of the murderous innocence of the sea', 'the artifice of eternity', 'monuments of unaging intellect'. The vigour and memorableness of the lines are partly due to music and rhythm, as in these lines that seem to sing and dance:

May she become a flourishing hidden tree
That all her thoughts may like the linnet be,
And have no business but dispensing round
Their magnanimities of sound . . .

('A Prayer for my Daughter')

In the best sense of the word Yeats is a rhetorician. His poetry works in ways rejected by many twentieth century poets. Edward Thomas, for example, wanted to 'get rid of the last rags of rhetoric'. D.H. Lawrence said: 'The essence of poetry with us in this age of stark and unlovely actualities is a stark directness. . . . Everything can go, but this stark, bare, rocky directness of statement, this alone makes poetry to-day.' He himself often begins a poem with a burst of casual speech, such as this:

O! start a revolution, somebody!
not to get the money
but to lose it all for ever.

And again:

How beastly the bourgeois is
especially the male of the species . . .

It is clear that Lawrence is not thinking at all of poetic form, or of music and rhythm.

Robert Frost is much more conscious of poetic form, but he still begins a poem in a casual conversational way:

My long two-pointed ladder's sticking through a tree
Toward heaven still,
And there's a barrel that I didn't fill
Beside it . . .

Compare these with a characteristic opening by Yeats:

Suddenly I saw the cold and rook-delighting heaven
That seemed as though ice burned . . .

This is forceful, dramatic, arresting. In comparison with Frost's line it is rhetorical, but not, to my mind in any pejorative sense. Those who dislike this rhetorical style have accused Yeats of getting on stilts to express his thoughts and feelings. Professor Yvor Winters, in a notable attack (*The*

Poetry of W.B. Yeats, 1960), calls his poetry 'inflated' and 'bardic in the worst sense', implying that there is excess, over-dramatisation, distortion of truth and reality. Yeats may be guilty of a little fustian, but at his best his mode of utterance — musical, eloquent, dramatic — is surely not a distortion of the truth, but rather a sharpening of the edge of truth to make it sink in.

In 'Nineteen Hundred and Nineteen' he expresses his sense of the change that has taken place in Ireland, transforming idealism into brutality, in a vivid image:

> We, who seven years ago
> Talked of honour and of truth,
> Shriek with pleasure if we show
> The weasel's twist, the weasel's tooth.

The dramatic force of this stark statement with its violent image, echoing the last line of verse five — 'Who are but weasels fighting in a hole' — is strengthened by the change of rhyme and rhythm in this stanza.

The powerful rhetoric that Yeats employs is rarely empty. The heightened expression is matched by intensity of thought and feeling. But there are many aspects of Yeats's view of the world that it is easy to mock by contrast with mundane reality. Winters writes wittily of his concept of what would be the ideal society in Ireland:

> The dominant class would be the landed gentry; the peasants would also be important, but would stay in their place; a fair sprinkling of beggars (some of them mad), of drunkards, and of priests would make the countryside more picturesque. The gentlemen should be violent and bitter, patrons of the arts, and the maintainers of order; they should be good horsemen, preferably reckless horsemen (if the two kinds may exist in one); and they should be fond of fishing. The ladies should be beautiful and charming, should be gracious hostesses (although there is a place for more violent ladies — *videlicet* Mrs French of *The Tower*), should if possible be musicians, should drive men mad, love, marry, and produce children, should not be interested in ideas, and should ride horseback, preferably

to hounds. So far as I can recollect, the ladies are not required to go fishing . . .

When we turn to Yeats's last message to the younger poets we must have some doubt about its relevance and reality:

> Irish poets, learn your trade,
> Sing whatever is well-made,
> Scorn the sort now growing up
> All out of shape from toe to top,
> Their unremembering hearts and heads
> Base-born products of base beds.
> Sing the peasantry, and then
> Hard-riding country gentlemen,
> The holiness of monks, and after
> Porter-drinkers' randy laughter;
> Sing the lords and ladies gay
> That were beaten into the clay
> Through seven heroic centuries;
> Cast your mind on other days
> That we in coming days may be
> Still the indomitable Irishry.

This is superb rhetoric, and there is a fine zest and energy in the ringing couplets. It is without any doubt 'memorable speech', and yet — is it not a kind of nonsense? Some would call it semi-Fascist nonsense and link it with Yeats's sympathy with the Blueshirt movement. Certainly no Irish poets can be said to have taken any notice of Yeats's advice.

At the end of this poem, 'Under Ben Bulben', we have the famous epitaph that is carved on Yeats's tombstone in Drumcliff churchyard:

> Cast a cold eye
> On life, on death.
> Horseman, pass by!

At times I feel myself reacting unfavourably to these lines, to what seems the deliberate striking of an attitude. Is there not an affectation in the address to a 'horseman'? How many horsemen will ever pass by Yeats's grave? I thought this when I last visited the grave and watched a Japanese student taking a photograph of it. And yet if we re-wrote the last line to read 'Tourist, pass by' the epitaph would collapse.

Not far north of Drumcliff there is another Irish poet's grave, in the churchyard at Ballyshannon. This belongs to William Allingham, whom Yeats admired and praised. His own valedictory poem, 'Under the Grass', ended with a much more modest address to the living, who would pass his resting place:

> And be the thought, if any rise, of me
> What happy soul would wish that thought to be.

But it is Yeats's not Allingham's lines that will be remembered. This struck me forcefully when I was going through a shelf of books left by a dead cousin in Belfast. I had thought of her as a cheerful, pious, exemplary old maid, who sang in the church choir and spent most of her spare time working for church charities. Among her books was Yeats's *Selected Poems* in an early Golden Treasury edition, and on the flyleaf she had inscribed his epitaph in a bold, clear hand.

'Under Ben Bulben' is something of an extreme case. In most other poems it is easier to demonstrate how the rhetoric speaks home to our human condition. Yeats was writing of himself in 'The Circus Animal's Desertion', of the destruction of his own youthful myths and dreams, but his final words find an echo in many hearts:

> Now that my ladder's gone,
> I must lie down where all the ladders start,
> In the foul rag-and-bone shop of the heart.

Recently these lines were quoted to me by a woman of fifty who had left her husband and home and country of her birth. She came to London with another man but before long he left her to fend for herself, an immigrant without citizenship or security. I had known her long years before as a student, romantic, idealistic, eagerly anticipating all that life offered of joy and beauty. She told me that Yeats's lines exactly described her own condition, utterly stripped of all the ideals and illusions of the past.

A few months ago I was undertaking in my late sixties a solitary long-distance walk. It was a considerable physical adventure and I was uncertain of the outcome, but as the days passed I became physically more confident. I thought a lot about old age and how far it was possible to keep the body young. Suddenly I found the powerful chorus lines of 'A Song' echoing in my head:

O who could have foretold
That the heart grows old?

Here, as so often, Yeats throws a rhetorical question at the reader. By doing so he puts a bold finger on the essential point. What matters ultimately is not the strength or fitness of the body, but the response of the heart.

I am aware that I have slipped into a dubious form of criticism — citing personal examples to show the force of a poet's words. What I am suggesting is that Yeats's memorable lines have not only music and style, but also the wisdom of experience that illuminates for all of us our own human condition.

Another quality that helps to give resonance and force to Yeats's poetry is his capacity for excitement. Joseph Hone in his biography of Yeats tells us that when a doctor was checking Yeats's blood pressure he asked if he had had any over-excitement of late. Yeats replied: 'I have lived a life of excitement.' This is something that actually seems to have grown stronger as he grew older. He states it openly in 'The Tower':

Never had I more
Excited, passionate, fantastical
Imagination, nor an ear and eye
That more expected the impossible —

More important than this direct statement is the tension of excitement that energised so much of his verse, from a startling single line like 'I spit into the face of time' to whole poems such as 'An Irish Airman Foresees his Death' or 'The Second Coming'. A fine example is the second part of 'A Dialogue of Self and Soul':

I am content to live it all again
And yet again, if it be life to pitch

Into the frog-spawn of a blind man's ditch,
A blind man battering blind men;

I am content to follow to its source
Every event in action or in thought;
Measure the lot; forgive myself the lot!
When such as I cast out remorse
So great a sweetness flows into the breast
We must laugh and we must sing,
We are blest by everything,
Everything we look upon is blest.

Not long after Yeats's death on 28th January 1939, W.H. Auden wrote a poem 'In Memory of W.B. Yeats'. It is still one of the best statements of his qualities as a poet. Here are the last three verses:

Follow poet, follow right
To the bottom of the night,
With your unconstraining voice
Still persuade us to rejoice;

With the farming of a verse
Make a vineyard of the curse,
Sing of human unsuccess
In a rapture of distress;

In the deserts of the heart
Let the healing fountain start,
In the prison of his days
Teach the free man how to praise.

Auden rightly emphasises Yeats's belief in joy and praise. More than any other twentieth century poet he does indeed 'persuade us to rejoice'. 'The arts', he wrote in *Explorations,* 'are all the bridal chambers of joy.' In her *Journals* Lady Gregory reports him as saying: '. . . there is no good literature without praise.' Certainly there is praise in his best poetry, praise of beauty, courage, nobility, love. The poem 'Beautiful Lofty Things' is a paean of praise. It could have become a sentimental, nostalgic lament for the past, but it is saved by its energy. We even accept the word 'arrogant' as a term of praise:

> Maud Gonne at Howth station waiting a train
> Pallas Athene in that straight back and arrogant head:

From one point of view Yeats was a crank, dabbling in the occult and fashioning an obscure mythological system out of cycles of history and the phases of the moon, but underneath all this he had a profound faith in human energy:

> Whatever flames upon the night
> Man's own resinous heart has fed. ('Two Songs from a Play')

In 'The Tower' he declares passionately his faith in man:

> I mock Plotinus' thought
> And cry in Plato's teeth,
> Death and life were not
> Till man made up the whole,
> Made lock, stock and barrel
> Out of his bitter soul . . .

Memorable speech, superb rhetoric, romantic bombast? Call it what you like, but the words do ring out like clear bells, and they do re-affirm and sustain our belief that human life is worth living.

16

John Millington Synge

My image of Synge is that of a lonely wanderer in remote places, watching the sea, watching the peasants at work, walking through the night like his own Christy Mahon: 'passing small towns with the lights shining sideways . . . or going in strange places with a dog noising before you and a dog noising behind . . . '. I have gathered this impression from Synge's own writings and from the records of those who knew him. James Stephens, in his brief reminiscences, describes him as follows: 'A silent, an aloof, a listening man! Listening to and watching all that which had never been completely his, and from which he should soon be parted. He would stand on a headland that jutted steeply on the sea, and he would look and look and look at the sparkling waters below.' In *Vale* George Moore records Synge's taste for a wandering, irregular life:

> Synge had gained the good-will of a certain tinker and his wife, and was learning their life and language as they strolled along the lanes, cadging and stealing as they went, squatting at eventide on the side of a dry ditch. Like a hare in a gap he listened, and when he had mastered every turn of their speech he left the tinker and turned into the hills, spending some weeks with a cottager, joining a little later another group of tinkers accompanied by a servant-girl who had suddenly wearied of scrubbing and mangling, boiling for pigs, cooking and working dough, and making beds in the evening. It would be better, she had thought, to lie under the hedgerow; and in telling me of this girl, Synge seemed to be telling me his own story. He, too, disliked the regular life of his mother's house, and preferred to wander with the tinkers, and when tired of them

to lie abed smoking with a peasant, and awake amid the smells of shag and potato-skins in the corner of the room.

Synge was born at Newtown Little, Rathfarnham, Co. Dublin, of Anglo-Irish stock. His father was a Dublin barrister, who had inherited some property in Co. Galway. His mother was the daughter of a Church of Ireland rector in Co. Cork. His ancestors included bishops and canons and missionaries, and the family trend was towards a rather narrow evangelicism. In his biography, *My Uncle John* (edited by Andrew Carpenter, 1974), Edward Stephens, his nephew, writes revealingly of family attitudes. Mrs Synge had taken her sons, John and Sam (who later became a missionary) to stay with her sister-in-law in the Isle of Man. Here there were crowds of trippers instead of the lonely Irish shore that John was used to, but in the house the atmosphere was familiar. The grownups, his uncle and aunt and his mother, talked as the grownups did at home:

> All three regarded an Irish crowd as composed mostly of Roman Catholics who believed in something that was definitely wrong. The Isle of Man crowds they looked on as composed mostly of Protestants who were indifferent as to what they believed — careless about God. Their stay in [their aunt's] household tended to confirm in the minds of John and Sam the tacit assumption that they belonged to a minority that was in the right, entitled to regard most people as forming the majority which was in the wrong. John's creed suffered profound changes as years passed, but this assumption remained unshaken.

Synge was educated privately and spent much of his boyhood wandering the countryside. He had a passion for natural history. Later he went to Trinity College, where he read languages and history. He also developed a passion for music and he studied at the Royal Irish Academy of Music, playing the piano, flute and violin. Later he had thoughts of becoming a professional musician and he went to Germany for further study, where he found a way of life very different from the narrow home circle. He eventually gave up music and turned to literature, though he continued to play the fiddle.

At about the age of eighteen he became an agnostic and

ceased to attend the family church. This naturally isolated him from the group he belonged to, and his mother never ceased to grieve over his loss of faith. When, some years later, he proposed to a girl he knew in the home circle, Cherry Matheson, daughter of a leading spirit in the Plymouth Brethren, she refused him, largely on religious grounds.

He lived for a time in Paris, and it was here that he had a famous encounter with Yeats, who said to him: 'Give up Paris, you will never create anything by reading Racine, and Arthur Symons will always be a better critic of French Literature. Go to the Aran Islands. Live there as if you were one of the people themselves; express a life that has never found expression.' Synge had already visited Aran, and he had wandered in many remote parts of rural Ireland. His interest in folk-lore, in the Irish language and Celtic culture had been stimulated by lectures he attended in Paris, so he was ready to accept Yeats's advice. He made long visits to the Aran Islands and later he published a journal, *The Aran Islands* (1907). Meantime he was writing plays for the National Theatre, and he later became involved in the management of it. He fell in love with one of the actresses, Molly Allgood (Maire O'Neill), but he was already a sick man, and the relationship was a troubled one. He died on 24 March, 1907, and was buried in the family tomb at Mount Jerome, Dublin.

At first sight it may seem strange that a solitary and intro-spective intellectual, who translated French and Italian poetry, should turn to peasant drama. A glance at Synge's own poems, and another at his journal, will help to show the movement of his mind. He reacted against the preciousness and aestheticism of much poetry written in his time, and against the misty romanticism of the Celtic Twilight. In 'The Passing of the Shee' he turned his back on those he called 'the poets of the fancy land':

Adieu, sweet Angus, Maeve and Fand,
Ye plumed yet skinny Shee . . .
We'll stretch in Red Dan Sally's ditch,
And drink in Tubber Fair,
Or poach with Red Dan Philly's bitch
The badger and the hare.

He wanted poetry, and drama, to be human and earthy, not remote and 'fey'. He remarked in his brief preface to the poems that 'it is the timber of poetry that wears most surely, and there is no timber that has not strong roots among the clay and the worms'. Humanity includes a touch of the brutal, and his disarmingly simple little ballad, 'Danny', brings a shock to the reader:

Then Danny smashed the nose on Byrne,
He split the lips on three,
And bit across the right-hand thumb
Of one Red Shawn Magee.

But seven tripped him up behind,
And seven kicked before,
And seven squeezed around his throat
Till Danny kicked no more.

Then some destroyed him with their heels,
Some tramped him in the mud,
Some stole his purse and timber pipe,
And some washed off his blood.

What drew Synge to the Arans was partly an impulse away from the intellectual and the sophisticated towards the simple and primitive, where traditional folk ways and folk arts still gave a style and dignity to men's lives that was absent in Paris or Dublin or London. A part of his journal, (omitted from the book published in 1907) shows that he approached Inishmaan, his favourite island, with something of the enthusiasm and jealousy of the collector, and he uses a sexual imagery that is perhaps revealing:

With this limestone Inishmaan however I am in love, and hear with galling jealousy of the various priests and scholars who have lived here before me. They have grown to me as the former lover of one's mistress, horrible existences haunting with dreamed kisses the lips she presses to your own. The thought that this island will gradually yield to the ruthlessness of 'progress' is as the certainty that decaying age is moving always nearer the cheeks it is your ecstasy to kiss. How much of Ireland was formerly like this and how much of Ireland is today Anglicised and civilized and brutalized . . .

Although *The Aran Islands* is coloured by Synge's own emotions — 'it gave me a moment of exquisite satisfaction to find myself moving away from civilization in this rude canvas canoe' — he is a keen observer, and by no means simply a romantic literary man enthusing over the quaint and simple peasants of the west of Ireland. He may have neglected the religious and spiritual aspects of the people he wrote about, as Corkery and others have complained, but in most other ways he gives us a vivid picture of life on the Arans. His journal is probably the best introduction to his drama. He took some of his plots from stories he heard in the Arans, and the people there gave him impressions for the world he wanted to create in his plays. But the plays he wrote are not simply sketches of peasant life; they are works of imagination, close to myth and fairy-tale. He uses a peasant background and a peasant idiom to create something new in drama.

When his plays were first performed at the Abbey Theatre they met with much hostile criticism because they offended Irish national sentiment. Maud Gonne and Arthur Griffith walked out of the first performance of *The Shadow of the Glen* in shocked protest. The first performance of *The Playboy of the Western World* caused riots in the theatre. Lady Gregory sent a famous telegram to Yeats, who was lecturing in Aberdeen at the time: 'Audience broke up in disorder at the word "Shift". Arthur Griffith described *The Playboy* as 'a vile and inhuman story told in the foulest language we have ever listened to from a public platform'.

Many years later W.R. Rodgers remarked that Synge 'was a tumbler who unrolled his carpet in front of a marching army'. The marching army of Irish patriots did not want to laugh at Synge's peasants; they wanted all Irish writing to reflect national ideals, to promote the dignity of Ireland and to further the cause of Irish independence. In his reflections on the death of Synge (*Autobiographies*), Yeats wrote:

When a country produces a man of genius he is never what it wants or believes it wants; he is always unlike its idea of itself. In the eighteenth century Scotland believed itself religious, moral and gloomy, and its national poet Burns came not to speak of these things but to speak of lust and drink and drunken gaiety. Ireland, since the Young Irelanders, has given itself up to apologetics. Every impression of life or impulse of imagination has been examined to see if it helped or hurt the glory of Ireland, or the political claim of Ireland. A sincere impression of life became at last impossible, all was apologetics. There was no longer an impartial imagination, delighting in whatever is naturally exciting. Synge was the rushing up of the buried fire, an explosion of all that had been denied or refused, a furious impartiality, an indifferent turbulent sorrow. His work, like that of Burns, was to say all the people did not want to have said.

Ireland has now had more than fifty years of independence and Irish people can laugh at themselves more freely than they were able to in the early years of this century. Synge is no longer attacked for letting down the national dignity, though he may still be regarded with some suspicion as an outsider. This was why Patrick Kavanagh attacked him. 'Imagine him sitting in the Aran cabin taking his superficial notes while the people were out at Mass on a Sunday.'

Synge knew the Aran people better than Kavanagh suggests but this has little to do with his power as a dramatist. He is not a social realist; his plays demand extravagance and fantasy. There are elements of farce, melodrama and the grotesque in them, as well as poetry.

The Shadow of the Glen dramatises a European folk-tale and popular fantasy, the story of the aging husband who pretends to be dead in order to catch out his young wife with her lover. Synge heard a version of this story in Irish from old Pat Dirane, a blind shannachie in the Aran Islands, and he recorded it in his book. The basic situation in the play is farcical — not even the dreamiest Nora would in reality mistake a living husband for a dead one — and the comic crisis comes when old Dan Burke leaps out of bed in his nightshirt. At the same time there is more than farce in the play. There is pathos and melancholy in Nora's loneliness and longing for a life of greater richness and excitement than can be found in the desolate glen, where there is 'nothing but the mists rolling down the bog, and the mists again and they rolling up the bog.' In the play Synge is beginning to find an idiom to suit his dramatic purposes, a speech that has colour and rhythm. The tramp, praising Darcy, who had a way with mountain ewes, says: 'That was a great man, young fellow – a great man, I'm telling you. There was never a lamb from his own ewes he wouldn't know before it was marked, and he'd run from this to the city of Dublin and never catch for his breath.'

Riders to the Sea is the play that springs most directly out of Synge's life on the Arans. A simple but tragic statement of the harsh fate that overtook so many of the island fishermen, it dramatises the conflict between the islanders and the sea. While Synge was on the islands the bodies of drowned men were washed ashore. He heard the people making coffins, and he attended an island funeral where the women rocked themselves in the wild grief of the keen.

At the centre of the play is Maurya, the old mother. The sea has already taken her husband and five sons, and she is anxious to stop Bartley, the youngest, from crossing to the mainland when the weather is threatening. But Bartley has horses to sell and he must get to the fair on the mainland. He is knocked into the sea and drowned while trying to get his horses on to the hooker, and at the end his body is carried into his mother's cabin in a sailcloth. The play ends with a moving ritual of grief. It is saved from sentimentality by being anchored in a homely reality. The common substances of life and death play a significant part – turf, a bit of rope, a knitted stocking, a cake of home-made bread, boards and nails for a coffin. It has something of the stark and simple strength of one of the old Scottish ballads.

Synge wrote one other tragedy, *Deirdre of the Sorrows*. This was left unrevised at his death and published posthumously. This is Synge's attempt to dramatise the famous epic story of the sons of Usna, a story of love defeated by treachery. His play is not without the power to move, and it has moments of intensity, such as Deirdre's speeches at the edge of Naisi's grave, but much of it seems melancholy rather than tragic, and there is some monotony. The monotony is felt in the rhythm, where there is a tendency to the repetition of similar phrases – a poor thing, a hard thing, a queer thing, a strange thing, and so on. The charge of 'Synge-song' is at times justified.

Synge's third play, *The Tinkers' Wedding*, is farce. It presents the conflict between a settled conventional society where marriage in a church is the norm, and the priest sanctifies traditional moral laws and beliefs, and the wild, free natural life of the tinkers, where the ritual of marriage seems irrelevant. Sarah Casey, a handsome tinker woman, takes a fancy to legitimise her union with Michael Byrne, by a proper wedding ceremony performed by a priest. The local priest agrees to wed them for ten shillings and a new tin can. But Mary Byrne, Michael's mother, 'an old flagrant heathen would destroy the world' steals the can to exchange it for drink, and substitutes, in the sack which was keeping it protected from the dew, three empty bottles. When the priest opens the sack that is handed to him he indignantly refuses to perform the ceremony. The play ends in a quarrel and the tinkers tie up the priest in the sack to prevent him calling the police. He promises not to do so and is finally left in command of the stage, pronouncing a Latin malediction while the tinkers flee for their lives.

The play is an amusing little farce, but there has been considerable objection to the portrayal of the priest, and to the brutality of forcing him into a sack. It is not easy to present the play on the stage with the right note of distance and extravagance and lightness of touch. There is some vigorous 'flyting' and some vivid speech in the play, and the unregenerate Mary, the dominant character, has a vitality that breathes imaginative life into the farce.

The Well of the Saints is wider and deeper in its range. Using material from folklore and hints from a fifteenth century French farce, Synge dramatises a theme that always haunted his imagination, the clash between dream and reality. Martin Doul, a blind beggar, fondly believes that he and his blind wife Mary are a handsome couple, and that the visible world is a beautiful place. When the couple recover their sight, after the application of holy water brought by a wandering saint, they are sadly disillusioned. Martin at first mistakes Molly Byrne, 'a fine-looking girl with fair hair', for his wife, whom he eventually discovers to be 'a dirty, wrinkled-looking hag'. He spurns Mary, but he in turn is spurned by Molly. Martin and Mary, with sight restored, are forced to work hard for a meagre living, like Adam and Eve turned out of Paradise. Martin expresses his disillusion with the brave new world of sight. The great day of his cure becomes

> a bad black day when I was roused up and found I was the like of the little children do be listening to the stories of an old woman, and do be dreaming after in the dark night that it's in grand houses of gold they are, with speckled horses to ride, and do be waking again, in a short while, and they destroyed with the cold, and the thatch dripping, maybe, and the starved ass braying in the yard.

In the end, when their sight is failing again, and the saint comes to complete the cure by a second application of holy water, Martin deliberately spills the water, and the blind couple go out hoping to recover something of the kinder world they once knew.

The play is basically a morality play, neatly constructed, and the poetry of disillusion that echoes in the words of Martin is moving, but Synge's greatest gift was for comedy, for what is superb and wild in reality, and this makes *The Playboy of the Western World* his finest work and the one on which his reputation will finally rest. In *The Playboy* the element of fantasy, of extravagance, is strongly present. The whole play is built on a half-grotesque myth. Christy Mahon, the ignorant, humble son of a crusty old farmer, who calls him 'a poor fellow would get drunk on the smell of a pint', arrives in a remote village on the coast of Mayo. He is fleeing from the law after killing his father in a quarrel, with the blow of a spade. Instead of rejecting him the people receive him as a hero, because they desperately need a myth to give colour and excitement to their barren lives. In the warmth of their admiration, especially that of Pegeen Mike, Christy changes from a timid, bashful coward to become a hero, a poet and a bold lover. When his father re-appears, with no more than a head-wound, to chastise his fleeing son, the myth has already done its work, and although the people reject him, he goes out in triumph, pushing his father before him and confident that he will henceforth go 'romancing through a romping lifetime'.

At the beginning of the play Synge is very careful to build
up the sense of spiritual and mental poverty in the lives of his
Mayo peasants. There is so little to excite their imaginations,
to give colour to their drab existence, that we hear of Sara
Tansey driving ten miles to see a man who had bitten a lady's
nostril. The best they can do for local heroes are Daneen
Sullivan who 'knocked the eye from a peeler' and Marcus
Quinn who 'got six months for maiming ewes'. Even these are
heroes of the past, and now there is 'none but Red Linahan,
has a squint in his eye, and Patcheen is lame in his heel, or
the mad Mulrannies were driven from California and they lost
in their wits.' Pegeen Mike is preparing to marry Sean Keogh
in despair that a likelier man will ever appear upon the scene.
It is against this background that the people make a hero out
of the mysterious stranger who appears in the village one
evening with a story of a wild murder done in 'a windy
corner of high distant hills'.

Early objections to *The Playboy* were often made on the
ground that the Irish people would never make a hero out of
'a lad who had murdered his da', but later criticism has been
more concerned with his dialogue and how far he is what St
John Irvine called him: 'a faker of peasant speech'.

In his preface to *The Playboy* Synge boldly asserts: 'In a
good play every speech should be as fully flavoured as a nut
or an apple.' This rightly calls attention to the importance of
vivid speech, but it also opens the door to a self-conscious
attempt to impart flavour and rhythm to speech. At times
Synge's dialogue becomes florid (Corkery's word for it), over-
elaborate, too obviously rhythmic, a 'Synge-song'. When
Christy is wooing Pegeen in a famous love-scene that has
considerable power and poetry, he remarks, *'with rapture'*:
'If the mitred bishops seen you that time, they'd be the like
of the holy prophets, I'm thinking, do be straining the bars of
Paradise to lay eyes on the Lady Helen of Troy, and she
abroad, pacing back and forward, with a nosegay in her
golden shawl.' The image used here seems too literary and
too self-conscious to be wholly right. And when Christy
says later: 'If I wasn't a good Christian, it's on my naked
knees I'd be saying my prayers and paters to every jackstraw
you have roofing your head, and every stony pebble is paving

the laneway to your door', the alliteration and the rhythm seems a little too deliberate to be true. Compare the naturalness of old Mahon's speech: 'It's Christy by the stars of God! I'd know his way of spitting and he astride the moon.' In general the speech of old Mahon, the widow Quinn and Michael James is more convincing, less obviously poetic, than the speech of Christy. Perhaps it is easier to be relaxed and natural in the language of abuse than in the language of love.

Although Synge claimed that his wildest fancies had been heard from the lips of real people, it is clear that the dialogue in the plays has been 'touched up', even if only slightly, for the theatre. We can see this if we compare a phrase as reported in *The Aran Islands* with the same phrase in a play. Synge records old Mourteen as saying that an unmarried man is 'like an old jackass straying on the rocks'. In *The Playboy* the phrase becomes 'like an old braying jackass strayed upon the rocks.' This is a very small change, but it immediately heightens the consciousness of rhythm.

In his journals Synge records many snatches of dialogue. Some of these may be his own renderings of the original Irish, though in many cases the speakers used English. The speech is sparer and more economical than much of his dramatic speech, but it is racy and vivid. Here are a few examples. There was a noisy fight one evening in an Aran cabin between two near relations. Synge writes: 'About ten o'clock a young man came in and told us that the fight was over. "They have been at it for four hours," he said, "and now they're tired. Indeed, it is time they were, for you'd rather be listening to a man killing a pig than to the noise they were letting out of them."'

On another occasion, this time in the Glens of Wicklow, Synge listened to an old woman, with whom he was slightly acquainted, bewailing the recent death of her husband:

'The poor old man is after dying on me,' she said, 'and he was great company. There's only one son left me now, and we do be killed working. Ah, avourneen, the poor do have great stratagems to keep in their little cabins at all. And did you ever see the like of the place we live in? Isn't it the poorest, lonesomest, wildest, dreariest, bit of a hill a person ever passed a life on?' When she stopped a moment, with tears streaming on her face, I told a little about the poverty I had seen in Paris.

'God Almighty forgive me, avourneen,' she went on, when I had finished, 'we don't know anything about it. We have our bit of turf, and our bit of sticks, and our bit to eat, and we have our health. Glory be to His Holy Name, not a one of the childer was ever a day ill, except one boy was hurted off a cart, and he never overed it. It's small right we have to complain at all.'

Had Synge kept closer to the kind of speech and dialogue he reports in his notebooks, he would not have indulged in the occasional overwriting, the excesses of rhythm and diction that sometimes call attention to themselves, and make him an easy target for parody.

In spite of this fault, Synge is a playwright whose work will endure. As Jacques Barzun says, it makes little difference whether anyone actually spoke the dialogue that a playwright uses so long as it has strength of style and animation. There is no doubt about Synge's animation in *The Playboy*: it is indeed the gayest of his plays, and it confirms his belief, stated in the preface, in 'the rich joy found only in what is superb and wild in reality'. It is neither morbid nor cruel, and it has little in common with contemporary black humour and the theatre of cruelty.

Although Synge had a deep vein of melancholy, his plays affirm a basic joy in life. Even after the great disillusion that befalls Martin Doul in *The Well of the Saints*, he goes out at the end, blind once more, with courage and hope. 'Keep off now, and let you not be afeard: for we're going on the two of us to the towns of the south, where the people will have kind voices maybe, and we won't know their bad looks or their villainy at all.' The tramp, going off with Nora at the end of *The Shadow of the Glen*, has a jauntiness and gaiety, though the gayest of all is Christy, leaving his blessings with the fools of Mayo.

Vivien Mercier speaks of the 'cruel humour' of *The Playboy*, but it seems to me that the zest and extravagance and richness of the humour make the word 'cruel' inappropriate. Yeats, recalling a Gaelic curse, in which a poet damns the devil waiting for his soul, the worms waiting for his body, and his children waiting for his wealth, with the words: 'O Christ, hang all in the same noose!': comments: 'I think those words were spoken with a delight in their vehemence that took out of anger half the bitterness with all the gloom.' In the same way the vehemence of Christy's threats, just before he bites Sean Keogh's leg, gives them an air of gaiety and fantasy instead of cruelty. 'If I can wring a neck among you, I'll have a royal judgment looking on the trembling jury in the courts of law. And won't there be crying out in Mayo the day I'm stretched upon the rope, with ladies in their silks and satins snivelling in their lacy kerchiefs, and they rhyming songs and ballads on the terror of my fate?'

In a letter to a young man about *The Playboy* Synge points out 'that the wildness, and if you will, vices of the Irish peasantry are due, like their extraordinary good points of all kinds, to the *richness* of their nature — a thing that is priceless beyond words.' It is this richness that transforms Synge's people, making them lively, humorous characters instead of the brutal uncouth beings that early nationalist critics saw in them. Synge's laughter is astringent but it is without malice; the irony is not morbid or destructive, and Synge expected that even *The Tinkers' Wedding* would be accepted in the spirit of humour with which it was offered. He writes in the preface to this play: 'In the greater part of Ireland, however, the whole people, from the tinkers to the clergy, have still a life, and view of life, that are rich and genial and humorous. I do not think that these country people, who have so much humour themselves, will mind being laughed at without malice . . . '

Synge never forgets the worms and the clay, the pathos of old age and death, and the fading of beauty; but his view of life remains rich and genial and humorous and sane.

Supplement to Part Four

Notes on some other twentieth century writers: poetry, drama, prose.

I said in the preface that death makes an untidy line of demarcation amongst writers, but for the sake of convenience I am using it here. This supplement includes only writers who have died. A further supplement to Part five includes some more living writers.

Poetry

One of the best known and most picturesque literary figures of the early century was AE (George Russell, 1867–1935). Born in Lurgan, he spent most of his life in Dublin and was a lifelong friend of Yeats. Poet, painter, economist, mystic – he was a delightful personality, enthusiastically supporting the literary revival, encouraging young poets, discovering new ones, editing, talking, promoting co-operatives. But I find his poetry disappointing, too insubstantial to leave much impression.

Joseph Campbell (1879–1944) was a minor poet caught up in the enthusiasm of the revival and encouraged to write on Irish themes. He writes mostly of country tasks and country people. Born in Belfast, he contributed to *Uladh*, a Northern offshoot of the revival, started in 1904, when the Ulster Literary Theatre was founded. Austin Clarke, in a foreword to *The Poems of Joseph Campbell* tells how, like Sean O'Casey, he took an Irish name: 'The early books of Joseph Campbell were published under the Irish form of his name, Seosamh MacCathmhaoil. He told me, with a chuckle, that he abandoned the Irish form when he heard a young woman asking for the poems of 'Seo-sam MacCatwail.'

Campbell collaborated with Herbert Hughes, who collected traditional Irish airs. The words of the popular song 'My Lagan Love' are his. For a time he was secretary of the Irish Literary Society in London. Then he took a small farm in Wicklow. The titles of his collections, *The Rushlight, The Gilly of Christ, The Mountainy Singer, Irishry, Pedlar's Pack*, indicate the world he wrote about. He wrote simply, though he experimented with imagist techniques.

One of the poets 'discovered' and encouraged by AE was Padraic Colum (1881–1972), who wrote plays for the Abbey Theatre. Like Campbell he was in close touch with folk-song and he wrote the words for the popular tune 'She Moved through the Fair', and 'A Cradle Song.' His best work is in *Wild Earth* (1907). He takes a romantic view of the people in the fields and on the roads, and of the elemental simplicities, as the opening lines of 'Plougher' reveal:

> Sunset and silence! A man; around him earth savage, earth
> broken;
> Beside him two horses, a plough!

Francis Ledwidge (1891–1917) was killed in Flanders before he had time to develop fully as a poet. A farm labourer and road-overseer in Co. Meath, he brought out his first volume in 1916 with the help of Lord Dunsany. The title, *Songs of the Fields*, indicates the bent of the poems. Dunsany called him 'the poet of the blackbird'. Most of his verse owes more to English pastoral tradition than to Irish influences, but there are signs of change at the end. His poems about the Easter Rising, 'Lament for Thomas MacDonagh' and 'The Blackbirds' are linked to Gaelic traditions.

Mention of the Easter Rising reminds us that there were three poets among the small group of patriot-rebels who seized the Post Office and were executed in 1916 — Patrick Pearse (b. 1879), Thomas MacDonagh (b. 1878) and Joseph Plunkett (b. 1887). Pearse's poems reveal so clearly his ruling passion for blood-sacrifice, that it is difficult to judge his work as literature. Plunkett shows a strong vein of religious mysticism. MacDonagh shows considerable skill in his version of 'The Yellow Bittern' from the Irish, and his poem 'John-

John' shows that he can work easily in the ballad and folk tradition.

F.R. Higgins (1896–1941) was a friend of Yeats and he played a part in the management of the Abbey Theatre in the thirties. He had a genuine lyric gift and he left some memorable poems, such as 'Father and Son'. He took an over-romantic view of the Irish peasantry and of the role of an Irish poet. Kavanagh called him 'the gallivanting poet'. He lacked intellectual discipline.

This could not be said of Denis Devlin (1908–1959), who looked to Europe rather than to the west of Ireland, or to London. At the time of his death Devlin was Irish ambassador to Italy. Though somewhat out of the main stream of Anglo-Irish poetry, he represents a European aspect that should not be forgotten. *The Heavenly Foreigner* (1967) contains some of his best work.

A very considerable poet, whom I felt unable to select for individual treatment, is Louis MacNeice (1907–1963). Although he is included in most anthologies of Irish verse, it seems to me that he really belongs with the English poets of the thirties, with Auden, Spender and Day-Lewis (also born in Ireland), rather than with the Anglo-Irish poets. He was born in Belfast, but was educated, lived and worked in England. However, he did re-visit Ireland quite frequently and he was, at least to some extent, haunted by Irish ghosts. He wrote some poems about Ireland, such as 'Carrickfergus', 'Western Landscape', and a fine passage in his 'Autumn Journal' (XVI). But the poems I like best, 'Sunlight on the Garden', 'London Rain', 'Snow' and many other lyrics, lie outside the Irish dimension. I would like to claim him for Ireland, but in view of my own guidelines in the first chapter, I am unable to do so.

W.R. Rodgers (1909–1969) was born in Belfast and became a Presbyterian minister, serving in Loughgall, Co. Armagh, from 1934 to 1946. Later he left the ministry to work for the BBC in London. He produced some lively 'literary Portraits' of Yeats and other Irish writers, and some excellent talks. His own poetry shows the eccentricity of a poet intoxicated by words, brilliant at times, but lacking control. He loves assonance and alliteration, and seems in deliberate revolt against Ulster Protestant taciturnity and reserve:

> Who bristle into reticence at the sound
> Of the round gift of the gab in Southern mouths.

Terence Brown called him a 'Romantic Calvinist'. His themes are often erotic, as in *Europa and the Bull* and 'The Net'. Derek Mahon assessed his work neatly in one sentence: 'His work contains an unusual mixture of humorous religiosity and sexual high jinks; and in this, as in other respects, the poet he most resembles is Dylan Thomas.'

Drama

Lady Gregory (1852–1932) played a major part in the founding and running of the Abbey Theatre, and she also wrote plays, providing comedy because that was what was most needed. She observed village life around her home at Coole Park in Co. Galway, and she adapted the idiom of local speech in her plays. *Spreading the News* is a one act farcical comedy based on the quick spreading of a rumour of quarrel and murder in a small town fair. Bartley Fallon, the perpetually unlucky man, has this mournfully amusing conversation with his brisk and sensible wife at the beginning of the play:

> *Bartley:* Indeed it's a poor country and a scarce country to be living in. But I'm thinking if I went to America it's long ago the day I'd be dead!
>
> *Mrs Fallon:* So you might, indeed.
>
> *Bartley:* And it's a great expense for a poor man to be buried in America.
>
> *Mrs Fallon:* Never fear, Bartley Fallon, but I'll give you a good burying the day you'll die.
>
> *Bartley:* Maybe its yourself will be buried in the graveyard of Cloonmara before me, Mary Fallon, and I myself that will be dying unbeknownst some night, and no one a-near me. And the cat itself may be gone straying through the country, and the mice squealing over the quilt.
>
> *Mrs Fallon:* Leave off talking of dying. It might be twenty years you'll be living yet.

Bartley: (With a deep sigh.) I'm thinking if I'll be living at the end of twenty years, it's a very old man I'll be then!

Hyacinth Halvey and *The Workhouse Ward* are neatly turned comedies of the same kind, based on the inveterate Irish weakness for myth-making. *The Rising of the Moon* presents a patriotic motif. It is simple, almost naive, and yet strangely moving. She wrote many other plays and she wrote out versions of the old Irish sagas in her peasant idiom, or Kiltartanese, as it is sometimes a little unkindly called. *Cuchulain of Muirthemne* (1902) was a great source book, and much admired and used by the writers of the revival. Synge told Lady Gregory that it was part of his daily bread. She continued the same work in *Gods and Fighting Men.* She also wrote a valuable first-hand account of the dramatic movement, *Our Irish Theatre* (1913). Possibly her most interesting work is in the journals that were edited by Lennox Robinson and published after her death, *Lady Gregory's Journals* (1916–1930). Her vivid personal account of life in Ireland during the 'troubles' makes fascinating reading.

Another early champion of the national theatre was Edward Martyn (1859–1923). A wealthy Catholic landlord from Co. Galway, he was an eccentric and a recluse, yet he did much to promote the literary revival and encourage the Irish language and Irish music. *The Heather Field,* his first and best play, has more in common with Ibsen than with Yeats. Carden Tyrell, an idealist and dreamer, married to an unimaginative wife, has plans to turn his wild heather field into pasture, but difficulties accumulate; the field goes wild and Tyrell goes mad. In spite of some faults, the play has considerable power.

The Abbey soon attracted a kind of peasant drama unlike that provided by Synge and Lady Gregory. It was more realistic and dealt with contemporary problems. Padraic Colum (1881–1972) wrote *Broken Soil* (1903), *The Land* (1905) and *Thomas Muskerry* (1910). His best play, *The Land,* is set in the Irish midlands and deals with the peasant farmer's passion for the land. He calls it 'an agrarian comedy' but the mood is tragic, 'the tragedy', as Ellis-Fermor sums it up, 'of wasted effort, broken dreams and divided lives'.

William Boyle (1853–1922) from Co. Louth was a more pedestrian writer but his satiric humour and his ability to construct a play made *The Building Fund* (1905) and *The Eloquent Dempsey* (1906) amusing and effective on the stage.

T.C. Murray (1873–1959), a teacher from Co. Cork, helped to found the Cork Little Theatre with Terence McSwiney (the Republican Mayor of Cork who died on hunger strike in 1920), Daniel Corkery and others. *Birthright* was performed at the Abbey in 1910, a plan reflecting faithfully the manners and speech of a farming family in West Cork. *Maurice Harte* (1912), perhaps his best play, presenting the conflict between devoted parents, whose life's ambition is to see their son a priest, and the son who doubts his vocation, has intensity and deep sincerity. *Autumn Fire* (1924) is a powerful tragedy of frustrated love.

George Fitzmaurice (1878–1963), son of a country clergyman in Co. Kerry, was one of the most original of the Abbey dramatists. After a well constructed comedy, *The Country Dressmaker* (1907), he turned increasingly to dramatic fantasies and folk plays. His work is little known, but Ernest Boyd called him 'the greatest folk-dramatist since the death of Synge', and a reviewer in *The Times Literary Supplement* wrote: 'His work is a direct product of Kerry legend, speech and ordinary life, translated into a fantastic world of his own where cottagers, mountebank doctors, priests and creatures of folklore can meet on the same plane. At the lowest estimate he was the best writer of Kerry dialect Ireland ever had.' *The Pie Dish, The Magic Glasses* and *The Dandy Dolls* will give readers a good sample of his work.

Drama after 1916

Lennox Robinson (1886–1958) was manager, and one of the directors, of the Abbey Theatre for many years. Born in Douglas, Co. Cork, he was drawn to the stage after seeing the Abbey Theatre company perform in Cork. His first play, *The Clancy Name* (1908), was produced at the Abbey and ran for three months. It presents a strong and convincing picture of peasant life in which Mrs Clancy struggles for the family farm and the family honour. *The White-Headed Boy* (1916) was even more enthusiastically received. I think this is his best play, but *The Big House, The Far-Off Hills* and *Drama at Innish* (a very funny play about the impact of a visiting drama group on a small Irish town) are all worth seeing.

Paul Vincent Carroll (1900–1968), born in Blackrock near Dundalk, and educated in Dublin, was devoted to the Abbey Theatre in his youth but emigrated to Glasgow to escape from Irish provincial life. He maintained contact with the Abbey which produced his plays. *Shadow and Substance* (1937) deals with the dramatic consequences of the religious visions of a priest's housekeeper. There is vigorous dialogue, effective characterisation and some sharp satire. *The White Steed*, first produced in New York, won the New York Drama Critics Circle award for the best foreign play of 1938–9, but it was rejected by the Abbey management because they feared its anti-clerical implications. Two priests are presented in sharp clash and contrast, the elderly paralysed Canon Lavelle, and the young hot-headed idealist-cum-bigot, Father O'Shaughnessy.

George Shiels (1881–1949), born in Ballymoney Co. Antrim, turned to playwriting after a railway accident in Canada that crippled him for life. He returned to Ireland and became one of the Abbey's most popular and prolific playwrights. He is simple and direct and warm-hearted. Lennox Robinson called him 'the Thomas Moore of the Irish Theatre'. Most of his plays are comedies – *Paul Twining, Professor Tim, The New Gossoon* – but he wrote some serious plays. *The Rugged Path* (1940) and *The Summit* (1941) deal with the problems of law and justice in rural Ireland. The problem is real and the plays are genuine and compel attention. Shiels is still one of the most popular playwrights with amateur dramatic societies in Ireland.

The example of the Abbey encouraged a group of actors and writers in Belfast to form the Ulster Literary Theatre in 1904. Unlike their Dublin counterparts, however, they were never able to acquire a theatre. But they did stimulate local drama. One of the chief writers was Rutherford Mayne (his real name was Samuel Waddell, brother of Helen Waddell, writer and scholar), and his play, *The Drone* (1908), is still remembered.

I have not yet mentioned Bernard Shaw (1856–1950) whom many readers may consider to be the greatest Irish dramatist of the twentieth century. In my first chapter I said that he was inescapably an Irishman, but in spite of this he rarely wrote from inside his Irish experience. Only two of his plays deal with Ireland, the short *O'Flaherty, V.C.* and the longer *John Bull's Other Island*. The latter is a lively, amusing and provocative play that everyone interested in Anglo-Irish literature should read, but Shaw's main work as a dramatist lies outside the scope of this book.

During the last ten years of his short but eventful life Brendan Behan (1923–1964) must have been the best known Irishman in the world. This was not primarily due to his talent as a dramatist, though he had talent, but to his filling so aptly the role of 'the rollickin' Irishman', mid-twentieth century version. Born into the world of the Dublin working class, he left school at thirteen, joined the IRA at fifteen, was arrested two years later and sentenced to three years in Borstal. Later still he spent four years in Mountjoy jail for shooting at the Irish police. It was this last experience that gave him the material for his one fine play, *The Quare Fellow* (1956). This dramatises life in a prison during the last twenty-four hours before a condemned murderer is executed. Much of it is comedy, but the final effect is grimly ironic and moving. More than anything else I have read or seen, this play persuaded me that capital punishment was wrong. But it is not a propagandist play. Through dialogue that presents the thoughts and feelings of prisoners and warders, Behan makes us vividly aware of the physical reality of hanging. Many small details contribute to this, such as the hangman's borrowing a warder's cap before he looks in at the prisoner, to size up his physique and estimate the drop required. *The Hostage* (1958) is lively and amusing and popular with audiences, but the comedy is anarchic. It is less a play than an extravaganza, with farce, melodrama and comic songs thrown in.

Prose

Canon Patrick Sheehan (1852–1913) belongs to a milieu very different from the Big House world of Somerville and

description of a happy childhood by the shore of Lough Foyle, it has greater unity and simplicity than *Castle Corner* and brings to life a world of eager children.

Eimar O'Duffy (1893–1935), born in Dublin, played an active part in the Irish Volunteers, but in the mid-twenties he moved to England and devoted himself to writing. He is probably best known for his satirical fantasy, *King Goshawk and the Birds* (1926), which is directed against Big Business and Power. Cuchulain and his son and a Philosopher are ranged against King Goshawk who wants to buy up all the world's singing birds. The book is still amusing but perhaps the novelty has worn off with time.

Brinsley MacNamara's real name was John Weldon (1890–1963). Born in Co. Westmeath, he joined the Abbey Theatre for a time and later succeeded James Stephens as Registrar at the National Gallery of Ireland. He wrote some plays, including a comedy, *Look at the Heffernans,* but is best known as a novelist. *The Valley of the Squinting Windows* (1918) led to bitter controversy and caused a violent reaction in Delvin, his home village, where the book was publicly burned. It is a harsh exposure of the meanness and gossip in the village, where the postmistress steams open letters, and the chief pleasure of the village is to see someone humiliated. The meanness of human nature seems overstressed, though the detail is authentic. Less bitter, less well known, but perhaps a better book, is *The Various Lives of Marcus Igoe* (1929).

Kate O'Brien (1897–1974) was born in Limerick and educated there and at University College, Dublin. She lived and worked abroad for many years. She wrote mainly of the Irish provincial middle class. *Without My Cloak* won literary prizes. *The Ante-Room* and *Mary Lavelle* (1936) followed. *The Land of Spices* (1941) is a sensitive study of the reverend mother of a convent, and Ben Kiely said of it: 'If there is any sense at all in talking about a Catholic novel, *The Land of Spices* is a Catholic novel.' In spite of this it was banned, because of a brief reference to homosexual love.

Elizabeth Bowen (1899–1973), born in Dublin and inheriting a family seat at Bowenscourt in Co. Cork, is still mainly an 'outsider', closer to Oxford and London and the Bloomsbury group than to Ireland. There is, however, an Irish dimension to some of her work. *The Last September* (1929) describes life in a Big House during 'the troubles', but the main characters are wrapped in the 'cocoon' of their own world. 'Nothing for me but clothes and what people say,' says Lois, the heroine and Elizabeth Bowen writes in the preface that this period of her youth was for her 'mainly a period of impatience, frivolity, lassitude or boredom.' The peasants and the IRA are shadowy, peripheral figures. This is not to imply that the novel is superficial. She writes subtly and beautifully of the world that she knew. She also wrote a family history, *Bowens Court* (1942) and a fine short story 'Summer Night', set in Co. Cork.

Francis MacManus (1909–1965) was born in Kilkenny, went to University College, Dublin, taught for a time and then worked for Radio Eireann in Dublin. He wrote a trilogy of novels based on the life of Donnacha Rua MacConmara, a Gaelic poet of the eighteenth century, *Stand and Give Challenge* (1934), *Candle for the Proud* (1936) and *Men Withering* (1939). These novels deal with the dark, hidden Ireland of the eighteenth century, with poverty, land-hunger and apostasy. *This House was Mine* (1937) deals with land-hunger in more recent times. *The Greatest of These* (1943) is one of the few good novels about the Catholic clergy. It tells how a bishop, with true Christian charity, wins back a rebellious and isolated priest to the community of the church.

PART FIVE

Some Living Writers

17

Sean O'Faolain

Sean O'Faolain's name is often coupled with that of Frank O'Connor. Both were from humble families in Cork, both took the Republican side in 1921, both fought against censorship and puritanism in the Free State, both had their books banned. John Montague, observing the sexual freedoms of the young at the Fleadh Cheoil in Mullingar, in the early sixties, commented:

Puritan Ireland's dead and gone
A myth of O'Connor and O'Faoláin.

O'Faolain, too, was a disciple of Daniel Corkery, and O'Connor, in his autobiography, records a pang of jealousy:

But Corkery's greatest friend was Sean O'Faolain, who was three years older than I and all the things I should have wished to be — handsome, brilliant, and, above all, industrious. For Corkery, who loved application, kept on rubbing it in that I didn't work as O'Faolain did. Once the three of us met on Patrick's bridge after Corkery and O'Faolain had attended a service at the Cathedral, and when O'Faolain went off in his home-spun suit, swinging his ash-plant, Corkery looked after him as I had once seen him look after Terence McSwiney and said: 'There goes a born literary man!' For months I was mad with jealousy.

O'Faolain was indeed a literary man, and a very industrious one. He was also very versatile and he had what Richard Fallis called a 'fine-honed mind'. When Maurice Harmon wrote a study of his work as far back as 1966, he listed thirty-eight major works and eight pages of minor works. O'Faolain founded *The Bell* in 1940 and edited it for six

years, six difficult years when Irish government censorship
was in its worst phase and intellectual life in Dublin was hard-
pressed. In the course of his writing life he has written novels,
short stories, biographies of Daniel O'Connell, the Countess
Markievicz and Hugh O'Neill, Earl of Tyrone, an autobiography, books of criticism, a study of the Irish, travel books
and innumerable articles and reviews. He has continued to
write into his old age. In 1979 he published another novel,
And Again, about a man who is selected by the Gods for an
experiment in rejuvenation. He grows backwards, becoming
steadily younger.

O'Faolain was born at 5, Half Moon Street, on 22 February
1900. His father was a police sergeant in the Royal Irish
Constabulary and his mother took in as lodgers the visiting
actors and actresses who were appearing at the old Opera
House nearby. He went to local schools and finally won his
way into University College, Cork. But in those days the
College offered a very limited intellectual life, and O'Faolain,
eager to talk, would seek out Corkery, though knowing how
busy he was with his own concerns:

> He never turned me away. After I got to know Frank
> O'Connor, he became an alternative victim. But he was
> three years my junior, fifteen to my eighteen, and he was
> so poor that I could not have counted on a fire in his
> house, or even a room to sit in, any more than he could
> have in my house, still full of lodgers and with, as with
> him, no other living room than the communal kitchen. If
> I did call on him we would walk around in the rain,
> sheltering in doorways, talking literature.

After 1916 he was slowly drawn into the growing current
of nationalist idealism. *Vive Moi,* a lively autobiography of
his early life, gives a vivid picture of the enthusiasm of those
years. In chapter eight he describes a summer school near
Gougane Barra in West Cork, where he, and the girl he loved
and was later to marry, Eileen Gould, went to improve their
spoken Irish. They stayed in a large farm-house belonging to
Irish speakers:

> We proved to be a company of about twenty or thirty men
> and women, youths and girls, all as light-hearted as child-

ren. Their gaiety was something I have never experienced before or since. The women and girls shared rooms in the house. The men slept in the dry stone loft, which had been turned for the summer into a simple dormitory. We ate in separate sittings, about ten at a time, at the long table in the dining room, and we always ate well. We spoke only Irish, often asking for a word or a phrase, or a correct pronunciation from the more practised. We had come from all parts of Ireland. They were clerks, students, craftsmen, carpenters, masons, an electrical engineer. Two, who were more serious than the rest of us, had been in the Rising in Dublin and had been released from jail in the general amnesty of the year before; but all of us were reborn of the Rising and all that led to it, so that the language acted both as a matrix to the tissues of our political faith and as its sign and password. Our zeal to speak Irish bound us into a community, a new glowing, persecuted, or about-to-be-persecuted, political sect. One small sign of this was that we all adopted, and, like myself, most retained for the rest of their lives the ancient, original Gaelic forms of our anglicised names, so from being Whelan, I became and remain, as my children do, O'Faolain. It is pronounced Oh-Fay-láwn.

He fought on the Republican side in the Civil War and remained an active Republican for some time, but finally he left to study at Harvard. He lectured for a time in America and England, but he finally settled down in Ireland as a professional writer, working as a free-lance journalist as well as writing stories. His first short story collection, *Midsummer Night Madness* was published in 1932. The book, as Brian Cleeve puts it, 'earned critical praise and clerical disapproval, a common fate in Ireland'.

In a study of the Irish short story (*Irish Press,* 17 June 1978) Walter Allen pays tribute to the work of O'Faolain and O'Connor, not only in the short story. 'Between them,' he writes, 'they have perhaps done more than any other Irishmen to interpret Ireland to the outside world.' O'Faolain certainly did much to inform the rest of the world about Ireland. His biographies of Daniel O'Connell and Hugh O'Neill are significant studies of two great figures in Irish history. His little introduction, *The Story of Ireland* (1943), is one of the best brief guides to Irish history, and *The Irish* offers an intelligent and witty analysis of the Irish people. But it is for his short stories that he is likely to be chiefly remembered.

In his own foreword to *The Stories of Sean O'Faolain* he criticises the youthful romanticism of his early stories. They were, he said, 'full of romantic boss-words like *dawn*', and the style was too lavish and rhetorical. He thought that he had perceived and remembered truly, but he did not sufficiently understand the experiences he was writing about. At the same time he declined to re-write the stories in the light of his later maturity and understanding: 'To re-write years afterwards is a form of forgery.'

In spite of romanticism and some overwriting, the early stories do convey vividly a sense of the revolutionary and confused times he is writing about. In 'Midsummer Night Madness' the story of old Henn and his mistress Gipsy, the tinker girl, whom the violent Stevey, the undisciplined guerilla, forces him in the end to marry, is wholly convincing. So is the burning of the Blake's house and the general mood of lawlessness. At times the writing is self-conscious, particularly in descriptive passages: 'A frightened bird fluttered in the woods; a star fell in a graceful, fatal swoop, vanishing in mid-air as if a mighty hand had scratched the sky with light.' The simile here seems unnecessary, a little forced. But such details do not destroy the total impact of the story.

In many ways I find 'Midsummer Night Madness' more convincing than a much cleverer and more controlled story such as 'Teresa'. This story, written some fifteen years later, is charming, amusing and urbane. It tells the story of a pilgrimage made by two nuns to Lisieux. The elderly Sister Patrick is accompanying the young and large-eyed novice Teresa — 'lovely as a black wallflower' — on a visit to the home of her patron saint in the hope of confirming her vocation as a nun. The story is deftly and wittily told, and the dialogue sparkles. The old nun is wholly convincing. She tries to quiet the scruples and complaints of the novice:

'Now, now, now' grumbled the old woman, 'you know you'll get peace and calm in Leesoo. The saint will reveal

your heart to you. You'll quieten down. You'll know that
all these scruples of yours mean nothing at all. Sure, we all
had them!' In spite of herself she became impatient. Her
soothing voice gradually took on an edge. 'And anyway,
goodness knows, you were eager enough to come! And let
me tell you it isn't every reverend mother would let you.
And it's not a holiday you're on, miss. It's thinking of the
holy saint you should be and not of gillygooseys in Dublin.'

The novice withdrew into herself. She was too tired to
pray; from sheer repetition the words were becoming
meaningless.

Presently the old nun said, as if she were thinking aloud:
'And even if I have an aunt . . . ha! . . . I suppose she won't
know me.'

She stopped again and folded her hands deep into her
sleeves.

'Thirty-one years,' she mused to the window.

The autorail rattled along for several miles. Then Patrick
leaned over and said comfortably:

'A terror for the hot milk at night. She'd drink two
pints of it. Sure, 'twas enough to kill a plough-horse.'

The volatile Teresa, who wants to be a saint, first rejects
the idea of the Carmelite order, then she fasts and sleeps on
bare boards and decides she wants to join them. But after
returning home to her convent in England, she leaves next
morning through a ground-floor window and takes the milk-
train to London.

O'Faolain makes no comment on Teresa. The shallowness
of her desire to be a saint is revealed by what she says and
does, including a telling brief scene with her husband at the
end when she revisits the convent. His handling of the whole
story is deft, clever and amusing, but I find it very hard to
believe in the reality of Teresa.

I don't have the same difficulty with other later stories.
'Sinners', 'Discord', 'The Man Who Invented Sin' and 'Lovers
of the Lake' all seem to me wholly convincing. These are
among his best stories. The little serving-girl in 'Sinners' takes
on an immediate reality as she faces the irascible canon in the
confession box, 'her hands clasping and unclasping, as if her
courage was a little bird between her palms trying to escape.'

The canon, too, irritated by Father Delaney's rows of penitents, and by Mrs Higgins' complaints about her missing boots, springs to life. Both the canon and the girl are 'sinners' and their confrontation in the confessional is ironic and amusing. We laugh at them but we sympathise too. When the canon has calmed his jàngled nerves and his jumping stomach by a long night walk, he comes suddenly on Mrs Higgins shouting down at the belated girl, and 'he felt the hound of his stomach jump from the kennel again'. He can only 'seek his dark presbytery deep among the darkest lanes'. The story is quite short but nothing is wasted. The tone is not anti-clerical, but we are left with a ruefully humorous side-light on the problems of the confessional.

Sin, in various shapes, figures a good deal in O'Faolain's stories, as it did, of course, in the Ireland he wrote about. 'The Man Who Invented Sin' throws a harsher light on the Church, and Lispeen, the officious, puritanical curate, cuts a sorry figure. The apparently conciliatory ending is sharply contradicted by the suggestion of the devil (the man who invented sin) in the final sentence: 'He bowed benevolently to every respectful salute along the glowing street, and, when he did, his elongated shadow waved behind him like a tail.'

Sin is dealt with in a different way in 'Lovers of the Lake'. This is a longer and later story; it is also more subtle and complex. It tells of two modern, middle class, sophisticated people whose extra-marital love affair is profoundly affected by a visit to the penitential island in Lough Derg (Co. Donegal). From the man's point of view the whole thing is seen as a joke at first, and he only agrees to go to humour a wayward impulse in the woman. But on the island, and on the journey home afterwards, subtle changes take place. At the end the lovers kiss passionately and go to their separate rooms.

Walter Allen, who knew nothing of the real Lough Derg and its significant place in Irish religious tradition, confessed to finding the story mysterious and disturbing. 'I also find it,' he wrote, 'perhaps against my will, convincing.' This is a striking tribute to O'Faolain's skill as a story-teller. What happens runs counter to many modern assumptions about human happiness and freedom, but I agree with Walter Allen that it is wholly convincing.

In the long run it is O'Faolain's stories, more perhaps than his histories and biographies and introductions, that will help to interpret Ireland to the rest of the world. The voice that speaks through his stories is one of the clearest and calmest and sanest among the Anglo-Irish writers of the twentieth century. There is a balance of irony and sympathy in his work. He can criticise priests or peasants or politicians, the Church or the State, but he can also make us understand and sympathise with people, and with their religion and institutions.

18

Mary Lavin

Mary Lavin belongs to a world rather different from that of O'Faolain and O'Connor. Born a decade later, in 1912, she spent the first ten years of her life in Walpole, Massachusetts, where her father, from Roscommon, was working for a wealthy American family. He had met his wife, the daughter of a middle class merchant in Athenry, on a return voyage from America to Ireland. Nora Lavin did not like living in America, and in 1921 she brought her daughter Mary back to Ireland, to live first with her parents in Athenry and later in Dublin. So Mary was not caught up in the early years of the national struggle in the way that O'Faolain and O'Connor were. With the sharp eyes and ears of a ten year old child coming from a different world, she observed the ways of life in Athenry, and the personalities of her relatives.

In Dublin she went to school at Loreto Convent and later studied French and English at University College, where she was awarded first class Honors for an M.A. thesis on Jane Austen. She taught French for two years at her old school, and she married William Walsh, a Dublin lawyer. They made their home at the Abbey Farm, Bective, in Co. Meath, where she still lives, though she also has a mews flat in Dublin.

Most of her stories are set in the Irish midlands and her basic concern is with human relationships. Seamus Deane, writing in *The Irish Short Story* (ed. Rafroidi and Brown) sees in her 'the authority of the artist as a woman', who is 'highly sceptical of the "male" worlds of politics and work'. And he aptly sums up the nature of her subject matter by calling it 'a deep and patient study' of 'the nature of love'. It does not follow from this that her stories are all of one kind. Love, and the lack of love, take on an immense variety of shapes. Marriage relationships, family tensions, relations between parents and children, between brother and sister, sister and sister, the relation of the individual to society and to the Church, are all explored in her stories. There is a great deal of variety in her method and manner of story-telling, and a wide range of human material. Her two island stories, 'The Great Wave' and 'The Green Grave and the Black Grave' are very different from 'The Will' or 'A Wet Day'.

Her approach to the short story, which she sees as a very different thing from an anecdote, is illuminated by some of the comments she has made in interviews. Speaking to Maev Kennedy (*The Irish Times*, 13 March 1976) she said:

> The real short story is possibly an idea, buried deep in the writer's consciousness, which he, miraculously at times, sees a chance of embodying in a story. I carry around a question in my mind, a question that teases and torments me for an answer, and then one day I think I see the answer in a person or an incident. But even then I don't rush and write it, it is only after I have encountered it a few times that I take the risk of inventing the story to house it in.

In another interview with Catherine Murphy (*Irish University Review*, vol.9, no.2, autumn 1979) Mary Lavin revealed that the source of 'The Great Wave' was something that Michael McLaverty told her. He had stayed a night with an old man who had survived the Cleggan fishing disaster. McLaverty noticed that he had only stumps for hands, and when he asked him what happened, he was told the story of the drownings and how he was the only man to survive. '"Weren't you the lucky man?" Michael said. The old man shook his head. "No. I was not lucky, because it was greed that saved me."' His hands had been torn off because he had clung to the nets full of fish. The same thing happens to Seoineen in 'The Great Wave'. Mary Lavin said in the interview: 'When Michael McLaverty told me of his adventure, I was fascinated by the paradox of a man having to live with the knowledge that his life had been saved by a vice not a virtue.'

Earlier in this interview Mary Lavin spoke of her desire to examine an incident or observe a character:

> I think short story writers try to break the continuity of life or at least slow life down. I think we try to break a life down into some of its components. When I said in the preface to my *Selected Stories* that, for me, story writing was looking deeper than usual into the human heart, I meant that I myself at times have had such a feeling of life's forever rushing past, that I wanted in my stories to arrest that onrush and examine an incident or observe a character in the same way that a scientist examines a specimen under a microscope, when you see the many small inner patterns below the large pattern of a whole life.

I would like to illustrate the kind of patterns that Mary Lavin observes in the lives around her by examining in more detail some of the individual stories. I begin with 'The Living'. The story opens with a conversation about dead people between two young boys who are out in search of some excitement:

> 'How many dead people do you know?' said Mickser, suddenly.
> Immediately, painfully, I felt my answer would show me once more his inferior.
> 'Do you mean ghosts?' I said, slowly, to gain time.
> 'No,' said Mickser, 'I mean corpses.'

The boys go to visit a cottage where there is a wake. The retarded, invalid son of the woman who opens and shuts the level crossing gates has died. But Mickser's boldness quickly turns to fright when the woman takes them in to see the body of her dead son and asks them to comb his hair. This suggests perhaps a story of macabre humour. But in fact the emphasis has shifted from corpses to the woman's love for her simple-minded son, and her coming loneliness. Another woman tries to comfort her:

> 'Hush now, you'll feel different as time goes on.'
> 'Will I?' said the mother, looking wonderingly at the other one. 'That's what's said to everyone, but is it true? I'll feel different, maybe, sometimes when I look at the

clock and have to pull off my apron and run out to throw back the gates. I'll feel different, maybe, when some woman stops to have a word with me, or when I have to take a jug and go down the road for a sup of milk. But in the middle of the night, or first thing when the jackdaws start talking in the chimney and wake me out of my sleep, will I feel different then?'

Before long the scene changes from the cottage by the railway to the home of Mickser's friend, the 'I' of the story. The boy, excited by his first view of a dead body, thinks of discussing corpses with his mother, but at home he finds a scene of pulsing life. In the family kitchen his brother is mending a puncture with his bike upended, his father is washing his feet by the fire, while his mother is scrubbing the floor. The warmth of family life is strongly felt, and the love of husband and wife is revealed in playful sparring, in a frankly sexual embrace, and in the sudden concern of the man for his wife's health. The boy is moved:

And all the things I had wanted to ask her about the poor fellow at the level-crossing came back into my mind. But I didn't feel like asking her then at all. And do you know what came into my mind? It was a few words of the prayer we said every night of our lives.

' . . . the living and the dead . . .' Over and over we'd said them, night after night, and I never paid any heed to them. But I suddenly felt they were terrible, terrible words . . .

But the kettle began to spit on the range, and my mother ran over and lifted it back from the blaze.

'How about us taking our tea in the parlour?' she cried. 'All of us. The kitchen is no fitter than the backyard with you.'

And in the excitement I forgot all about the living and the dead. For a long time.

A lively humour flashes here and there in the story, but it reveals delicately and beautifully the grain of the living, and the precarious closeness of life to death.

Attitudes to death play a large part in 'The Will' and 'A Happy Death', and we can see how important religion is in the world of her stories. 'The Will' is about the exclusion of Lally, the youngest daughter of the Conroy family, from any bequest in her mother's will. Her mother disapproved of Lally's marriage and had never forgiven her. Lally is not upset by her omission from the will but she is upset by the thought that her mother died without forgiving her. She is afraid for her mother's soul, and on her way to catch a train back to town, she calls on the local priest to arrange for masses to be said for her mother's soul.

Lally, impetuous, warm-hearted, unworldly, is set against her brothers and sisters, who are concerned with keeping up appearances. They want Lally to give up her boarding-house. 'It's not a very nice thing', says her sister Kate, 'for us to feel that our sister is a common landlady in the city.' And very quickly their sympathy with her for being excluded from the will changes to hostility and dislike because she will not accept their arrangements and their advice. At the same time the obvious signs of her aging, accentuated by hardship, remind them of their own decay:

> A chill fell on them. A grudge against her gnawed at them.
>
> 'I begin to see', said Matthew, 'that Mother was right. I begin to see what she meant when she said that you were as obstinate as a tree.'
>
> 'Did she say that?' said Lally, and her face lit up for a moment with the sunlight of youth, as her mind opened wide in a wilful vision of tall trees, leafy, and glossy with light, against a sky as blue as the feathers in a young girl's hat.

This passage aptly reveals the skill and subtlety of Mary Lavin's writing. The image of the trees suggests Lally's natural energy and spontaneity, which is set against the cold prudence and prejudice of the rest of the family who are 'gnawed' by a grudge against her. And the reference to the blue feathers picks up the earlier conversation about the feathers that Lally wore in her hat on her wedding day. The passage works by implication and suggestion, rather than by statement. This is true of the details, and it is also true of the total moral wisdom of each complete story. As Seamus Deane remarks: 'The stories are not morality tales; they adjudicate by implication not by pronouncement.'

This may be seen very clearly in 'A Happy Death', one of her longer stories. It is the story of a marriage between Robert and Ella, that began in a green glade of sunlight and happiness and intimacy, but turned sour and bitter with frustration and nagging, as Ella is forced to let rooms for money and Robert, weak and sick, suffers the indignity of being downgraded from his post of assistant librarian to become a library porter, because his coughing disturbs readers. One morning he stays at home and his moaning in the kitchen disturbs the youngest child and one of the lodgers. But Ella deliberately avoids the kitchen until she begins to take comfort from the fact that Robert is not going to work, that he will have to give up his job, and that she will be able to put into operation her own plans for him. Feeling that she has won her long fight with him and is about to reap her reward she goes to see him:

> Even Robert would have to see that she had been acting for the best. She had been making a way for them both out of the dark forest in which they had been imprisoned, and together now they would flash out into the open glade. That it would be like the green glades of their early youth she did not for a moment doubt.
>
> She stood up. As her tiredness and misery had given way to excitement and exultation, so these emotions had in turn given way to an infinite feeling of peace. She moved toward the back door that led into the house. She would tell him her plans.
>
> But as she entered the mean hallway, her nostrils were assailed by imprisoned odours of the stale past, and she heard him move his feet on the broken cement floor of the kitchen. And immediately her spirits were dampened. She felt tongue-tied. The habits of years were not to be broken so easily. How would she begin? What would she say? For she would now have to deal with the real Robert; the bodily Robert, and whereas it had seemed in her mind, as long ago it had seemed in her heart, that they were one person, indissoluble in intimacy, who could say or do whatever they liked to each other, she had no sooner heard him cough and scrape his foot on the floor than she was aware again that two people never are one, and that they

were, as they always were, and always would be, two separate beings, ever at variance in their innermost core, ever liable to react upon each other with unpredictable results. She was uneasy. She had lost her surety before she had crossed the threshold.

And when she heard him call her name in a strange voice as if trying to penetrate some incredible distance between them while she was actually within a few yards of him, with her hand on the kitchen door, all her old irritation came back.

'I'm here,' she said, 'There's no need to shout.' She went into the house.

'Didn't you hear me moaning?' he asked feebly and without accusation. Her antagonism gathered.

'Are you ever doing anything else?' she asked. The bright flock of hopeful thoughts had taken flight again.

So deep has the division between Ella and Robert become that she is unable to understand how ill he is, but finally she is forced to get a doctor and Robert is removed to die in hospital. Soon her anxiety is that he shall die 'a happy death' after confession and absolution. For a long time he is in a coma, but when he does briefly regain consciousness his thoughts are on his early courtship of Ella. He does die a happy death — '"Just the two of us!" he said, the look of rapturous happiness returning to his face.' — but not in the religious sense that Ella wanted. She realises that the waiting priest has only been able to give Robert the blessing of conditional absolution, and the story ends with deep irony as she is led screaming from his death-bed:

And as she was led out of the ward a few minutes later she was still screaming and sobbing, and it was utterly incomprehensible to her that God had not heard her prayers, and had not vouchsafed to her husband the grace of a happy death.

In 'A Wet Day' the moral implication is made very clear, though it is still implication not pronouncement. The story, one of her finest, is a devastating exposure of selfishness. The central figure is Father Gogan, an elderly parish priest, who suffers from diabetes and is greatly concerned with his own health and comfort, but the story is not anti-clerical. Father Gogan is judged as a man not as a priest. The story begins with talk of lettuce as the niece-narrator, her aunt and the priest walk down a wet garden path. The priest's doctor has told him to eat plenty of lettuce, and Mike the aunt's gardener, loads his car with lettuce before he leaves. After his departure the niece takes a walk and returns with a good appetite for her dinner:

> And when I came back I was hungry. I was looking forward to my dinner. When Ellen came in with a bowl of salad I hoped my aunt would not take too big a helping because I felt I could eat the whole bowlful. But what do you think? Before the girl had time to set the bowl before us my aunt rapped on the table.
>
> 'Take away that lettuce,' she said. 'We don't want any tonight.'
>
> I was going to protest when I caught her eye and held my tongue. We didn't mention Father Gogan or the big red-haired farmer from Mullingar — either then or since — but isn't it a funny thing, I have been on better terms with my aunt since that day. We get on better. And we have less fights about books and politics and one thing and another.

The aunt's rejection of the salad is wholly explicable after the story told by the priest, where he reveals to aunt and niece that his concern for his own comfort and domestic peace allowed him to send away the big red-haired farmer to his death from pneumonia. A bare summary of the story like this can do little justice to its art. The force of the revelation is largely due to the casual way it starts in conversation with Mike the gardener, and then continues in the priest's chatty narrative in which he seems quite unaware of what he is revealing about himself. When the young farmer's fiancée, a nurse, asked for a thermometer, the priest protested that he hadn't got such a thing. Another turn in the conversation brings out the truth:

> 'Don't tell me you had one all the time?' my aunt said and I'll say this for her — she said it very falteringly.

'Three!' said the old priest. 'I had three of them, no less, but I wasn't going to let on to her that I had . . . '

The writer's skill in the use of words is shown here by the choice of 'falteringly'. The niece's comment illuminates the relationship between all three people.

Mary Lavin's stories can be read and re-read many times, and each reading brings new insights. The trivial and the local take on universal significance as William Trevor has pointed out: 'Writing about provincial Ireland, about ordinary people and events that are parochial and unremarkable, she manages to create small worlds that are perfect microcosms of the greater one.'

19

Francis Stuart

'I believe in romantic love, in God, in angels and in the
immortality of the soul. And I do not believe in humani-
tarianism divorced from religious belief. Above all I do not
believe that the temporal happiness and material prosperity
of man on this earth must be our goal. I believe that man-
kind has a divine destiny.

'I recall a wet road, nothing more than a cart-track
really, that winds across an Antrim Bogland. It is evening,
and the surface of the black pools of water with their sheer
sides cut deep into the turf are red with the dying sun. I
see myself as a boy sitting by that roadside on such an
evening in summer looking across the flat bogland to
where Knocklade and the Antrim hills drape the horizon
with their sweet, soft curves. And I wonder how much it
is a desire to remain faithful to the dreams I cherished then
that now makes me loathe so much of the grown-up,
practical, mechanically efficient world.'

The passage above was written by the first person narrator,
clearly Stuart himself, in his novel *The Angel of Pity* (1935).
In a bleak world of the future destroyed by war, with only
two survivors left on a desolate battlefield, he feels the need
to declare his faith, to write it down on a piece of paper. The
passage, of which this is the beginning, reveals something of
Stuart's temperament and attitudes, and also reminds us of
his link with Northern Ireland.

His father, Henry Irwin Stuart, was born near Dervock in
Co. Antrim, and his mother, Elizabeth Montgomery, belonged to a neighbouring family. Henry emigrated to Australia,
where he had a sheep station, and it was in Townville that his
son, Henry Francis Montgomery Stuart, was born in 1902.

225

A few months later his father died in a mental home, so mother and son returned to Ireland. The family lived first near Drogheda and then in Dublin. Francis began his education in Monkstown but was sent to various boarding schools in England, and finally to Rugby. At the age of eighteen he married Iseult Gonne, the natural daughter of Maude Gonne. He took the Republican side in the Civil War, was captured and interned. After his release he turned to writing. He published a small volume of poems and several novels. Early in 1939 he accepted an invitation to lecture and give readings from his novels in Germany, under the aegis of *Die Deutsche Academie*. This visit led to an appointment the following year with the *Englische Seminar* at Berlin University. He went, in spite of the outbreak of war; his marriage had already proved a failure. In Berlin he met Gertrud Meissner, whom he eventually married, after the death of his first wife in 1954. He remained in Berlin during the war, and he gave some broadcast talks over the German radio, but finally he found that he could not take the line the German authorities wanted and he ceased to broadcast. He was never a Fascist, but he had little love of British imperialism and he disliked the moralistic tone of British propaganda. A full account of his attitudes will be found in *Black List, Section H.*

Stuart moved south in the hope of leaving Germany with Miss Meissner, but they were arrested by French occupation troops and imprisoned until July 1946. After some time in Freiburg, they moved to Paris, then to London, and finally to Ireland, where they have been since 1957.

As a novelist Stuart has been compared with D.H. Lawrence and Dostoievsky. He writes, not as a detached observer of the social scene, but as a man obsessed with certain themes, a man on an urgent quest for the salvation of his soul through the acceptance of guilt, suffering, despair, and the love that blossoms on the far side of despair, on 'the flowering cross', which he takes as the title of one of his novels. All his novels are to some degree autobiographical but his book, *Things To Live For: Notes for an Autobiography*, provides some explicit statement of his attitudes and beliefs:

To love, that is all that matters, to lavish love even on objects unworthy of it is infinitely better than living a cold ordered life in a study, in an office, or even in a garden tending flowers. It is only through opening one's arms to life that one will find the ultimate peace and security. Only through suffering and loving. There is no short cut. Protecting oneself against life is not peace but death. Of all the strange varied people I have met it has not been the sinners, the degraded, the drunkards, the gamblers, the crooks, the harlots, who have made me shudder, but the dead, the respectable dead; cut off like a branch from the tree.

Later in the book (chapter IV) he gives an image of 'the respectable dead', three people eating a meal in a 'Board Residence' at a small summer resort on Belfast Lough, where he and his friends stop for tea. While they are waiting, they overhear the three residents speaking a few sparse words in dead voices:

It was enough to suggest to me a living death. There they must live month in and month out in that 'board residence' eking out their existence broken only by their three dreary meals at tables from which nothing but asphalt and lamp-posts and, beyond, the wintry sea could be seen. And even the sea was not the wild open sea, but a particularly ugly lough.

Our arrival was like the sudden entry of three mortals, three beings of flesh and blood, into the abode of the lost. But they did not even eye us curiously as slum dwellers or street urchins would, they were not interested, or perhaps too genteel for that. I felt nothing could raise a flicker of life in those dead faces. Even Brian's conversation, spoken in his beautiful but never lowered voice, only made them draw back their shoulders a little more stiffly as though a warm human breeze was an unwelcome thing in this chill place. I felt they were beyond happiness or suffering and such a state struck me as so terrible, such an antithesis of all I believe in, that I became depressed.

Stuart looked for intensity in life, as he explains in a note he provided for Fred B. Millett's *Contemporary British Literature* (1935). This is quoted in Harry T. Moore's postscript to the Southern Illinois University Press edition of *Black List, Section H*:

> I am interested in life where it is most intense; in sport because I see in a race or a football match a better reflection of the real drama of living than in many books. Besides I like boxers, jockeys, gamblers much more than most writers and painters with their narrow limits of the studio and the library. It does not matter what people do so long as they love and suffer, hope and fear, as long as they are sentient to life and not dead, not withdrawn and smug and secure . . .

His reference here to 'the narrow limits of the studio and the library' is typical. 'The literary atmosphere kills life,' he remarks in *Things To Live For*, and again, 'Even a hard-boiled girl is better than an article on a poet — a remark that gives me pause while I am writing a chapter on him.

Stuart believed that the artist should ally himself not with the winners in life, the powerful, the respectable, the successful, but with the losers, the despised and rejected, the maimed and the suffering. Speaking at the International Yeats Summer School in 1974, he said:

> What a growing number of readers want is to feel that the writer is at least as vulnerable as they are to all kinds of human experience and relationships, and that he is communicating to them from the most exposed positions. Indeed, the more desperate his position, the more complete his exposure to misfortune and danger, the more intently they listen. That is why Camus, Genet, Beckett, Kavanagh, Berryman, Mailer, to name some, have such a fascination.

Stuart himself was fully exposed, especially towards the end of the war and during the years that followed. He knew hunger, fear, imprisonment, uncertainty and endless waiting, and he learnt patience, endurance and humility. He speaks through Louis Clancy, a Canadian sculptor, in *The Flowering Cross*, who says: 'Real life isn't lived behind a veil of riches, in lightness and ease. It's being exposed to all that happens in patience and faith, waiting in solitude through the succession of setbacks and disappointments, letting all things touch, till gradually you learn the gentleness of the touch of life.'

Even Stuart's early novels, written before his experiences in war-torn Europe, present desperate situations, where his heroes are fully exposed. In *Pigeon Irish* (1932) Ireland is engaged in a semi-allegorical war against a super-civilisation, an unknown, rationalistic, totalitarian power. The narrator, Frank Allen, takes command of the Irish Home Guard during the absence of his friend, Joe Arigho, at the front somewhere in Europe, and proposes a plan that precipitates mutiny. The plan is to surrender Dublin to the superior forces of the enemy and to set up secret colonies of resistance in the country, where the traditional spirit of Ireland can survive. Frank, though saved from death by the return of Joe, who is executed in his place, is disgraced. His wife leaves him, but Joe's daughter, Catherine supports him, and they remain to symbolise hope in defeat and humiliation.

There is a kind of lyrical fable as sub-plot, dealing with three pigeons (hence the title) who are used to carry messages to and from the battle front. The pigeons have religious over-tones, and when one of them dies after faithfully bringing back an urgent message, his dead body is gently lifted to heaven by the fingers of Archangels, 'fingers rinsed in the wet blueness of infinite space'.

The Coloured Dome is kept closer to earth than *Pigeon Irish* but it deals with a similar spiritual quest. Garry Delea is searching for a way of salvation, something that will give meaning to his life and death, and he finds it through the way of the cross: 'To share in himself the anguish of the broken heart of the world. To look through the coloured dome at the white unstained snows of light beyond it. That was the fulfilment towards which he darkly groped.' He offers himself for execution in a bid to end a civil war, but another is shot in his place. His end is not to be dramatic, but humble and squalid, in a cell for the drunk and disorderly: 'He was at last utterly humble, lost to the eyes of the world and to his own eyes.'

Although Stuart had already suffered imprisonment, there is something a little tentative and theoretical in these two early novels. The later novels that treat a similar theme of love through suffering have a greater strength and sureness. *A Pillar of Cloud* (1948) carries the weight and conviction of Stuart's own experience in the war and its aftermath: 'All these years when I ate my regular three or four meals a day, when I lived in a house whose kitchen and larder were stacked with supplies, I knew nothing about food! Without hunger, without starvation, you cannot know what food is, you cannot really know what life is or what your body is. Wait till the hole beneath your ribs comes to ache and to have no bottom to it.'

The story is set in a war-damaged town in French-occupied Germany, after the war. Dominic Malone, an Irish poet, is arrested, imprisoned and interrogated at length by the French authorities who suspect him of collaboration with the Germans. He is befriended by Halka Mayersky, a girl who bears the marks of Nazi whips on her breasts. She has plumbed the depths of humiliation and suffering. Forced into prostitution by necessity, she was imprisoned in a concentration camp and later in an asylum. Dominic learns to love Halka with so deep a love that he can give her up in order to help her younger sister, Lisette, who has advanced tuberculosis. There is some hope that she may live if Dominic can take her back to Ireland, which he can only do by making her his wife. He marries her but she dies before they can get the necessary papers to leave. Dominic is now free to take Halka as his wife to Ireland, but for the time being they stay: 'They had not sought to save themselves in the world, to save their lives, and life was being given to them.'

The story is a kind of Christian parable, but tied closely to earthly reality, to the harsh details of life in war-torn Marheim. Although the setting is Germany, Ireland is strongly present in Dominic's mind through images of his Uncle Egan, and his former life with him.

In spite of its dark background the book has a grace and tenderness, a lyrical flow that gives it beauty as well as power. The following passage, where Dominic and Halka visit an old graveyard, one of their favourite places in battered Marheim, gives some idea of the tone and style of the book:

In the afternoon Dominic took Halka to the old graveyard. He loved the still, greenish light in the long, overgrown alleys of sycamores with their smooth, peeling barks and the grey, half-hidden tombstones along the edges of the wild lawns. Never was she so close to him as here and never had she been so close as on this evening. 'Whoever seeks to save his life shall lose it and whoever is ready to lose it shall save it.' And life was all that was precious. Now when he was prepared to lose her their union was growing and blossoming.

'Does this remind you of your graveyard at home near the lake? Is that why you like it so much?' she asked him.

'A little, perhaps . . . '

'Look. There is our blackbird,' she said.

On the topmost stone of the ruined chapel a blackbird perched and sang, like a small black tongue of flame that had descended out of heaven.

Redemption is also a largely allegorical novel, using a good deal of symbolism and offering an interpretation of the Christian belief in redemption. There are many echoes of the Bible in the language and imagery of the novel, and the priest, Father Mellowes, is at the centre of it. But the view of Christ and the Christian mystery that Stuart presents is given an individual slant. As epigraph to the book we find the lines of Blake:

The vision of Christ that thou dost see
Is my vision's greatest enemy.

In chapter XII, Father Mellowes has lunch with Ezra Arrigho, who is, at least in part, a Stuart persona, the outsider returned from the bombed cities of Germany, estranged from his wife, disillusioned with the unreal 'duck-pond' quality of small-town life. Mellowes asks Ezra what shape Christ has taken in his imagination, and although reluctant at first to be drawn into this discussion, he presents at some length his vision of Christ, a vision that he describes with a smile as 'the gospel according to St Ezra'. Ezra, in fact, sees Christ as a figure very like Father Mellowes himself:

'He has appeared to me, as you put it, Father, to some extent as you appear to me,' said Ezra. 'As a man who would have accepted my invitation to lunch to-day just as you have accepted it. And not come picking and sipping at the food or drink either. And just such a girl as Annie would have been ready to serve Him, would have come running with bowls of water for his feet and dried them on her hair. He liked anyone who let themselves be carried away, especially if they were carried away in his direction, of course. But better be carried away in any direction and become a prodigal son or a lost sheep than not be carried away at all, that seems to have been His point of view. And like you, Father, He sought the mad, the possessed, and the sick and dying, they being in a sense nearest Him and most likely not to be appalled and scandalized by the extravagance of what He was going to do and be at the end, when His hour came. Anything to get away from the calculators, the adders-up and subtractors, the moralists for whom the ordinary fleshy communion was already a little suspect and for whom therefore what He meant to offer would be an outrage.'

This lunch-time conversation takes place in the shadow of a murder. In a room above, the local police have called to interview Kavanagh, a fish-monger, a violent, sensual, selfish man, who has murdered Annie, his shop-assistant and the girl he slept with, in a fit of lustful, jealous rage.

The book is largely about the varied shapes of violence and evil. Ezra talks of his experiences in the war when the Russians had occupied a German town: 'They had come. The Apocalyptic rider on the pale horse had dismounted and come through the door into the hall and gone on into the wards.' But Altamont, too, has its shapes of violence. Kavanagh murders Annie, Ezra violates the virginal Romilly, the priest's sister. It seems as though evil must overwhelm good, and the priest has an hour of despair in the dirty, dishevelled hotel bathroom, not yet cleaned after a dance the previous night. But in the end there is redemption. At the invitation of the priest, a little group joins him in a fraternal community in the flat above Kavanagh's fish shop. There is Kavanagh himself, until he is taken to prison, Romilly, Ezra and Margareta, the girl he thought was killed in a bombing raid. She survives, with a damaged hip, and searches him out

in Altamont. Ezra suggests to his wife, Nancy, from whom he
has long been estranged, that she might join them, but she
declines. Her Aunt Nuala, however, does eventually allow
herself to be taken to join the group. A queer company,
certainly, but there is finally 'the taste of the fruit of friendship.'

Before Kavanagh leaves, to face trial and execution,
Romilly marries him, so that he will have at least one person
to visit and befriend him before death. It is a self-sacrifice
on her part, and a response to human need in extremity, but
it brings her peace and her brother's blessing. In the final
short chapter, after Romilly has returned from her last visit
to Kavanagh, with despair on her face, Ezra asks Father
Mellowes: 'All the destructive pain . . . what can come of it?
All the pain that cannot be borne or submitted to. What condemned men go through and children and others. Can there
be any point in it or isn't it the sign of chaos?' Father
Mellowes' answer is not in words but in his smile, which has
become familiar and re-assuring. One closes the book with a
sense that the Christian mystery of redemption has indeed
taken place.

It is a highly original and a fascinating novel, with its odd
mixture of allegory and symbol and carefully recorded
naturalistic detail. *The Pillar of Cloud* I find easy to accept
because the background is strange, foreign, set in the stress
of war and war's aftermath. But in Altamont, we are in the
familiar streets and pubs of a small Irish town, with people
drinking Guinness and talking and going to the dog-races.
Chapter XI, for example, paints vividly the scene and the
conversation in a pub, with an amusing detached irony:
'There was some quiet talk going on at the counter about the
murder and about the dog-races. Nothing loud or excited, but
damped down by plenty of good stout and plenty of good
time.' I find myself acutely conscious of the different planes
of reality in the book, admiring the boldness that brings them
together, but not quite certain of its complete success.

The figure of Aunt Nuala is a case in point. Although she
only appears late in the book she is fully and vividly presented, with her house and farm, her vibrant voice and her
waspishness. She is more fully realised than Nancy, Ezra's

wife, or even Romilly, who remains a somewhat shadowy figure. When Ezra finally goes to visit Aunt Nuala she vents her spleen on him. She resents his living in a hotel:

> The idea of living in a hotel without responsibilities and duties roused rage and fear in her — the ever-present fear that others might be enjoying life without paying the price while she was always paying the price and not enjoying it.
>
> 'I'm sharing a house with some other people,' Ezra said. 'I wanted Nancy to come there too, but it didn't appeal to her.'
>
> 'Didn't appeal to her? By the hoaky, I don't suppose it did!'
>
> She sat there in her mannish and worn clothes and her heavy boots and talked at him, and he felt the core of her grudge, like a small, hard growth in her, somewhere in her bowels or her womb.

And yet Aunt Nuala submits to being massaged by Margareta, the strange foreign woman who accompanies Ezra, who speaks to her in German which she cannot understand; and she finally agrees to leave her house and farm and go with them to the flat. I am not wholly convinced that Aunt Nuala would do this.

Two of the crucial actions in the novel are both real and allegorical — the murder of Annie and the violation of Romilly. On the level of reality both deeds seem insufficiently motivated; but perhaps this does not matter since they fit so clearly into the book's allegorical and symbolic structure.

In spite of the doubts that I have just raised, I think that *Redemption* and *The Pillar of Cloud* represent a fine achievement and reveal Stuart's powers as a novelist at their height. To these I would add the autobiographical *Black List, Section H.* I have not space to discuss it here, but it combines the interests of autobiography and fiction. It helps us to understand Stuart and the world he belonged to. It is also an absorbing study of an artist's struggle to pursue his own path against the tide of the times, his lonely and obstinate struggle to keep faith with his own vision.

Stuart seems to have found a renewal of creative energy in his seventies. He has published two novels set against a background of the 'troubles' in Northern Ireland, *Memorial* (1973) and *A Hole in the Head* (1977). Both novels show his constant concern not to withdraw from suffering and evil. The protagonist in the later novel, clearly a Stuart persona, goes to a clinic in Belbury (Belfast) after an attempted suicide, and finally offers himself as a hostage in a kidnapping siege, in exchange for the two children of a paramilitary leader. He remarks at one point in the book: 'I needed fairly complex and even desperate situations to get my system, such as it is (neurological, psychological, physical), into top gear. And that, as I now know, went for my writing too.' The novel is, perhaps, a little too close to a clinical case-history, and a little too explicit in its symbolism and moral philosophy.

I prefer *Memorial*, where the characters have a richer humanity. The book is a daring one, dealing with the sexual relationship between a man of seventy and a girl of sixteen. The unlikely couple, with a sympathetic but alcoholic governess, move into a community centre in the 'no-go' area of a Northern town. The girl, who gets help from a British soldier for her sick hare, is accidentally shot. The story carries conviction and is free from sentimentality, though the writing lacks the easy flow of earlier books.

Stuart is very much his own man, an original writer by any standards, a solitary wrestling with the forces of darkness that surround him in a world of war and violence, but he has deep roots in Irish experience that give him a secure place in the ranks of Anglo-Irish novelists.

20

Brian Moore

Brian Moore has now written a dozen novels and he has already an international reputation. I intend to examine three of these novels, the first two he wrote, both of which are set in Belfast, and the later *Catholics* set in the west of Ireland. I choose these three, not only because they all deal with aspects of Irish experience, but because I think they are his best.

Moore was born in Belfast in 1921, the son of a well-known surgeon at the Mater Hospital. His father was fifty when he married, and his son has described him as 'Edwardian'. He was an intensely religious man and Moore had a traditional middle class Catholic upbringing, attending St Malachi's College, a local Catholic school. The second World War was on when he left school and he joined an ARP unit in Belfast. This led him to service later as a civilian employee of the British Ministry of War Transport in North Africa, Italy and France. Later he served with UNRRA and became a freelance reporter in Scandinavian countries. He said in a radio interview that the war broke him loose from Ireland. He emigrated to Canada and eventually became a Canadian citizen. In Canada he did various jobs, including proof-reading and reporting. He also wrote some pulp fiction to earn money. Finally, after the success of his early books, he became a full-time serious writer, and he now lives in California.

He still goes back to Ireland every year, and thinks of it as 'The Moscow of my mind'. But he goes, not to Belfast, but to the west and south, where he had spent family holidays as a boy. When he made a film for the BBC series on 'Writers and Places' the setting he chose was in Connemara.

In an interview in 1967 with the editor of *Studies in the Novel* Moore revealed something of the genesis of his first serious novel, *The Lonely Passion of Judith Hearne*. He spoke of the immense influence that Joyce had had on him. *A Portrait of the Artist as a Young Man* seemed to him the story of his own early life: 'It's our generation's *Catcher in the Rye;* our *Huck Finn* — all those things.' So when he came to write a novel he deliberately avoided the autobiographical approach:

> When I came to thinking about writing a novel, one thing I didn't want to do was an autobiographical novel because I thought, 'Who can compete with *Portrait*?' Most Irish novels are autobiographical. As Sean O'Faolain once said, at the end of an Irish novel the hero gets on a boat and goes to England. So I didn't want my character to do that . . . I wanted to write something about the ordinary person losing the faith, not the intellectual losing the faith; the intellectual thing's been done by so many people. So I said why don't I do a woman. Women are much more emotionally Catholic than men; it would be more shattering for a woman. [And in a later interview for *The Irish Times* (11 Sept. 1976) he added] What if one of my mother's friends in Belfast, one of the sodality ladies, lost her faith?

All the odds are stacked against Judith Hearne. She is one of those destined to be an 'outcast from life's feast', to use the phrase from Joyce's story, 'A Painful Case'. Judith Hearne's case is also a painful one, and Moore describes it with something of the 'scrupulous meanness' that Joyce aimed at. The Belfast background is a bleak and loveless one, symbolised in 'the staring white ugliness of City Hall':

> There, under the great dome of the building, ringed around by forgotten memorials, bordered by the garrison neatness of a Garden of Remembrance, everything that was Belfast came into focus. The news vendors calling out the great events of the world in flat uninterested Ulster voices; the drab facades of the buildings grouped around the Square, proclaiming the virtues of trade, hard dealing, and Presbyterian righteousness. The order, the neatness, the floodlit

cenotaph, a white respectable phallus planted in sinking Irish bog. The Protestant dearth of gaiety, the Protestant surfeit of order, the dour Ulster burghers walking proudly amongst these monuments to their mediocrity.

The novel begins with Judith unpacking her few belongings in a seedy bed-sitter in a run-down part of Belfast. She is thirty-seven, unattractive, poor, without talents of any kind. She places on the mantelpiece in her new room, in the position of honour, a framed silver photograph of her aunt. She was an orphan and her aunt had brought her up. But it was largely her aunt's selfishness that kept Judith back from any prospect of a decent job or a possible husband. Under the pressure of emotional blackmail, she promises not to let her aunt be taken to an institution, even though she has suffered a stroke and her mind has been affected:

> She had given her word: she did not go back on it. Her aunt lived five years after that promise, fighting and raving her way through every ghastly day, until one Sunday morning in 1947, Judy found her sitting straight up in bed, eyes open, her bloated hawk face fixed in its habitual frown of reproof as life suddenly deserted her.

Judith is left alone with very little money, and no prospects. It is not surprising that she turns to alcohol and to fantasy. In the end she is driven to question the existence of God.

The other picture that she had unpacked in her new room, and put over the head of the bed, is a 'coloured oleograph of the Sacred Heart'. This symbolises the traditional Catholic piety in which she had been brought up: 'She had never missed Sunday Mass in her life, except from real illness. She had made the Nine Fridays every year for as long as she could remember. She went to evening devotions regularly and never a day since her First Communion had she missed saying her prayers.' But her religion has no deep spiritual roots; it is a matter of pious ritual, and so it fails to support and strengthen her in loneliness and frustration. In her personal crisis she loses her faith in God; his Tabernacle seems empty.

The work 'passion' in the book's title has several shades of meaning. There is the passion, or craving, for alcohol. There is the romantic and sexual passion for James Madden, her landlady's brother returned from America, whom she mistakenly thinks has made her a proposal of marriage. Most important, there is passion in its original sense of suffering. Judith suffers loneliness, humiliation, rejection; she reaches a point where, like Jesus in His passion on the cross, she is saying: 'My God, my God, why hast thou forsaken me?'

Requested to leave her new boarding-house, after she had been noisily drunk, she draws out her meagre savings, takes a room in a hotel, and buys drink. Drunk, she calls on her friends, the O'Neills, who only tolerate her Sunday visits out of pity. She begins to realise that she is just a nuisance to them, and goes on to her confessor and priest, Father Quigley, who tells her sharply to go home and sober up. Finally she enters the almost empty church and walks up the aisle, seeking a sign from God.

And now? What will become of me, am I to grow old in a room, year by year, until they take me to a poor-house? Am I to be a forgotten old woman, mumbling in a corner in a house run by nuns? What is to become of me, O Lord, alone in this city, with only drink, hateful drink that dulls me, disgraces me, lonely drink that leaves me more lonely, more despised? Why this cross? Give me another, great pain, great illness, anything, but let there be someone to share it. Why do You torture me, alone and silent behind Your little door? Why?

'I hate You', she said, her voice loud and shrill in the silence of the church. And she waited. Now, surely now, in His anointed, consecrated place, a thunderbolt, striking down, white and terrible from the vaulted roof.

But God gives no sign, and after this she tries to open the tabernacle. Then, in a moment of hallucination, she thinks God has come out 'terrible, breathing fire', accompanied by Mary and Joseph. It is, in fact, Father Quigley and two elderly parishioners.

Judith is removed to a home where her room is paid for by the O'Neills. Her revolt against God has not set her free or revealed any way out for her. After a period of depression she turns again to her old habits of piety and attends Mass: 'If you do not believe, you are alone.' And the story ends where it began, after the Nursing Sister has arranged the picture of her Aunt and the Sacred Heart on her dressing table: 'Funny about those two. When they're with me, watching over me, a new place becomes home.' This last sentence is identical with the last sentence of chapter one, but the word 'home' now has an even sadder irony.

The novel has the strength of unity and simplicity. The narrative technique is fairly straightforward, though from time to time it slips into the stream of Judith's consciousness in order to reveal her thoughts and fantasies. In one chapter Moore gives shots of Judith as seen in the private language of the other inmates of the boarding house. These provide a sharp contrast with the way Judith sees herself.

In writing on 'The Simple Excellence of Brian Moore' in the *New Statesman* (18 February 1966), Christopher Ricks remarks: 'He is, if you like, a "conventional" novelist, quite without experimentalism and gimmicks. In none of the novels is anything concealed except the art by which they transmute "an ordinary sorrow of man's life" into something we care about. He does not, in fact, need the services of the literary critic . . . '

Certainly this novel speaks for itself. The loneliness of Judith is strongly felt, and although we are made aware of her weaknesses we feel a deep pity for her. Moore's imagination is actively working as he writes; small symbols and significant details of description combine to produce a kind of poetic intensity. When Judith leaves the O'Neill's house to catch her bus home, attended to the bus stop by the polite but embarrassed son of the house, he writes: 'The bus whirled off, to the last stop, the lonely room, the lonely night.'

Moore, like Francis Stuart, is more interested in the losers than the winners. 'I think that failure is a more interesting condition than success,' he writes: 'Success changes people; it makes them something they were not and dehumanizes them in a way, whereas failure leaves you with a more intense distillation of that self you are.' Diarmuid Devine (usually known as 'Dev'), the central figure of Moore's second novel, *The Feast of Lupercal*, is one who fails to take the opportunity offered to him. He fails to respond to love, and lapses back at the end of the book into the closed world of his school and his digs. He is a pitiful figure, a virgin at the age of thirty-seven, whose sexual adventures have been confined to his imagination. When Una Clarke, on the rebound from an unhappy affair with a married man in Dublin, goes back to Dev's lodgings with him and offers him her body, his acute embarrassment, his ingrained puritanism and his lack of experience make him impotent.

The title of the novel, *The Feast of Lupercal*, (which was changed in some later editions to *A Moment of Love*) refers to a Roman feast of expiation and atonement, which is mentioned at the beginning of Shakespeare's *Julius Caesar*. After the disastrous night which Una spent at his lodgings, Dev finds himself explaining the Lupercalia to the boys in his class. The priests of Lupercus ran through the streets of Rome, striking all they met with thongs: 'Barren women placed themselves in the path of the flogging priests, believing that by means of the strokes, the reproach of barrenness would be taken away from them.'

Una Clarke is a niece of Tim Heron, one of the senior lay masters at St Michan's. When he finally learns from Dev that Una spent the night at his lodgings he raises his cane and flogs him. Later Dev tells Una about the caning and says: 'It's a form of expiation, I suppose. Funny thing — we were reading about it in class today.' The cane is the cornerstone of discipline at St Michan's. Those in authority are literally 'flogging priests'. Authoritarianism and puritanism have a tight grip on Dev, and when news of his adventure with Una gets to the Dean he is in danger of losing his job, but in the end the President, for reasons of his own, comes to his rescue.

The odds are certainly stacked against Dev, but he is weak and ineffective. When Una's eyes are opened to his weakness, and she is about to break off her relationship with him, she says: 'We're completely different types. I want to fight against what life's doing to me, and you're afraid to. Live and let live is your motto.'

The story of Dev, like that of Judith, is 'a painful case', and Moore tells it again with scrupulous meanness. All the details of incident and image are convincing. Although it is painful, the episode when Una stays the night in Dev's digs is realised in such vivid detail that it is comic as well as pathetic. Each thinks the other experienced in sex and love, whereas both are virgins. Una thinks her inexperience has been to blame for the night's failure, so that later, when Dev confesses his virginity, she bursts out: 'O God, . . . if it wasn't so pitiful it would be funny. Funny!' When Dev bends to kiss Una he finds his spectacles in the way and misses her mouth. When she lies prone on his carpet her head nearly touches his dirty old slippers in their cardboard box and he awkwardly pushes them away. When she starts undressing and sends him into the bedroom to do likewise, he is terrified. 'And he, what should he do? Undress? Be in bed and waiting? Or just sit here? With shame, he thought of his naked body. He would look awful, his turned-in knees, his narrow chest, and, *merciful God*! long white underwear. A comedian in long drawers, someone to be laughed at.'

But the comedy is sad comedy. We may despise Dev for his weakness and lack of courage, but we can hardly laugh at him. At the end of the book we are left with the image of a harnessed, blinkered horse. Dev, knowing he will see Una no more, runs out into the street to watch her turn the corner. Absently he puts his hand on the neck of a waiting horse: 'Horse and man looked down the avenue, and there was no one there. The horse, harnessed, dumb, lowered its head once more. The man went back into the house.'

I jump over several later novels now to the brilliant novella, *Catholics.* It is not that the other novels are weak or lacking in interest; Moore is versatile and inventive, but he seems to me to be at his best in *Catholics*, and the book is very different from his first two novels. There is, perhaps, a greater detachment in *Catholics* than in most of his other books. In an interview for *The Irish Times* (11 September 1976) he said: 'I write about the Church as an outsider but at the same time I was once an insider.' He has some emotional involvement with the Belfast Catholic environment of his first two novels. In *Catholics,* although he is deeply interested in the problems the Church faces in adapting itself to a changing world, he is able to distance himself from both Father Kinsella and the Abbot of Muck.

Father Kinsella, an Albanesian monk, is sent by the Father General of his Order to bring the disobedient Abbot into line with the current ecumenical policy of the Church. The story is set in the future 'when interpenetration between Christian and Buddhist faiths is on the verge of reality', as the Father General explains in his letter to the Abbot. The Abbot has defied his superiors and gone counter to general Church policy by continuing to use Latin in the celebration of the Mass, and to hold private confessions. His continuance of the old practices has been high-lighted by television, and now pilgrims and tourists are flocking to Cahirciveen, where the monks hold Mass at an ancient Mass rock. The publicity embarrasses Rome on the eve of the ecumenical approach to Buddhism, so Kinsella is sent to put a stop to it.

Kinsella is the new type of ecumenical Catholic priest. Instead of a priest's collar and robes or dark suit, he wears 'grey-green denim fatigues', and carries a 'paramilitary despatch case'. His model and hero is Gustav Hartmann, who 'had taken Holy orders as an Albanesian monk . . . not for the obvious condition, but as a means towards social action . . . The Church, Hartmann taught, despite its history and its dependence on myth and miracle, exists today as the quintessential structure through which social revolution can be brought to certain areas of the globe.'

One of the humorous episodes of the book — there is a good deal of lurking humour in it — is the refusal of the boatman, sent over from the island to fetch the priest, to let Kinsella come aboard. In spite of his declaration — 'I *am* a priest.' — he is ignored, the boat returns without him, and he is forced to hire a helicopter.

There is a deeper irony in the fact that both Kinsella and the Abbot are, at heart, agnostic: though in different ways and for different reasons. For Kinsella religious belief is symbolic, a means to a social end. The Abbot, deeply disillusioned by his experience at Lourdes, finds that prayer, attempts at invoking God, lead him into the void, the null. At the end, to save his community, he leads them in the prayer that is fatal to his own peace of mind: 'He entered null. He would never come back.'

The confrontation between Kinsella and the Abbot is fascinating. Kinsella, pursuing an exercise in diplomacy, with flash-backs in his mind to Hartmann's lectures in Boston, is set against the elderly, practical Abbot, anxious to preserve his small community, his only ambition to join the previous fifty-one Abbots of Muck who are buried under a wall of the Abbey: 'I feel at home here. I am at home nowhere else.'

Kinsella has very different feelings about the place he has come to. After failing to get the boat to the island he calls at a pub to telephone. He emerges to find a thunderstorm and a rainbow. A sense of the strangeness of this Ireland, and its kinship with the supernatural, is revealed in the following passage, which illustrates, too, the quality of Moore's style in the book, at once taut and suggestive:

> He felt cold. He thought of Hartmann in the rain forests of Brazil. He looked again for the rainbow, but it had vanished, shimmering, in that sudden rain. It had appeared, then disappeared, in this lonely place, a place which now, in its noon darkness, made him think of a Beckett landscape, that place in which Vladimir and Estragon might have waited for Godot. The rainbow had seemed to end, down there, in the centre of the white cross formed by two concrete ribbons of road. In such phenomena people once read signs of God's hand. He turned and went back into the pub.

Apart from this short book, I have not discussed Moore's later novels. These certainly extend the range and originality of his achievement. The rift between dream and reality that we find in Judith Hearne is found too in Ginger Coffey (*The Luck of Ginger Coffey*), but in a wholly different character and in a wholly different setting. In his later novels, however, I do not find a real increase in the depth and complexity and subtlety of his work, though the central characters may be more intellectual than Judith Hearne. I thought both *The Great Victorian Collection* and *The Mangan Inheritance* were interesting and original, but ultimately unsatisfactory.

Moore may yet have more and greater novels to write, but the three I have examined show that he is a novelist of considerable power and skill. He has a quick eye for image and symbol, and a simple honesty in the presentment of scene and character, so that we feel a strong sympathy for his failures and misfits, his dreamers and fantasists.

21

John McGahern

John McGahern writes novels and short stories, and I find most of his work compulsive reading. His vision of life is intense and dark. A character in one of his later short stories, 'The Beginning of an Idea', quite casually tosses off this simile: 'as once alive it is better to go on than die, the best not to have been born at all'. Much of his fiction explores the pain of living and the purposelessness of life's journey to nowhere. A recurring image in his work is that of the wheel. The first story in *Nightlines* is called 'Wheels', and it tells of a son making a painful visit to his father's house in the country. He had previously made it clear that he did not wish to share a house with his elderly father and his step-mother, if they moved to Dublin:

> I knew the wheel: fathers became children to their sons who repay the care they got when they were young, and on the edge of dying the fathers become young again, but the luck of a death and a second marriage had released me from the last breaking on this ritual wheel.

As the son returns to Dublin on the train, he thinks of his youthful days on the Shannon river, and the turning wheel of life brings him little to hope for:

> The farther flows the river the muddier the water: the light was brighter on its upper reaches. Rustle of the boat through the bullrushes as we went to Moran's well for springwater in dry summers, cool of watercress and bitterness of the wild cherries shaken out of the white-thorn hedge, black bullrush seed floating in the gallons on the floorboards, all the vivid sections of the wheel we watched

so slowly turn, impatient for the rich whole that never came but that all the preparations promised.

In his latest novel, *The Pornographer,* the protagonist, returning in a taxi with a young nurse to the hospital where his aunt lies dying of cancer, thinks again of the wheel:

The wheel had many sections. She had reached that turn where she'd to lie beneath the window, stupefied by brandy and pain, dulling the sounds of the whole wheel of her life staggering to a stop. I was going past that same window in a taxi, a young woman by my side, my hand on her warm breast. I shivered as I thought how one day my wheel would turn into her section, and I would lie beneath that window while a man and woman as we were now went past into the young excitement of a life that might seem without end in this light of the moon.

It might seem from what I have said so far that McGahern is a writer akin to Beckett, seeing life as painful, pointless and absurd. And yet this is not so. McGahern's writing is rooted firmly in the actual, in the vivid and particular detail of everyday life, in a way that Beckett's is not. As I read him the effect of Beckett's fiction is often to diminish life; this is not the case with McGahern. A reviewer of *Nightlines* in *Hibernia* put this point aptly: 'He writes from a personal anguish which can hurt and horrify but never repel.'

John McGahern was born in Dublin in 1934, the son of a police officer, but he spent much of his boyhood in Cootehill near Roscommon. He went to Presentation College, Carrick-on-Shannon, and later to St Patrick's, Drumcondra, and to University College, Dublin. For some ten years he was a teacher, but after the publication of his second novel, *The Dark*, which was banned by the Censorship Board, he lost his job. He held several fellowships at American and British universities, and he won a number of literary awards. He now lives mainly in Ireland and continues to write.

So far he has published five novels and two collections of short stories, and he seems equally skilled in both forms of fiction. I still like his first novel the best, so I propose to illustrate his work by looking first at this and then at his first collection of short stories.

The Barracks is set in a small Irish town where the Reegan family lives. The 'barracks' of the title is not a military base but a rural police station. Sergeant Reegan has a fierce hatred of his superintendent, and he works compulsively at turf cutting so that he can leave the police and be independent. But it is his second wife, Elizabeth, who is at the centre of the book. She marries Reegan, a widower with three children, after she has had many years of independence working as a nurse in London. Her new life does not bring her the fulfilment she had hoped for. She falls ill and the dark shadow of cancer forces her to question the meaning of her life. After the children have gone to school she sits in the kitchen to rest and think:

> This'd be the only time of the day she might get some grip and vision on the desperate activity of her life. She was Elizabeth Reegan; a woman in her forties; sitting in a chair with a book from the council library in her hand that she hadn't opened: watching certain things like the sewing-machine and the vase of daffodils and a circle still white with frost under the shade of the sycamore tree between the house and the river: . . . with a life on her hands that was losing the last vestiges of its meaning and purpose: with hard cysts within her breasts she feared were cancer . . .

Elizabeth visits a doctor, goes to hospital for examination, has a painful operation and finally comes home to rest and convalesce. She realises that the chances of recovery are against her, but she goes on with her domestic tasks until she is too weak and has to stay in bed. She still struggles to make meaning of her life and impending death:

> 'I am Elizabeth Reegan and another day of my life is beginning,' she said to herself. 'I am lying here in bed. I've been five weeks sick in bed, and there is no sign of me getting better. Though there's little pain, which is lucky, and the worst is fear and remorse and often the horrible meaninglessness of it all. Sometimes meaning and peace come but I lose them again, nothing in life is for ever resolved once and for all but changes with the changing life . . . '.

In the end Elizabeth slips quietly into death, and soon afterwards Reegan escapes from the police force. Life goes on for the living and the domestic routine continues. The book ends as it had begun with the children lighting the oil lamp and pulling down the blinds.

As he reads the novel, the reader comes very close to the thoughts and feelings of Elizabeth, and shares her sense of bewilderment at the way life eludes explanation and control. Her story is a sad one, and yet there is much in the book that redeems it from darkness. There are vivid and detailed descriptions of rural and domestic tasks, such as spraying the potatoes and making blackcurrant jam, so that the world of things takes on a solidity and order that balances Elizabeth's despair. There are rituals, small and large, secular and religious, that give shape to the passing days. Elizabeth responds to Christmas and the special solemnity of the Christmas dinner:

> Reegan carved the turkey and handed out the helpings. The children's faces shone throughout and they cried for more and more. The delf was tidied away at the end and they stood to repeat with Reegan, *We give thee thanks, O Almighty God, for all thy benefits, who livest and reignest, world without end. Amen.*
>
> At so many tables over the world, at this moment, the same words of thanksgiving were being uttered, as the Mass in the same way was being celebrated, and it couldn't be all blind habit, a few minds must be astonished by such as *World without end.* Never did the tablecloth appear so bright as on this day, not until this day next year would they have roasted meat, and it was unlikely that they'd sit to a meal for another year at which such marvellous courtesy and ceremony were observed. Even the children said, 'Please pass me this and that'; everybody was considered and waited on; there was even a formal exactness in the way they lifted the salt and pepper cruets, and the meal began and ended in the highest form of all human celebration, prayer. It was a mere meal no longer with table and tablecloth and delf and food, it was that perfectly, but it was above and beyond and besides the wondrous act of their reality. All other meals throughout the year might

be hurried and disjointed, each one eating because of their animal necessity, but this day and meal were put aside for celebration.

Not only rituals and high moments are vividly realised. McGahern presents deftly and convincingly the routine of life in the barracks and in the village. He catches tones and turns of speech, sometimes fatuous or banal, and there is often a keen comic or satiric edge to the picture he presents. I can think of few novels that convey so effectively the feel of provincial life in rural Ireland.

Nightlines, as the title suggests, portrays forces of darkness. I have already mentioned the first story 'Wheels', which carries a sharp tang of disillusion, as the inexorable wheel of time turns. Growth and experience seem to bring pain, disgust and boredom, a sad journey through a waste land. At the same time there is a deep compassion for the different kinds of people who figure in the stories, and who are caught in various nets of circumstance. 'Coming into his Kingdom' tells of a young boy's first discovery of sex and the 'facts of life', after he had accidentally fallen on to a girl in the road and the other children cheered and jeered. He bribes an older girl with a toffee and a clock wheel to explain the mystery to him. The simple story could be banal, but it isn't. The subtle mingling of disgust and desire in the boy's consciousness is truthfully and delicately portrayed, and the revelation is firmly anchored in the common reality of the children's world:

'Can you not think?' the girl was urging.

'Is it like the bull and the cow?' he ventured. It couldn't be, it would be too fantastic, and he waited for her to laugh.

Instead she nodded her head vigorously: he had struck on how it was.

'Now you've been told,' she said. 'That was why they cheered when you fell on Nora.'

Suddenly it was so simple and so sordid and so all about him that it seemed he should have discovered it years before.

They were silent now as they went downhill home, a

delicate bloom on the clusters of blue sloes along the road, the sudden gleam of the chestnut, or the woollen whiteness of the inside of a burst pod in the deal leaves their shoes went rustling through. 'They're in love! They're in love!' coming again to his ears but it was growing so clear and squalid that there was hardly anything to see.

'Korea' is a tense little story of the wary relationship between a father and a son. The father is bitter about his life in Ireland and suggests to his son that he might go to America. Later the son overhears him talking to a neighbour about the American government's provision for those drafted to Korea and realises what was in his father's mind:

He'd scrape the fare, I'd be conscripted there, each month he'd get so many dollars while I served, and he'd get ten thousand if I was killed.

In the darkness of the lavatory between the boxes of crawling worms before we set the night line for the eels I knew my youth had ended.

I rowed as he let out the night line, his fingers baiting each twisted hook so beautifully that it seemed a single movement.

The style and method of this passage is characteristic, with its taut, bare statements and careful exact detail of description. Most of the conversation between father and son takes place in the boat while they are fishing for eels. The story is very short but it sets up powerful resonances, and every word tells until the very end.

In 'Hearts of Oak and Bellies of Brass' there is an almost raw, grating quality. It is a sketch of life on a London building site where most of the labourers are Irish. The boredom, the frantic shovelling of sand and gravel — 'shovel or shite, shite or burst' — the latent violence, the crude animal satisfactions of beer and sex (the latter provided by elderly prostitutes living in a row of condemned houses) add up to a grim picture. Equally grim, in a different way is the seaside guest house in 'Strandhill, The Sea', and the tortured claustrophobic relationship between the couple living in Spain in 'Peaches'.

McGahern believes, as he once wrote to me, that 'the YEA

and the NAY are equal (even Melville sang the NAY as the carpet-bagger in Europe). All that counts is the quality of the saying.' I sometimes find it hard to accept the view that the negative is as valid as the positive in literature, though it is impossible to refute the logic of it. If literature is concerned with extending our knowledge of good and evil, as Auden once phrased it, then we must accept the portrayal of squalor and nullity and the dark. I do not mean to suggest that McGahern's work is only concerned with the NAY. This is very far from the case. Even his second novel, *The Dark*, is not wholly negative, though there is an intense absorption in pain, humiliation and frustration. At the end of the novel the boy 'has finally emerged from the dark into the light of the maturity of acceptance'. The words are those of Michael Foley in a perceptive review of McGahern's first two novels in *The Honest Ulsterman* (no.5, September 1968). Foley rightly stresses the idea of acceptance in the novels. Speaking of Elizabeth Reegan's life, he calls it: 'a life in the main a mystery without meaning or purpose but lived in the dignity of acceptance which is love and lit up by the flashes of joy which only acceptance can bring.'

There is room for argument about how far McGahern's work concentrates on the NAY rather than the YEA, but there can be no doubt about the quality of his saying. His mainly simple and straightforward prose often achieves the intensity and concentration of poetry. This may be seen in some of the passages I have already quoted, but I would like to give one further short example. This is how he opens the story 'Wheels': 'Grey concrete and steel and glass in the slow raindrip of the morning station, three porters pushing an empty trolley up the platform to a stack of grey mail-bags, the loose wheels rattling, and nothing but wait and watch and listen . . . ' Mood and scene are skilfully and economically evoked in these few opening lines.

McGahern has a perceptive and accurate ear for speech at all levels. Here, in a passage from 'Swallows', a story in his second collection, *Getting Through*, is Mrs Kilboy in full spate:

'Something will have to be done about Jackson's thieving ass, Sergeant, it'll take the law to bring him to his senses, nothing less, and those thistles of his will be blowing again over the townland this year with him dead drunk in the pub, and is Biddy's hens laying at all this weather, mine have gone on unholy strike, and I hear you were measuring the road today, you and a young whippersnapper from Dublin, not even the guards can do anything unknownst in this place, and everybody's agog as to how the case will go, the poor woman's nerves I hear are in an awful condition, having to pass that wooden cross twice a day, and what was the use putting it up if it disturbs her so, it won't bring him back to life, poor Michael, God rest him, going to Carrick for his haircut, the living have remindedness enough of their last ends and testaments without putting up wooden crosses on the highways and byways, and did you ever see such a winter, torrents of rain and expectedness of snow, it'll be a long haul indeed to the summer.'

This passage is a reminder that there is much humour and irony in McGahern's writing, as well as disillusion and bitterness.

22

John Hewitt

In 1978, when John Hewitt was writer-in-residence at Queen's University, Belfast, Landseer Productions made a short film of his life and work for the Arts Council of Northern Ireland. The title of the film, taken from one of his poems, was 'I Found Myself Alone'. The words give us a leading clue to his life and work. In his anthology, *Irish Poets of the Nineteenth Century*, Geoffrey Taylor referred to William Allingham as 'that almost impossible thing, an Irish Liberal'. Hewitt was a follower and admirer of Allingham, and he edited a selection of his verse. We might perhaps adapt Taylor's label for Hewitt and call him that 'almost impossible thing, an Ulsterman without a church or creed'. In an autobiographical sketch in *The Bell* (vol. 18) Hewitt confesses that he was never baptised because his father disliked the local Methodist minister: 'This has given me a sense of liberation, spiritually I have felt myself to be my own man, the ultimate Protestant.'

He was born in Belfast in 1907, son of a school teacher with liberal views, except in the matter of strong drink. A life-long abstainer, he even returned the wedding presents sent him by a lady connected with the liquor trade. His own father had been equally staunch in this matter, resigning from his Orange Lodge when it was agreed to permit the consumption of alcohol. It is not surprising that John Hewitt reflects a little ruefully on 'the vigorous element of teetotalism which still has power to nudge my elbow in any bar'.

The Hewitt family came from Kilmore in South Armagh, where they seem to have been settled for several centuries. The name Hewitt is English in origin but there seem to have been some links with Scotland. His grandfather lived in Glasgow for a time, and Hewitt recalls a Scots timbre in his father's speech. Growing up in Belfast, the young Hewitt made friends with a boy of his own age from a Catholic family that moved into the house next door. Willy Morrisey, son of an officer in an Irish regiment, lent him his magazine, *Our Boys*, which 'carried exciting stories of Cuchullain and Colmcille and Red Hugh O'Donnell and Owen Roe O'Neill and the Penal Days and the Famine ... So began my fifty years' involvement with our country's past and the rights and wrongs of it.'

He attended Methodist College and went on to Queen's University. Here he wrote an M.A. thesis on 'Ulster Poets 1800–1870'. From 1930 to 1957 he worked for the Belfast Museum and Art Gallery, progressing from Art Assistant to Deputy Director. When the Directorship fell vacant he was passed over for the appointment because his political views were somewhat suspect and he was not considered to be a safe man. A candidate from outside was appointed in his place. He tells us in *Threshold* (no. 23) that the Unionist chairman of the appointing committee insisted that 'besides being a Communist, I had numerous Catholic friends, play-actors and the like'. Not long after this he was made Art Director of the Herbert Art Gallery and Museum in Coventry, and he remained in this post until his retirement, when he returned to live and write in Belfast.

In the thirties Hewitt had found himself moving to the left: 'It was a dead German Jew who gave me my guide-lines. It was an English poet who, for me, most movingly evoked the quality of the Good Society in his *News from Nowhere*.' His affection and respect for William Morris and for the English Radical tradition has remained ever since. Hewitt and his wife, together with two Professors of Queen's University, became involved with the National Council for Civil Liberties in an investigation of the Stormont Government's Special Powers Act: 'This was my first acquaintance with the nature of state authority and its techniques of the opened letter and the tapped telephone.' Later he belonged to the Left Book Club and the Belfast-based Peace League.

He first began to publish poetry in the thirties. His voice as a poet is a quiet, even one, and he uses traditional forms and metres for most of his verse. Some people think at first glance that his poetry is dull. He can be dull at times, but at his best he has a rare vitality and perceptiveness. It often takes a little time to get tuned in to his wavelength, so that he needs to be read with care and quiet patience. These are the qualities he looks for in his readers, as he makes clear in a brief poem, 'I Write for . . .' from *Scissors for a One-Armed Tailor* (Belfast 1974):

> I write for my own kind,
> I do not pitch my voice
> that every phrase be heard
> by those who have no choice;
> their quality of mind
> must be withdrawn and still,
> as moth that answers moth
> across a roaring hill.

The second poem in his *Collected Poems* (1932–67) is entitled 'Frost' and it would be easy to pass it by as a pleasing but slight sketch of winter. Look again, however, and you see that the second verse presents a remarkable image of old age. Here is the complete poem:

> With frost again the thought is clear and wise
> that rain made dismal with a mist's despair,
> the raw bleak earth beneath cloud-narrowed skies
> finds new horizons in the naked air.
> Light leaps along the lashes of the eyes;
> a tree is truer for its being bare.
>
> So must the world seem keen and very bright
> to one whose gaze is on the end of things,
> who knows, past summer lush, brimmed autumn's height,
> no promise in the inevitable springs,
> all stripped of shadow down to bone of light,
> the false songs gone and gone the restless wings.

The key image is the 'bone of light' in the penultimate line. It suggests a paring down of all growth and texture, all earthy and fleshly covering, down to the hard bony skeleton. At the same time this brings light and illumination. Frost and clear air show us the naked reality of the earth's surface — 'a tree is truer for its being bare'. We may wish to argue this point, but the poem makes us vividly aware of the possibility of it, and of the way in which the world might 'seem keen and very bright / to one whose gaze is on the end of things'. Whatever else it may be, this is certainly not a pedestrian poem.

A strong leading theme in Hewitt's poetry has been the search for an Irish identity. He is acutely aware of his special position as an Ulsterman of planter stock. His ancestors were strangers in Ireland, colonists, but surely now, after more than three centuries, their descendants have earned a place in the Irish story. An early poem 'Once Alien Here', expresses this view:

> So I, because of all the buried men
> In Ulster clay, because of rock and glen
> and mist and cloud and quality of air
> as native in my thought as any here . . .

Hewitt is deeply read in Irish history and literature, and he has a keen awareness of Irish traditions that stretch back to Oisin and St Patrick. In some autobiographical sketches entitled 'Planter's Gothic' written for *The Bell* (vol.18, 1953) under the pen name of John Howard, he wrote:

> When I discovered, not long ago, that the old Planter's Gothic tower of Kilmore church still encloses the stump of a round tower and that it was built on the site of a Culdee holy place, I felt a step nearer to that synthesis [of Scots and English with basic Irish]. It is the best symbol I have yet found for the strange textures of my response to this island of which I am a native. I may appear Planter's Gothic, but there is a round tower somewhere inside, and needled through every sentence I utter.

As a young man he came to realise that Dublin was the literary capital of Ireland, and he was proud to have a poem printed in *The Irish Statesman*, edited in Dublin by AE. Later on, in the forties he went through a phase of enthusiasm for Ulster regionalism, and contributed to a Belfast literary annual, *Lagan*. But this phase ended, and 'The Colony', written in 1949, uses a Roman analogue to affirm the wider view that Ulstermen, though once colonists, have now become natives of Ireland:

this is our country also, nowhere else;
and we shall not be outcast on the world.

Hewitt's sense of Irish identity owes much to his love of the countryside. Although born and bred in the city he is deeply attached to the country, especially to the glens of Antrim, where for many years he and his wife had a country cottage near Cushendun. In 'Conacre' he writes:

I'd give the collar of an Irish king
for one wet catkin jigging loosely in the spring

And later in the same poem he states:

This is my home and country. Later on
perhaps I'll find this nation is my own;
but here and now it is enough to love
this faulted ledge, this map of cloud above,
and the great sea that beats against the west
to swamp the sun.

In his poem 'Because I Paced My Thought' Hewitt explains how he found himself alone in the city world of political debate because he paced his thought 'by the natural world, the earth organic . . . rather than the city'. If anyone listened, it was to disagree with him: 'The day is urgent. The sun is not on the agenda.' But in the country also he frequently found himself alone. He is acutely conscious of his difference from the people of the hill farms, and he has expressed it vividly in the poem 'O Country People':

I would be neighbourly, would come to terms
with your existence, but you are so far;
there is a wide bog between us, a high wall.
I've tried to learn the smaller parts of speech
in your slow language, but my thoughts need more
flexible shapes to move in, if I am to reach
into the hearth's red heart across the half-door.

. . . .

I know the level you accept me on,
Like a strange bird observed about the house,
or sometimes seen out flying on the moss

that may to-morrow, or next week, be gone,
liable to return without warning
on a May afternoon and away in the morning.

To a large extent a poet is always an outsider, a watcher,
whether in a field or in a city street. The nature of his
activity makes him an observer, standing to one side, rather
than a man caught up in the life of a farm or a factory.
Although Hewitt was troubled by the gap between himself
and the country people, he nevertheless observes the life of
the countryside with love and sympathy. He patiently watches
a badger, a hedgehog, an owl, and then records, in sober,
quiet and skilful verse, not only the animal or bird, but the
scene and mood. Birds and animals only figure occasionally
in his verse; he writes of places and people, of the changing
seasons and of his own reflections on hill, in glen or by the
shore.

Although he preferred the country to the city, his poetry
is by no means confined to country themes. It ranges widely
over different times and places, wherever personal reminiscences and reflections lead him. He responds quickly to the
life around him, and when the present 'troubles' began in
Ulster, although he was then living and working in Coventry,
his mind and spirit were drawn into them. He published a
small volume of poems, *An Ulster Reckoning*, in 1971, which
was privately printed in Belfast. In the foreword he writes:
'To one living outside Ireland the impact of the terrible days
of August, 1969, was heartbreaking. As I could not readily
walk among the barricades with my white flag, I found
release for my sense of frustration in verse.' The second poem
in the collection, 'A Dilemma', states his position with an
honest anguish. Neither a Unionist nor a Republican, he
cannot readily take sides:

So, since this ruptured country is my home,
it long has been my bitter luck to be
caught in the cross-fire of their false campaign.

In spite of a sense of helplessness to influence the course
of events in Ulster, Hewitt wrote some telling poems at this
time. 'The Coasters' is an effective satire on those who go
easily with the tide and so assist the drift to disaster and

violence. 'Conversations in Hungary' reveals the difficulty of explaining sectarian riots in Ulster to foreigners. But perhaps Hewitt's most characteristic response to the troubles in Ulster is to be found in a later poem from *Out of My Time*. 'Neither an Elegy nor a Manifesto' is addressed to 'the people of my province and the Rest of Ireland':

> Bear in mind these dead:
> I can find no plainer words.
> I dare not risk using
> that loaded word, Remember . . .
>
> So I say only: Bear in mind
> those men and lads killed in the streets;
> but do not differentiate between
> those deliberately gunned-down
> and those caught by unaddressed bullets . . .

The poem insists, perhaps over-insists, on a plain low-profiled approach to the violence in Ulster, but it seems to me an honest and moving poem.

Hewitt's poetry has a considerable range and variety. He can write long discursive, meditative poems in heroic couplets, like 'Conacre' and 'A Country Walk in May', that recall the Augustan mode of Goldsmith and Crabbe, and he can write brief unrhymed pensées, such as he offers in *Scissors for a One-Armed Tailor*.

Seamus Heaney, reviewing his poetry in *Threshold* (no. 22) referred to 'a typical Hewitt area, half-way between statement and evocation'. When Hewitt describes a scene or an incident, or recalls a memory, he often does it in a way that evokes resonances, ripples of thought and feeling that spread when the poem has ended. 'The Distances', which I give below to end this introduction to his work, has this effect on me. He recalls a very simple, ordinary scene, in language that is only differentiated from prose by a delicate pause and rhythm, and yet the distances of loneliness are hauntingly suggested:

> Driving along the unfenced road
> in August dusk the sun gone from
> an empty sky, we overtook
> a man walking his dog on the turf.

The parked car we passed later,
Its side-lights on, a woman
shadow in the dark interior
sitting upright, motionless.

And fifty yards further a runner
in shorts pacing steadily;
and I thought of the distances
of loneliness.

23

Seamus Heaney

Unlike John Hewitt, Seamus Heaney had no need to search for an Irish identity. By birth into a rural Catholic family in south Derry and by education at a Catholic school in the city of Derry, he inherited naturally an Irish tradition, as well as the 'split culture' of Ulster. He was born in 1939 on a farm at Mossbawn, near Castledawson, and after attending the local Anahorish Primary School, he became a boarder at St Columb's College in Derry. He took a degree in English at Queen's University, Belfast and trained as a teacher. He subsequently taught at a school in Ballymurphy, then became a lecturer, first at St Joseph's College, then at Queen's University. In 1972 he moved from Belfast to Ashford in Co. Wicklow, to devote himself for some years to writing. Since 1975 he has been teaching again, at a Dublin Teacher's Training College, and he now lives near Dublin.

Heaney wrote about his own background in an article he contributed to *The Guardian* (25 May, 1972) on 'The Trade of an Irish Poet':

At school I studied the Gaelic literature of Ireland as well as the literature of England, and since then I have maintained a notion of myself as Irish in a province that insists that it is British. Lately I realised that these complex pieties and dilemmas were implicit in the very terrain where I was born.

Our farm was called Mossbawn. Moss, a Scots word probably carried to Ulster by the planters, and bawn, the name the English colonists gave to their fortified farmhouses. Mossbawn, the planter's house on the bog. Yet in spite of this Ordnance Survey spelling we pronounced it Moss bann, and ban is the Gaelic word for white. So might not the thing mean the white moss, the moss of bog-cotton. In the syllables of my home I see a metaphor of the split culture of Ulster.

Mossbawn lies between the villages of Castledawson and Toome. I was symbolically placed between the marks of English influence and the lure of the native experience between 'the demesne and the bog'.

The tangled mysteries of Irish history play a significant part in Heaney's poetry, but when we first look at his work other things are more immediately apparent. In the second of the 'Glanmore Sonnets' from his latest collection of poems, *Field Work*, he writes of 'Words entering almost the sense of touch', and it is this quality of vivid sensuous apprehension that strikes us most forcibly in his first book, *The Death of a Naturalist*. It is fully illustrated in the title poem, which describes a flax-dam:

> Bubbles gargled delicately, bluebottles
> Wove a strong gauze of sound around the smell.
> There were dragon-flies, spotted butterflies,
> But best of all was the warm thick slobber
> Of frogspawn that grew like clotted water . . .
> Right down the dam gross-bellied frogs were cocked
> On sods; their loose necks pulsed like sails. Some hopped:
> The slap and pop were obscene threats. Some sat
> Poised like mud grenades, their blunt heads farting.

'Blackberry Picking' and 'Churning Day' are sensuously evocative in a splendid way. When the butter is finally made after the churners have 'slugged and thumped for hours', they relax in a clean kitchen rich with piled butter:

> And in the house we moved with gravid ease,
> our brains turned crystals full of clean deal churns,
> the plash and gurgle of the sour-breathed milk,
> the pat and slap of small spades on wet lumps.

In 'Cow in Calf' we feel the tingling hand that slaps the big-bellied cow out of the byre:

> her belly is slung like a hammock

slapping her out of the byre is like slapping
a great bag of seed.

But even in his first collection there is much more to
Heaney's poetry than a vivid sensuous apprehension. There is
considerable variety of mood and mode. 'Mid-term Break',
with its simple, dramatic statement, is very different from
'Churning Day' and 'Blackberry Picking'. The love poems,
'Honeymoon Flight' and 'Scaffolding', are different again.
Heaney's strong sense of the Irish past appears in 'At a Potato
Digging' and 'For the Commander of the "Eliza"', where
dark and bitter memories of the famine are evoked.

In the last poem of the collection 'Personal Helicon', he
uses images of his boyhood obsession with peering into dark
wells to focus his activity as a poet:

> I rhyme
> to see myself, to set the darkness echoing.

In an interview with the BBC (reported in *The Listener*,
5 February 1970) he said: 'The dark centre, the blurred and
irrational storehouse of insight and instincts, the hidden core
of the self — this notion is the foundation of what viewpoint
I might articulate for myself as a poet.' Heaney's gaze as a
poet is characteristically focused, not on the skies, on the
stars or clouds, but downwards, earthwards, on the bog, the
ditch, the dark well, the river, on graves and tombs.

His next volume of poems is appropriately entitled *Door
Into The Dark*. It begins with a 'Night-Piece' and a dark
dream of chopping a man's head:

> Before I woke
> I heard the steel stop
> In the bone of the brow.

It ends with 'Bogland', with a gaze downwards into the dark
bogs of Ireland where 'The wet centre is bottomless'. The
collection includes 'A Lough Neagh Sequence', a sequence of
seven poems dealing with eel-fishing in Lough Neagh and the
strange life-cycle of the eels. Worms are drawn out of the
earth for bait, and we are conscious of the underwater world
of the Lough:

A line goes out of sight and out of mind
Down to the soft bottom of silt and sand

Men, too, may go to the bottom. 'The Lough will claim a victim every year', say the fishermen, and 'There is a town sunk beneath its water.' In the last of the sequence, 'A Vision', a childish superstitious fear of being drawn by the hair into the water is echoed in the silent slimy movement of eels through the grass into the Lough:

To watch the eels crossing land
Re-wound his world's live girdle.

The theme of 'Bogland', the final poem, is picked up again in Heaney's third collection, *Wintering Out*. An important poem in this collection is 'Tollund Man'. Heaney had read P.V. Glob's book, *The Bog People*, about the excavation of iron age bodies preserved in the peat bogs of Jutland. The book contains vivid photographs of the Tollund man, who died two thousand years ago. He was evidently a victim sacrificed to the fertility goddess, Mother Earth. In Heaney's imagination he becomes a symbolic victim, recalling the many victims of tribal revenge in the Irish 'troubles', past and present:

I could risk blasphemy,
Consecrate the cauldron bog
Our holy ground and pray
Him to make germinate

The scattered, ambushed
Flesh of labourers,
Stockinged corpses
Laid out in the farmyards,

Tell-tale skin and teeth
Flecking the sleepers
Of four young brothers, trailed
For miles along the lines.

He contemplates a visit to Aarhus to see the peat-brown head of the Tollund man:

Out there in Jutland
In the old man-killing parishes
I will feel lost,
Unhappy and at home.

The themes of 'Tollund Man' proliferate and develop in
North, Heaney's next collection. There are more memories of
the peat-preserved Bog People, more 'bone dreams', and a
new dimension is added in the violence of the Vikings and
the Northern peoples generally with their history and legends.
As the dust-jacket puts it 'the idea of the north allows the
poet to contemplate the violence on his home ground in
relation to memories of the Scandinavian and English invasions which have marked Irish history so indelibly'. The
result is a group of powerful poems. Perhaps the finest is
'Punishment', where the 'little adulteress' of the Bog People,
punished by death, is linked with the modern victims of IRA
punishment, and the poet's role is that of the compassionate
but helpless onlooker:

Little adulteress,
before they punished you

you were flaxen-haired,
undernourished, and your
tar-black face was beautiful.
My poor scapegoat,

I almost love you
but would have cast, I know,
the stones of silence.
I am the artful voyeur

of your brain's exposed
and darkened combs,
your muscles' webbing
and all your numbered bones:

I who have stood dumb
when your betraying sisters,
cauled in tar,
wept by the railings,

who would connive
in civilized outrage
and yet understand the exact
and tribal, intimate revenge.

'Kinship' celebrates the treasure house of the bog that links past and present, and relates Ireland to Europe and the world:

I love this turf-face
its black incisions,
the cooped secrets
of process and ritual

. . .

Ground that will strip
its dark side,
nesting ground,
outback of my mind.

In following the theme of 'the dark centre' and the bog, which is certainly one part of the outback of Heaney's mind, I have perhaps overstressed this aspect. He is by no means always groping in the darkness of the bog or the grave or the past. I think the two poems I like best in *North* are the first and the last. The first celebrates sunlight and love, in the image of a woman baking bread in the kitchen on a sunny afternoon. The last is a very personal poem entitled 'Exposure'. The poet is at a climax in his own process of 'wintering out'. 'It is December in Wicklow' and he debates with himself his position as poet and his 'responsible *tristia*', aware of his move away from troubled Belfast:

I am neither internee nor informer;
An inner émigré, grown long-haired
And thoughtful; a wood-kerne

Escaped from the massacre,
Taking protective colouring
From bole and bark, feeling
Every wind that blows;

The poem has a cold clarity and simplicity that gives it steely edge and force.

From *Wintering Out* I selected 'Tollund Man' somewhat to the exclusion of other themes and interests. Before passing on to *Field Work*, Heaney's latest collection, I would like to mention one or two other poems from his third book. 'The Other Side' presents a clearly and delicately etched portrait of a Protestant neighbour:

> His brain was a whitewashed kitchen
> hung with texts, swept tidy
> as the body o' the kirk.

'The Wool Trade' and several poems about place-names show Heaney's sensitive response to the sounds of words and his love of the roots of speech. 'Limbo' and 'Bye-Child' reveal a compassionate imagination that finds simple and forceful expression in controlled imagery, tender but unsentimental.

Finally in *Field Work*, we see a poet mature and confident, using his talent in a number of different directions, not simply repeating himself or peering into the same patch of bog. There are some fine and original love poems. The otter, the skunk and the sandmartin, surely an unusual trio, are used effectively to illuminate different aspects of a husband's love for his wife. 'The Skunk' is perhaps the best poem, and it has been singled out for praise, but I like 'Homecomings', where the returning husband finds an analogue in the sand-martin's returning to 'the worn mouth of the hole' leading to his nest. The poem ends:

> Mould my shoulders inward to you.
> Occlude me.
> Be damp clay pouting.
> Let me listen under your eaves.

The 'Glanmore Sonnets' form an effective group at the centre of the book. Together they give a vivid picture of the way Heaney's imagination works. In number V he writes of the boortree (Ulster) or elderberry (English), as he has now learned to call it:

> I love its blooms like saucers brimmed with meal,
> Its berries a swart caviar of shot,

A buoyant spawn, a light bruised out of purple.
Elderberry? It is shires dreaming wine.
Boortree is bower tree, where I played 'touching tongues'
And felt another's texture quick on mine.

There is not only a vivid sensuous apprehension here but a wonderfully deft use of words. 'Quick' for example in the last line combines the two meanings of speedy (the darting tongue touching quickly) and alive (the sensitive moist tongue conveying the touch of another's warm life).

There are fine elegies to Sean O'Riada and Robert Lowell, but the one that seems to me most moving is written in memory of a compulsive drinker who broke the curfew after Bloody Sunday, and was blown to bits in a bar. It is entitled 'Casualty' and it throws a sharp sidelight on the troubles.

Heaney is still relatively young as a poet and we can expect a good deal more from him. Already he has been compared with Yeats, but it seems to me that such comparisons are premature and unhelpful. I find him the most talented and interesting of contemporary Irish poets, and I am content to leave it at that.

Supplement to Part Five

Notes on some other living writers: poetry, drama, prose.

Poetry

In the sixties, a number of poets from Northern Ireland began to publish their work. James Simmons (b. 1933) was born in Londonderry and educated at Leeds University. He taught English in a Lisburn school, then at a university in Nigeria, and he currently teaches at the New University of Ulster in Coleraine. In 1968 he founded, and edited for two years, *The Honest Ulsterman*, a lively literary magazine that still flourishes. In addition to being a poet, Simmons is a popular entertainer. He sings, plays the guitar and sets some of his work to music. His moving ballads about the bombing of Claudy (a small village in Co. Derry) and the shooting of Gerry Kelly, a Belfast newsagent, should be listened to rather than read, though they are moving even when read. But the lines are deliberately casual and simple, in the traditional ballad manner, without poetic density, and rightly so for Simmons' purpose:

> the small town of Claudy at ease in the sun
> last July in the morning, a new day begun.

A relaxed, casual quality is perhaps the dominant note in Simmons' poetry as a whole, a cheerful irreverence, a witty, humorous, deflating, *gamin* quality. If it is possible to do the opposite of getting up on stilts to express your thoughts, then Simmons does it. One might say that he writes with his fly-buttons undone. This is occasionally embarrassing, but it mostly succeeds in amusing and provoking us. Simmons is not simply a joker, who 'lets off poems like well-timed rude noises'. He has a keen and lively intelligence, and a serious respect for life, as he shows in 'Dangerous Bathing'.

> A wise man knows his father, knows the sea,
> Learns to endure our dangerous heritage,
> And use our weapons, love and poetry.

Derek Mahon (b. 1941) comes from urban Belfast, but went to Trinity College, Dublin, to read French and English. He has lived in England and America and has been called 'the most European of the Belfast poets, civilised and philosophical'. He looks ironically at Glengormley, the Belfast suburb where he was born, in the poem of that name, but at the end he admits wryly:

> By
> Necessity, if not choice, I live here too.

Michael Longley once suggested that you might divide the elements between Heaney and Mahon, giving Heaney earth and water, and Mahon air and fire. There is something in this division, though it should not be pushed too far. Imagery of light and air, and fire, too, is frequent in Mahon's verse. 'Recalling Aran' opens with the marvellous line, 'A dream of limestone in sea-light', the best one-line description of an Aran island that I know of.

In his preface to *The Sphere Book of Modern Irish Verse* Mahon has spoken of 'the metaphysical unease in which all poetry of lasting value has its source'. Certainly he himself finds no easy resting place in the universe. He questions his own roles. 'I Am Raftery' makes ironic and humorous reference to the Gaelic poet:

> I am Raftery, hesitant and confused among the
> cold-voiced graduate students and inter-
> changeable instructors.

He has a leaning towards outsiders, odd characters, gypsies, eccentric painters and men, like Bruce Ismay, who was put on trial for deserting his ship. In one of his finest poems, 'A Disused Shed in Co. Wexford', he uses the image of mushroom life in a long-abandoned shed to make a moving plea for the helpless victims of history, 'Lost victims of Treblinka

and Pompeii'. After three separate volumes, Mahon published his *Collected Poems* in 1980. Witty, intelligent, widely
read, with a command of style and music, critical of and yet
drawn to the Irish dimension that he inescapably belongs to,
Mahon is a poet who has much to offer.

Michael Longley (b. 1939), although a little older, was a
fellow student with Mahon at Trinity College. He too was
born and schooled in Belfast, and he continues to live and
work there as an Assistant Director in the Arts Council of
Northern Ireland. He once described himself as 'an Ulsterman, a Protestant and an Anglo-Irishman', but his Irish
identity is more complex than this definition suggests. He
too is sophisticated, witty, aware of the difficult and uncertain
role that a poet and a promoter of literature and the arts is
playing in contemporary Belfast. In 'Letter to Derek Mahon',
he sees himself and his friend as

> Two poetic conservatives
> In the city of guns and long knives.

In a poem preceding this, informing his friends of the birth of
a son, he had ended

> I who have heard the waters break
> Claim this my country, though today
> Timor mortis conturbat me.

Longley is somewhat uneven as a poet. 'Epithalamium'
begins beautifully but doesn't sustain its opening quality. But
in two different ways he often succeeds brilliantly. He can be
witty, amusing and relaxed, especially in some of his later
verses, as in 'Ars Poetica' and 'The Lodger':

> The lodger is writing a novel.
> We give him the run of the house
> But he occupies my mind as well —

He can also write poems that carry a strong lyrical impulse in
a simple straightforward style, like 'Swans Mating'. Equally
strong, though more complex, is his moving tribute to his
dead father in 'In Memoriam'. A selection of Longley's verse
was published in *Penguin Modern Poets* 26. He has so far
published four separate volumes.

Another poet from the north, who stands outside the group I have just mentioned, is John Montague (b. 1929). He was born in Brooklyn, New York, of Ulster Catholic parents, but brought up on a farm in Co. Tyrone. He attended local schools, then went to St Patrick's College, Armagh, and afterwards to University College, Dublin, where he took an M.A. in Anglo-Irish literature. He later went to Yale Graduate School and taught at Berkeley, California. For some years he was Paris correspondent of *The Irish Times*. He currently lectures in English at University College, Cork. It will be seen from this that he has a more European, indeed international, background than the other northern poets. But he has not forgotten his Ulster background, although he has moved away from it. His best work so far is *The Rough Field*, which is a poetic sequence about his home townland, Garvaghey (Irish for 'a rough field'.), and Ulster generally. 'I had a kind of vision,' he wrote, 'in the medieval sense, of my home area, the unhappiness of its historical destiny.' He uses a variety of forms in the sequence, including a technique of collage, quoting from historical texts and from contemporary sectarian propaganda. The poem could be seen as a cleverly designed piece of poetic journalism, but it goes beyond this. There is irony and wit, but the verse has power to move us too, and Montague has a flair for quick and vivid snapshots of life in rural Ulster:

> the sack-cloth pilgrimages under rain
> to repair the slabbery gaps of winter.

Apart from *The Rough Field* Montague has written a variety of shorter poems in several collections. 'The Trout' is a vivid and dramatic account of tickling a trout, and 'All Legendary Obstacles' is a fine love lyric.

Moving south again, and away to the west, we find Richard Murphy (1927–). His home is on the west coast of Connemara, where he bought a Galway hooker and restored it to take friends and visitors sailing. He writes of the sea, and of the Cleggan Disaster, in *Sailing to an Island* (1963), and he tells the story of the boat he bought in 'The Last Galway Hooker':

> We met here last summer, nineteen fifty-nine,

Far from the missiles, the moon-shots, the money,
And we drank looking out on the island quay

When his crew were in London drilling a motorway.
Old age had smoothed his barnacled will,
One calm evening he sold me the *Ave Maria*.

He has also written an historical sequence *The Battle of Aughrim* (1968). His style is mostly severe, simple, concrete.

Thomas Kinsella (b. 1928) was born and is still based in Dublin. He is certainly dedicated to the craft of poetry. After nineteen years as a civil servant in the Department of Finance, he became a free-lance lecturer, holding a Chair of English at Temple University in America for a time. He made a fine translation of *The Tain*, the old Irish epic; his version seems to capture the spirit of the original work much better than earlier adaptations. I find his own poetry puzzling. I like some poems, such as 'Before Sleep' and 'Folk Wisdom' which uses the images of toads fearing the harrow, and the toad changed into a prince, to express the transformation of pain into beauty.

> As when a man
> Clutches his ears, deafened
> By his world, to find a jewel
> Made of pain in his hands.

Other poems I can see are clever and skilful, but they don't come alive for me. His poem about Bloody Sunday, 'Butcher's Dozen', has been much admired and compared to Swift, but I find the satiric edge a little blunt and crude. I think his best volume is *Nightwalker and Other Poems* (1968) which contains the poems I have mentioned above, also 'A Lady of Quality'.

Pearse Hutchinson (1927–) was born in Glasgow of Irish parents, and lived for some years in Spain. He writes in Irish as well as English. His poetry has vigour, variety and originality. 'No Hands' and 'Connemara' are good examples. I quote a snippet from the latter:

In kelp cormorant fuschia foxglove country . . .
In these green fields I pray against barbed wire
And never forget to take my pills.

Brendan Kennelly (1936–) is a Kerryman, born in Bally-longford. He went to Trinity College, Dublin and did post-graduate work at Leeds University. He is now a professor of English at Trinity College. With astonishing energy and ebullience he has written verse and prose, edited *The Penguin Book of Verse*, lectured, taught, given readings and done reviews. Perhaps words come to him too easily. Sometimes his adjectives seem to be doing little work, and the writing seems flat and generalised. He is best when he keeps close to physical detail, as in 'Blackbird' and 'Bread'. In 'Up and At It' he uses the persona of Moloney with humour and gaiety:

'That was a gay night', he said,
'I went to a wake and hopped into bed
With the corpse; not a very nice
Thing to do, I suppose; cold as ice
Her belly and thighs;'

Drama

Denis Johnston (1901–) was one of the first dramatists to break away from Abbey traditions. Born in Dublin, he was educated there and in Edinburgh, and he took degrees at Cambridge and Harvard. He practised law in Dublin, directed the Gate Theatre, was a BBC war correspondent (1942–5), held fellowships and lectured in America. His first play – complex, allusive, expressionistic, miles away from the usual Abbey fare – was rejected by the management. He revised it, re-titled it *The Old Lady Says No* (the old lady being Lady Gregory, one of the Abbey directors), and it was produced at the Gate Theatre, which had been founded by Michael MacLiammoir and Hilton Edwards in 1928. In the play, an actor playing Robert Emmet is accidentally knocked unconscious, and this starts a dream sequence, moving back and forth in time, and allowing scope for satire and criticism and a sharp exposure of Irish sentimentality. As Richard Fallis puts it: 'After all the political talk and the unthinking nationalism of the decade, someone needed to set off a fire-cracker under Irish pretensions, and *The Old Lady Says No* does it with a bang.'

His next play, *The Moon in the Yellow River* (1931), is

more traditional in technique, but lively and original in its treatment of Irish people and problems. It is his best play, as witty as Shaw's *John Bull's Other Island* but more profound in its handling of Irish politics and patriotism. This was followed by other interesting and experimental plays, including *A Bride for the Unicorn*, based on J.W. Dunne's theory of time, and *The Dreaming Dust,* a play about Swift.

Samuel Beckett (1906–) will seem to many the greatest living Anglo-Irish dramatist. Although he was born near Dublin, educated at Portora Royal School, Enniskillen, and at Trinity College, Dublin, he is an 'outsider' in terms of my conception of Anglo-Irish literature. His plays belong more properly to a European than an Anglo-Irish tradition. *Waiting for Godot* was first written in French, and it can hardly be said to have an Irish dimension. *All That Fall* (1957), a radio play commissioned by the BBC, does have an Irish setting and Irish characters, and some of the dialogue has a distinctly Irish flavour, but the Irish location is not really important. The play's mood and mode is metaphysical, Beckettian. It would be flattering to include Beckett as part of the Anglo-Irish drama of the fifties but inappropriate. So with a nod of apology to the distinguished Irishman who takes his place alongside Yeats and Joyce as a winner of the Nobel Prize for Literature, I pass on to other writers whose Irish dimension is indisputable.

John B. Keane (b. 1928–) is probably the most popular contemporary playwright in Ireland. His plays are regularly chosen by drama groups all over Ireland. Born in Listowel in Co. Kerry, he still lives there and keeps a pub. In an invitation to the Listowel Writers' Week, now an annual event, he wrote: 'There isn't a Listowel man but could talk the hind leg off a pot, sober or in his cups.' Certainly the characters in his own plays have vivid and forceful speech. *Sive* (1959), his first play, was rejected by the Abbey but later the Listowel Drama Group won the All-Ireland Amateur Drama Final with a performance of it. The theme is unoriginal, a young girl's forced marriage to a senile old farmer, and the story melodramatic (the young girl commits suicide), but in spite of this the play has power. He has written many plays, some of them flawed by sentimentality or unreality. By far the best and strongest of them is *The Field*. Lust for money and lust for land are powerfully presented in this play, and some of the tensions in Irish provincial life are sharply revealed.

Brian Friel (b. 1929—) was a teacher in Derry who wrote short stories. When he had saved up £250 he gave up teaching to try his luck as a full-time writer. His courage was rewarded. For a time he worked with Tyrone Guthrie in Canada, and he turned increasingly to drama. He has now written some twelve plays. Of those that I have seen the best is undoubtedly *Philadelphia, Here I Come*. Gar, the chief character, is a young man who worked for some years in his father's shop in a small Donegal town and is now on the point of leaving for Philadelphia. The central dramatic device, that of splitting Gar into two people, Public and Private, succeeds brilliantly. Private Gar, 'the unseen man, the man within' is able to play a lively vaudeville of different roles, from fantasy to mimicry.

Lovers, two short plays thematically linked, like 'Winners' and 'Losers', is typical of Friel's vitality in handling character and dialogue, and of his power to move both laughter and tears. He is a daring and subtle writer who continues to experiment with themes and methods. His recent *Translations* (1980) is a fascinating play.

Prose

Peadar O'Donnell (b. 1893) and Liam O'Flaherty (b. 1896) both come from Irish-speaking peasant communities in the west. O'Donnell was born in Co. Donegal, and became an active nationalist and socialist, commanding the Donegal Brigade of the IRA in 1921. He fought on the Republican side in the Civil War, was captured, imprisoned and escaped. He has said that he was not primarily a writer but an agitator, and that he never used the pen except as a weapon. He was clearly more concerned to change the world than to interpret it, but he wrote some fine novels.

The Knife (1930) is one of the best novels I know about the Civil War. He wrote it partly from a desire to explore the Orange mind, and it gives a deep insight into the sources of Orange and Green divisions, and into the feelings of those Republicans who continued to fight against the Free State. *Islanders* (1927) and *The Big Windows* (1955) are two other novels that show O'Donnell's skill as a writer, as well as his intimate knowledge of the life of the poor peasant communities of the west.

O'Flaherty was born on Inishmore in the Aran Islands. He was educated with a view to the priesthood but found that he had no vocation. After a number of wandering years, doing various labouring jobs, he turned to writing and was encouraged by Edward Garnett to write of the life he knew in the Arans. He made his name with *The Informer* (1927) but *Skerrett* (1932) and *Famine* (1937), are much more impressive novels. His main literary achievement is as a short story writer. He writes about birds and animals, and simple country people, with extraordinary insight and sympathy. The stories are simple, mostly very short, and completely convincing. 'Three Lambs', for example, tells how a small boy goes early in the morning to watch a sheep lambing. To his amazement and delight she gives birth to three lambs, and he helps to clean them and put them to suck. Then, already on his way home, he goes back to check on the sex of the newly born lambs.

> He raced back to the lambs and examined each of them. 'Three she lambs', he gasped. 'Oh, you devil, that never happened before. Maybe father will give me half-a-crown.'
> And as he raced homeward, he barked like a dog in his delight.

Nothing could be simpler, but because of the authentic detail, and because of O'Flaherty's sympathy with his people and animals, the stories are absorbing and moving. *The Short Stories of Liam O'Flaherty* (1937) contains the best of his work.

I have already referred to Samuel Beckett (1906–) in the section on drama, and explained why I don't see him in an Anglo-Irish tradition. The same goes for his novels, in spite of the Irish flavouring in *Murphy* (1938), *Malone Dies* and *Molloy* (1959). I must also confess to a personal quirk of taste. In spite of their wit and humour and intelligence, I do not find Beckett's novels enjoyable to read, as I do Flann O'Brien's. I have to labour my way through them. Yet I know that many of my friends, whose literary opinions I deeply respect, find him enthralling, and think that even his nasty, slick stories, *More Pricks Than Kicks,* are worthy to be set alongside Joyce's *Dubliners.* So, with another brief nod of apology to Beckett, I pass on.

Michael McLaverty (b. 1907—) writes of an Ulster world that is fast disappearing, in which Belfast still has a rural air and a man can keep a game cock in his backyard. Although born in Monaghan, McLaverty has lived most of his life as a teacher in Belfast. He was trained as a scientist but turned to literature. He has published eight novels and two volumes of stories, and his work has been translated into German, Spanish and Italian. His novels, *Call My Brother Back* (1939), *Lost Fields* (1942), *In This Thy Day* (1954), deal mainly with rural Ulster. Both novels and stories have links with an oral tradition. There are many Ulster usages — 'haskey weather', 'the scrake of gulls', 'a plout of rain' — but McLaverty is much more than a purveyor of provincial, local colour. The scenes may be provincial and the local detail faithfully recorded, but themes, feelings, attitudes to life, are universal. The novels are all worth reading but his best work is in his short stories. My own favourites are 'The Game Cock', 'The White Mare' and 'The Poteen Maker'.

Mervyn Wall (b. 1908—) is a Dubliner who has worked in the Civil Service, with Radio Eireann and finally with the Arts Council. He is best known for his comic and satiric fantasy, *The Unfortunate Fursey* (1946). This delightfully gay, picturesque and inventive book tells the story of a humble lay brother in the medieval monastery at Clonmacnoise who gets involved in an assault on the holy monks by the devil and a company of demons. He is expelled from the monastery and forced into a world of sorcery and witchcraft. After various hilarious adventures, he escapes to England on a broomstick, 'the first of many exiles for whom a decent way of living was not to be found in their own country'. The book is not simply fey; the satire finds many targets in modern Ireland. *The Return of Fursey* (1948) continues the humour and fantasy, though in a somewhat different mood. *Leaves for the Burning* (1952) is a wholly different kind of novel, mostly realistic and set in contemporary Ireland.

Sam Hanna Bell (b. 1909—) was born in Glasgow of an

Ulster-Scots family but came to Co. Down at the age of nine. He has published stories, novels and books about Ulster. *December Bride* (1951) is a fine novel of rural life in Co. Down in the early years of this century. It faithfully reflects the life and work and speech of the people, a Presbyterian family on a farm, and the passions, silent but strong, of those caught in an unusual triangle. The story is simple and moving.

Brian MacMahon (b. 1909–) has written plays, poems and novels, but is best known for his short stories. He was born in Listowel, Co. Kerry and still lives there. He has an intimate knowledge of rural life, including the life of the tinkers (or Irish gypsies), whom he writes about in *The Honey Spike* (both novel and play). He has published two collections of short stories, *The Lion Tamer* (1948) and *The Red Petticoat and Other Stories* (1955).

Benedict Kiely (b1919–), novelist and short story writer, was born in Dromore, Co. Tyrone. He started training to become a Jesuit priest, but instead went to University College, Dublin and became a journalist. He has written six novels and two collections of short stories. He has considerable comic and satiric energy and inventiveness, and a wide experience of Ireland. As a story teller he is still in touch with the oral tradition, like William Carleton, whom he admired and wrote about. Probably his best novel is *The Captain with the Whiskers* (1960). His stories are collected in *A Journey to the Seven Streams* (1963) and *A Ball of Malt and Madame Butterfly* (1973).

James Plunkett (b. 1920–) is the pseudonym of James Plunkett Kelly, who is very much a Dubliner. He was born and educated in Dublin and has mainly lived and worked there since. Much of his fiction deals with life in Dublin. As a worker in the Gas Company he was an active member of the Workers' Union of Ireland and held office under Jim Larkin. He wrote a radio play, *Big Jim*, and a stage play, *The Risen People*, about Larkin. His best work is in his short stories and novels. His two collections of stories, *The Eagles and the Trumpets* (1954) and *The Trusting and the Maimed* (1959) reveal an ability to cover a wide range of diverse material, a skilful control of structure and language and a power to move the reader. *Strumpet City* (1969) recreates the life of

Dublin from 1907 to 1914 in terms of memorable and living characters, ranging from the clergy, all of them different, to the hungry, dirty and tenacious Rashers, haunter of the city's ashbins.

Edna O'Brien (b. 1930–) is probably the best-known and most popular woman writer from Ireland today, but I find her work a little facile. Born in Co. Clare and educated at the Convent of Mercy in Loughrea, and then in Dublin, she now mostly lives in London. *The Country Girls* (1960) is lively and amusing, and she clearly knows all about the country background of the girls she writes about. But her characters remain figures in a cleverly contrived comedy, and there is a certain artificiality about her writing. Her story 'Irish Revel', in *The Love Object* (1968) is one of her best pieces, but little of her work stands up to re-reading.

A good novelist whose work is less widely known is Jennifer Johnston (b. 1935–). The daughter of Denis Johnston and his first wife, Sheelagh Richards, she has a Dublin background and went to Trinity College, but she now lives in Londonderry. She has published five novels to date, starting with *The Captains and the Kings* (1972). Her last, *The Old Jest* (1979) is perhaps her best. She writes simply and sparely – her novels are all short – but with a powerful though delicate insight into the thoughts and feelings of lonely and isolated people, and with a gift for evoking place and time. With the exception of *Shadows on our Skin* (1978), dealing with a working class family in contemporary Derry, the people in her novels are the Anglo-Irish gentry, often living in Big Houses.

A Big House in decline is at the centre of a fine novel by Aidan Higgins (b. 1927–). *Langrishe, Go Down* (1966) tells of three middle-aged spinsters living on in an odour of rural decay in Springfield House. Higgins was born in Celbridge, Co. Kildare and became something of a wandering, impoverished artist. With his wife he joined John Wright's Marionette Company, touring Europe, Rhodesia and South Africa, then in Spain, Germany and England, but has returned to Ireland. He has also written a volume of imaginative short stories, *Felo de Se* (1960).

Select Bibliography

(Place of publication London, unless otherwise stated)

Historical and General
J.C. Beckett, *A Short History of Ireland*, 1952 (rev, 1966).
Brian Inglis, *The Story of Ireland*, 1956.
T.W. Moody and F.X. Martin, *The Course of Irish History*, Cork, 1967.
F.S.L. Lyons, *Ireland Since the Famine*, 1971.
Ruth Dudley Edwards, *An Atlas of Irish History*, 1973.
Edgar Holt, *Protest in Arms: The Irish Troubles 1916–23*, 1960.
Conor Cruise O'Brien, ed., *The Shaping of Modern Ireland*, 1960.
Cecil Woodham-Smith, *The Great Hunger*, 1962.
Sean O'Faolain, *The Irish*, 1947.
Malcolm Brown, *The Politics of Irish Literature*, Seattle, 1972.
Henry Boylan, *A Dictionary of Irish Biography*, Dublin, 1978.
Gill History of Ireland (11 vols) Dublin.

Literary History and Criticism
Ernest A. Boyd, *Ireland's Literary Renaissance*, New York, 1916.
Thomas MacDonagh, *Literature in Ireland*, 1916.
Stephen Gwynn, *Irish Literature and Drama*, 1936.
Frank O'Connor, *The Backward Look*, (*A Survey of Irish Literature*), 1967.
Richard Fallis, *The Irish Renaissance*, New York, 1977.
Herbert Howarth, *The Irish Writers, 1880–1940*, 1958.
Thomas Flanagan, *The Irish Novelists, 1800–1850*, 1958.

Andrew E. Malone, *The Irish Drama*, 1929.

Una Ellis-Fermor, *The Irish Dramatic Movement*, 1939.

Sean Lucy, ed., *Irish Poets in English*, Cork, 1973.

Benedict Kiely, *Modern Irish Fiction — a Critique*, Dublin, 1950.

Terence Brown, *Northern Voices, Poets from Ulster*, Dublin, 1975.

J.F. Foster, *Themes and Forces in Ulster Fiction*, Dublin 1974.

Brian Cleeve, *Dictionary of Irish Writers, vol. 1, Fiction*, Utrecht, 1966, Cork 1967.

Robert Hogan (ed.), *A Dictionary of Irish Literature*, 1979.

Diarmaid O'Muirithe, *The English Language in Ireland*, Cork, 1977.

Bibliographical

Harmon, Maurice, *Modern Irish Literature 1800—1967, a Reader's Guide*, Dublin, 1967.

Harmon, Maurice, *Select Bibliography for the Study of Anglo-Irish Literature and its Backgrounds*, Dublin, 1977.

Finneran, Richard, ed. *Anglo-Irish Literature, A Review of Research*, New York, 1976.

Rafroidi, Patrick, *L'Irlande et le romantisme*, Paris, 1972 (contains full bibliographies of Anglo-Irish writers, 1789—1850).

Fallis, Richard, *The Irish Renaissance, an introduction to Anglo-Irish Literature*, New York, 1977, Dublin 1978 (contains helpful 'Suggestions for Further Reading').

Writers selected for detailed discussion in this book.

I have not attempted to provide full bibliographies for each writer, but have listed the more important works, and some critical studies that might be helpful.

Maria Edgeworth

Castle Rackrent, 1800. Modern edition (ed. George Watson) 1964.

Ennui, 1809.

The Absentee, 1810.

Ormond, 1817. Modern edition (ed A.N. Jeffares) Shannon, 1978.

Memoirs of Richard Lovell Edgeworth, Esq., Begun by Himself and Concluded by his daughter, Maria Edgeworth. 2 vols. 1820. Modern edition, Shannon, 1970.

O. Elizabeth McWhorter Harden, *Maria Edgeworth's Art of Prose Fiction.* The Hague, 1971.
Patrick Murray, *Castle Rackrent,* Dublin, 1972.

Somerville & Ross
An Irish Cousin, 1889.
The Real Charlotte, 1894.
Some Experiences of an Irish R.M., 1889.
Further Experiences of an Irish R.M., 1908.
Irish Memories, 1917.
Mount Music, 1919.
The Big House of Inver, 1925.

John Cronin, *Somerville and Ross,* Lewisberg, 1972.
Violet Powell, *The Irish Cousins,* 1970.
Maurice Collis, *Somerville and Ross,* 1969.

George Moore
A Drama in Muslin, 1886.
The Untilled Field, 1903.
The Lake, 1905.
Hail and Farewell, 1911–1914. One vol. ed. Richard Cave, Gerrards Cross, 1976.

Joseph Hone, *The Life of George Moore,* New York, 1936.
Malcolm Brown, *George Moore: A Reconsideration,* Seattle, 1955.
Graham Owens, ed., *George Moore's Mind and Art,* New York, 1970.

William Carleton
Traits and Stories of the Irish Peasantry (2 vols.), Dublin, 1830.
Traits and Stories of the Irish Peasantry Second Series (3 vols.) Dublin, 1833.
Fardorougha The Miser, Dublin, 1839.
Valentine McClutchy, The Irish Agent, Dublin, 1845.

The Black Prophet, 1847.
The Tithe Proctor, 1848.
The Autobiography of William Carleton, (preface by Patrick
   Kavanagh) 1968.

Benedict Kiely, *Poor Scholar*, 1947.

Patrick Kavanagh
Collected Poems, 1964.
The Complete Poems of Patrick Kavanagh (ed. Peter
   Kavanagh), New York, 1972.
The Green Fool, 1938.
Tarry Flynn, 1948.
Collected Prose, 1967.

Peter Kavanagh, *Garden of the Golden Apples: A Bibliography
   of Patrick Kavanagh*, New York, 1972.
Alan Warner, *Clay is the Word*, Dublin, 1973.

Frank O'Connor
The Stories of Frank O'Connor, New York, 1952, London,
   1953.
Domestic Relations, New York and London, 1957.
Collection Three, 1959.
An Only Child, New York, 1961, London, 1962.
My Father's Son, London, 1968, New York, 1969.
Kings, Lords and Commons, New York, 1959, London, 1961.
The Saint and Mary Kate, London and New York, 1932.
Leinster, Munster and Connaught, 1950.

Maurice Sheehy, ed. *Michael/Frank: Studies on Frank
   O'Connor*, New York, 1969.

James Joyce
Dubliners, Dublin, 1914.
A Portrait of the Artist as a Young Man, New York, 1916.
Ulysses, Paris, 1922.
Finnegans Wake, 1939.
Stephen Hero, (ed. Theodore Spencer) 1944.
The Critical Writings of James Joyce (ed. Ellsworth Mason

and Richard Ellmann), 1966.
A Shorter Finnegans Wake (ed. Anthony Burgess), 1966.

Clive Hart (ed.) *James Joyce's Dubliners: critical essays*, 1969.
Kenneth Grose, *James Joyce*, 1973.
Stuart Gilbert, *James Joyce's Ulysses*, 1930.
Frank Budgen, *James Joyce and the Making of Ulysses*, 1934.
Richard Ellmann, *James Joyce*, 1959 (biography).
Anthony Burgess, *Here Comes Everybody*, 1965.
Harry Blamires, *The Bloomsday Book*, 1966.
Richard Ellman, *Ulysses on the Liffey*, 1972.

James Stephens
The Charwoman's Daughter, 1912.
The Crock of Gold, 1912.
The Insurrection in Dublin, Dublin, London and New York, 1916.
Collected Poems, 1926.
James, Seamus and Jacques (Unpublished writings of James Stephens, ed. Lloyd Frankenberg), 1964.
Letters of James Stephens (ed. Richard Finneran), 1974.
Here Are Ladies, 1913.
The Demi-Gods, 1913.
Reincarnations (transaltions from Irish poets), 1919.
Irish Fairy Tales, 1920.
Deirdre, 1923.
In the Land of Youth, 1924.
Hilary Pyle, *James Stephens: His Work and an Account of his Life*, 1965.
Augustine Martin, *James Stephens: A Critical Study*, Dublin, 1977.

Sean O'Casey
Two Plays, 1925. (*Juno and the Paycock* and *The Shadow of a Gunman*
The Plough and the Stars, 1926.
The Silver Tassie, 1928.
Within the Gates, 1933.

Red Roses for Me, 1942.
Cock-a-Doodle Dandy, 1949.
The autobiographies were published separately in six volumes
as follows:
I Knock at the Door, 1939.
Pictures in the Hallway, 1942.
Drums Under the Window, 1946.
Inishfallen Fare Thee Well, 1949.
Rose and Crown, 1952.
Sunset and Evening Star, 1954.

David Krause, *Sean O'Casey: The Man and his Work*, 1960.
David Krause (ed.), *The Letters of Sean O'Casey, vol. 1,
1910—1941*, 1975.

Austin Clarke
Collected Poems, Dublin, 1974.
Collected Plays, Dublin, 1963.
The Cattledrive in Connaught, 1925.
Pilgrimage, 1929.
Night and Morning, 1938.
Ancient Lights, 1955.
Flight to Africa, 1963.
The Bright Temptation (prose romance), 1932.
The Sun Dances at Easter (prose romance), 1952.
Poetry in Modern Ireland, Dublin, 1951.
Twice Round the Black Church (autobiography), 1962.
A Penny in the Clouds (autobiography), 1968.

Susan Halpern, *Austin Clarke, his life and works*, 1974.

Flann O'Brien
At Swim-Two-Birds, 1939; re-issue 1960.
The Hard Life, 1961.
The Dalkey Archive, 1964.
The Third Policeman, 1967.
The Best of Myles, 1968.
An Beal Bocht, Dublin, 1964 (translated by Patrick Power as
The Poor Mouth, 1973).

Anne Clissmann, *Flann O'Brien: a Critical Introduction to his writing,* Dublin, 1975.

W.B. Yeats
For further details of separate collections of poems, and separate plays, see the books listed below. Apart from the full bibliography by Wade, several critical studies contain useful shorter bibliographies.

The Collected Poems of W.B. Yeats, revised ed., 1950.
The Collected Plays of W.B. Yeats, 1952.
The Variorum Edition of the Poems of W.B. Yeats, ed. Peter Allt and Russel K. Alspach, 1957.
The Variorum Edition of the Plays of W.B. Yeats, ed. Russell K. Alspach, 1966.

Prose Writings.
Autobiographies, 1955.
A Vision, rev. edn., 1956.
Mythologies, 1959.
Essays and Introductions, 1961.
*Explorations,*1962.
Uncollected Prose by W.B. Yeats, vol. 1, ed. J.P. Frayne, 1970 (contains reviews and articles, 1886—1896).
Uncollected Prose by W.B. Yeats, vol. 2, ed. J.P. Frayne and C. Johnson, 1975 (contains reviews, articles, etc., 1897—1939).
Letters, ed. Allan Wade, 1954.

A Bibliography of the Writings of W.B. Yeats, ed. Allan Wade, rev. ed., ed. Russell K. Alspach, 1968.
Joseph Hone, *W.B. Yeats,* 1943; rev. ed., 1962 (biography).
A. Norman Jeffares, *W. B. Yeats: Man and Poet,* Yale 1949; rev. ed. 1962.
Louis MacNeice, *The Poetry of W.B. Yeats,* 1941.
T.R. Henn, *The Lonely Tower,* 1950.
Richard Ellmann, *The Identity of Yeats,* 1954.
Peter Ure, *Yeats the Playwright,* 1963.
William H. Pritchard, ed., *W.B. Yeats, A Critical Anthology,* 1972.

J.M. Synge
Riders to the Sea, 1904.
The Shadow of the Glen, (acted 1903) 1905.
The Well of the Saints, 1905.
The Playboy of the Western World, 1907.
The Aran Islands, 1907.
The Tinker's Wedding, 1908.
Poems and Translations, 1909.
Deirdre of the Sorrows, 1910.
In Wicklow, West Kerry and Connemara, 1911.
T.R. Henn ed. *The Plays and Poems of J.M. Synge,* 1963.
Collected Works, I Poems, ed. R. Skelton, 1962; *II Prose,* ed.
    A. Price, 1966; *III and IV Plays,* ed. A. Saddlemyer, 1968.

D.H. Greene and E.M. Stephens, *J.M. Synge, 1871—1909,*
    New York, 1959.
A. Carpenter ed. *My Uncle John, Edward Stephen's Life of*
    J.M. Synge, 1974.
Alan Price, *Synge and Anglo-Irish Drama,* 1961.
S.B. Bushrui, ed., *Sunshine and the Moon's Delight,* 1971.
    (Centenary essays on Synge, with extensive bibliography).
N. Grene, *Synge: A Critical Study of the Plays,* 1975.

Sean O'Faolain
Midsummer Night Madness and other stories, 1932.
Constance Markievicz, or the Average Revolutionary, A
    Biography, 1934.
Bird Alone (novel), 1936.
A Purse of Coppers: Short Stories, 1937.
The Autobiography of Theobald Wolfe Tone, 1937.
King of the Beggars, A Life of Daniel O'Connell, New York,
    1938.
The Great O'Neill, A Biography of Hugh O'Neill, Earl of
    Tyrone, 1550—1616, New York, 1942.
The Story of Ireland, 1943.
Teresa, and other stories, 1947.
The Irish, 1947.
The Short Story, 1948.
The Man Who Invented Sin, and Other Stories, New York,
    1949.

The Vanishing Hero, Studies in Novelists of the Twenties,
   1956.
The Stories of Sean O'Faolain, 1958.
Vive Moi!, Boston, 1964.

Maurice Harmon, *Sean O'Faolain, A Critical Introduction,*
   Notre Dame (Indiana, U.S.) and London, 1966.

Mary Lavin
The House in Clewe Street (novel), Boston and London,
   1945.
Mary O'Grady (novel) Boston and London, 1950.
The Stories of Mary Lavin, vol. I, 1964.
The Stories of Mary Lavin, vol. II, 1974.

Zack Bowen *Mary Lavin,* Lewisburg, 1975.

Francis Stuart
Pigeon Irish, 1932.
The Coloured Dome, 1933.
Try the Sky, 1933.
Things to Live For: Notes for an Autobiography, 1934.
The Angel of Pity, 1935.
The White Hare, 1936.
The Pillar of Cloud, 1948.
Redemption, 1950.
The Flowering Cross, 1950.
Angels of Providence, 1959.
Black List, Section H., Carbondale (U.S.) and London, 1971.
Memorial, 1973.
A Hole in the Head, 1977.

J.H. Natterstad, *Francis Stuart,* Lewisburg, 1974.
W. J. McCormack, ed., *A Festschrift for Francis Stuart on his
   Seventieth Birthday,* Dublin, 1972.

Brian Moore
The Lonely Passion of Judith Hearne, 1955.
The Feast of Lupercal, Boston, 1957 (title changed in later
   editions to *A Moment of Love*).

The Luck of Ginger Coffey, Boston 1960.
An Answer from Limbo, Boston, 1962.
The Emperor of Icecream, 1966.
I am Mary Dunne, New York, 1968.
Fergus, New York, 1970.
The Revolution Script, New York, 1971.
Catholics, New York, 1972.
The Doctor's Wife, 1976.
The Great Victorian Collection, New York, 1975.
The Mangan Inheritance, 1980.

Jeanne Flood, *Brian Moore,* Lewisburg, 1974.

John McGahern
The Barracks, 1963.
The Dark, 1965.
Nightlines, 1970.
The Leavetaking, 1974.
Getting Through, 1978.
The Pornographer, 1979.

John Hewitt
No Rebel Word, 1948.
Collected Poems, 1932—1967, 1968.
The Day of the Corncrake, 1969.
Out of My Time, Belfast, 1974.
Time Enough, Belfast, 1976.
The Rain Dance, Belfast, 1978.
Kites in Spring, 1980.
The Poems of William Allingham. Edited with an introduction by John Hewitt, Dublin, 1967.
Rhyming Weavers and other country poets of Antrim and Down. Edited and introduced by John Hewitt, Belfast, 1974.

Seamus Heaney
Death of a Naturalist, 1966.
Door Into the Dark, 1969.
Wintering Out, 1972.
North, 1975.

Field Work, 1979.

Robert Buttel, *Seamus Heaney,* Lewisburg, 1975.

Index

The index lists Anglo-Irish writers discussed or referred to in the book and critics whose views have been referred to. Individual works are listed under their authors' names.